PERGAMON INTERNATIONAL LIBRARY
of Science, Technology, Engineering and Social Studies
The 1000-volume original paperback library in aid of education, industrial training and the enjoyment of leisure
Publisher: Robert Maxwell, M.C.

Geography and Population

Approaches and Applications

PERGAMON OXFORD GEOGRAPHIES

General Editor W.B. Fisher

Other titles in this series:

Clarke, J.I.
Population Geography, 2nd Edition

Clarke, J.I.
Population Geography and the Developing Countries

Clout, H.D.
The Geography of Post-War France: A Social and Economic Approach

Clout, H.D.
Rural Geography: An Introductory Survey

Cooke, R. and Johnson, J.H.
Trends in Geography: An Introductory Survey

Coppock, J.T.
Second Home: Curse or Blessing?

Coppock, J.T. and Sewell, W.R.D.
Spatial Dimensions of Public Policy

Dennis R. and Clout, H.D.
A Social Geography of England and Wales

Dewdney, J.C.A.
A Geography of the Soviet Union, 2nd Edition

Eckholm, E.P.
Losing Ground: Environmental Stress and World Food Prospects

Goodall, B. and Kirby, A.
Resources and Planning

Johnson, J.H.
Urban Geography, 2nd Edition

Kerr, A.J.C.
The Common Market and How It Works, 2nd edition

Matthews, J.A.
Quantitative and Statistical Approaches to Geography: A Practical Manual

McIntosh, I.G. and Marshall, C.B.
The Face of Scotland, 3rd Edition

O'Connor, A.M.
The Geography of Tropical African Development, 2nd Edition

Sunderland, E.
Elements of Human and Social Geography: Some Anthropological Perspectives

Trewartha, G.T.
The More Developed Realm: A Geography of its Population

A Related Journal

GEOFORUM

The International Multidisciplinary Journal for the Rapid Publication of Research Results and Critical Review Articles in the Physical, Human and Regional Geosciences
Full details of all Pergamon publications and a free specimen copy of any Pergamon journal available on request from your nearest Pergamon office

Geography and Population

Approaches and Applications

edited by

JOHN I. CLARKE

Professor and Head of the Department of Geography
University of Durham, U.K. and Chairman of the International
Geographical Union Commission on Population Geography

PUBLISHED BY PERGAMON PRESS ON BEHALF OF THE
INTERNATIONAL GEOGRAPHICAL UNION
COMMISSION ON POPULATION GEOGRAPHY

PERGAMON PRESS

OXFORD · NEW YORK · TORONTO · SYDNEY · PARIS · FRANKFURT

U.K.	Pergamon Press Ltd., Headington Hill Hall, Oxford OX3 0BW, England
U.S.A.	Pergamon Press Inc., Maxwell, Fairview Park, Elmsford, New York 10523, U.S.A.
CANADA	Pergamon Press Canada Ltd., Suite 104, 150 Consumers Rd., Willowdale, Ontario M2J 1P9, Canada
AUSTRALIA	Pergamon Press (Aust.) Pty Ltd. P.O. Box 544, Potts Point, N.S.W. 2011, Australia
FRANCE	Pergamon Press SARL, 24 rue des Ecoles, 75240 Paris, Cedex 05, France
FEDERAL REPUBLIC OF GERMANY	Pergamon Press GmbH, Hammerweg 6, D-6242 Kronberg-Taunus, Federal Republic of Germany

First edition 1984

Library of Congress Cataloging in Publication Data

Main entry under title:

Geography and population.

(Pergamon international library of science, technology, engineering, and social studies) (Pergamon Oxford geographies)
Includes bibliographical references.
1. Population geography – Addresses, essays, lectures

I. Clarke, John Innes. II. Series.

HB1951.G42 1984 304.6 83-22028

0 08 028781 6 Hardcover
0 08 028780 8 Flexicover

Printed in Great Britain by A. Wheaton & Co., Ltd., Exeter

Contents

List of Contributors

D. M. Bohra, University of Jodhpur, India
W. A. V. Clark, University of California, U.S.A.
J. I. Clarke, University of Durham, U.K.
A. L. Convey, Trinity and All Saints College, Leeds, U.K.
P. Curson, Macquarie University, Australia
R. J. Fuchs, University of Hawaii, U.S.A.
G. A. Fuller, University of Hawaii, U.S.A.
M. E-S. Ghallab, Cairo University, Egypt
G. S. Gosal, Panjab University, India
W. T. S. Gould, Liverpool University, U.K.
A. Jagielski, University of Wrocław, Poland
H. R. Jones, University of Dundee, U.K.
L. A. Kosiński, University of Alberta, Canada
M. T. G. de MacGregor, Universidad Nacional Autónoma de Mexico, Mexico
P. Nag, National Atlas and Thematic Mapping Organisation, Calcutta, India
D. Noin, University of Paris 1, France
P. E. Ogden, Queen Mary College, University of London, U.K.
S. H. Ominde, University of Nairobi, Kenya
A. Otomo, Utsunomiya University, Japan
R. M. Prothero, Liverpool University, U.K.
R. J. Pryor, Numurkah, Victoria, Australia
P. H. Rees, University of Leeds, U.K.
R. E. Rossini, University of São Paulo, Brazil
D. T. Rowland, Australian National University, Australia
Sun Panshou, Chinese Academy of Sciences, Beijing, China
K. E. Vaidyanathan, UNESCO, Paris, France
A. C. Walsh, Massey University, New Zealand
E. Weber, Ernst Moritz Arndt University, Greifswald, G.D.R.
R. Woods, University of Sheffield U.K.

List of Figures

Introduction

The object of this edited volume is to reveal the variety of approaches and applications to population geography over time and space. Written by numerous authors from many parts of the world, it reveals how this field of geography has evolved and diversified particularly since mid-century. A variety of ecological, landscape, positivist, quantitative, behavioural and applied approaches can be discerned, with differing levels of demographic content. Moreover, so can a variety of national approaches, as population geographers are greatly influenced by their physical, cultural and political environments as well as by their educational systems. In some countries geographers are mostly trained to be teachers, and the process is very cyclical; in others, the training is much less canalized and more relevant to the problems of the country. Generally, population geographers focus upon the specific population processes, patterns and problems which surround them, and their approach to the subject is influenced by them. A population geographer working in Peru or Nepal is much more likely to be concerned with mountain population pressures and their ecological impact than in either demographic accounting models or intra-urban mobility, which are more common research interests in advanced industrialized countries, where the demographic conditions are so different and the data availability so much greater. In short, the context of studies of population geography greatly affects the nature of those studies, and that is why a thoroughly international team of authors has been asked to contribute to this volume, 27 authors from 15 different countries.

The multinational authorship has been assembled through the activities of the International Geographical Union's (I.G.U.) Commission on Population Geography, one of the 14 commissions of the I.G.U. during its 1980–84 session. Since 1956 there has always been an I.G.U. commission concerned with aspects of population, though its name and membership have varied over the years (Kosiński, 1980), initially being concerned with the World Population Map (1956–64), then with the Geography and Cartography of World Population (1964–68) and subsequently with Population Geography (1968–). Gradually, the activities of the Commission have increased and the variety of themes has multiplied, but always the main aim has been to stimulate international collaboration and cooperation in the study of population geography. During the current session the major theme has been population redistribution and the nine members of the Commission have organized symposia in São Paulo/Rio de Janeiro (Brazil), Khartoum (Sudan), Cagliari, Sardinia (Italy), Dunedin (New Zealand), Kathmandu (Nepal), Winnipeg (Canada) and Rouen (France) on diverse topics:

—the impact of development projects upon population redistribution in Africa (Khartoum)
—women, work and production space (São Paulo/Rio)
—the socio-economic policy of the state and its population (São Paulo/Rio)
—general aspects of population geography (São Paulo/Rio)
—women's role in population redistribution (Cagliari)
—mobility, identity and policy in the Island Pacific (Dunedin)
—mountain population pressures (Kathmandu)
—the problems and consequences of refugee migrations in the developing world (Winnipeg)
—migration and the city (Rouen)

Many of these meetings result in books and special numbers of journals published in different countries, and in addition the Commission is preparing an international volume on 'Census Mapping Surveys'. In these ways, the I.G.U. Commission on Population Geography is attempting to foster research and international involvement in population geography. As Chairman, I would like to pay tribute to its members—Murray Chapman (U.S.A.), Maudood Elahi (Bangladesh), Maria-Luisa Gentileschi (Italy), Mustafa Khogali (Sudan), Leszek Kosiński (Canada), Prithvish Nag (India), Rosa Ester Rossini (Brazil) and Egon Weber (G.D.R.)—for all their help, enthusiasm and advice.

The scope of a volume such as this could be extended. More theoretical and thematic aspects might be included, and more country case studies of the situation of population geography. In fact, late withdrawals of authors almost inevitably affect its character, and certainly their chapters would have accentuated the diversity of the position of population geography vis-à-vis geography and population studies in general. But the present series of cases reveals sufficient diversity, and I am grateful to all authors for their contributions to this volume. In addition, I owe much to Joan Dresser for dealing with typescripts from so many countries.

Durham, May, 1983 JOHN I. CLARKE

Reference

Kosiński, L.A. (1980) Population geography and the International Geographical Union, *Population Geography*, **2,** 1–20.

1

Geography, Demography and Population

JOHN I. CLARKE
(University of Durham, U.K.)

If we accept the early works of George (1951) and Trewartha (1953) some thirty years ago as initial codifications of population geography, there is little doubt that since then it has flourished and diversified, becoming a multi-faceted field of study, and accounting for more than one in ten of all published geographical papers. Of course, from the late nineteenth century a keen interest in population phenomena had been shown by many geographers of the ecological school, both determinists and possibilists, from Ratzel and Hettner to Vidal de la Blache and Sorre. But it is during the second half of the twentieth century that population geography has emerged and expanded. It was variously examined and structured in a number of basic texts during the period 1951–70 (George, 1951 and 1959; Clarke, 1965; Zelinsky, 1966; Beaujeu-Garnier, 1956–58 and 1966; Kosiński, 1967; Wilson, 1968; Trewartha, 1969; Griffin, 1970; Demko, Rose and Schnell, 1970) since when the field has diffused internationally and diversified thematically, so that today there are a large number of practitioners around the world utilizing different approaches, methods and applications.

An indication of the current diversity in approaches to population geography is revealed by the contents of four recently published textbooks. On the one hand, the Frenchman Noin (1979) and the Indians Chandna and Sidhu (1980) devote extensive coverage to spatial distribution of population, ethnic, demographic and socio-economic diversity of populations, spatial mobility and the relationships between population and resources, but give relatively little attention to fertility, mortality and population growth; on the other, the British authors Woods (1979) and Jones (1981) devote most of their texts to these last three themes, along with a consideration of population policies (in the text of Jones) and of models and population forecasting (in the text of Woods), but say hardly anything about the distribution and diversity of populations or their relationships to environment or resources. Woods and Jones have suggested that texts like those of Noin and Chandna and Sidhu exemplify a 'traditional' pattern-orientation in population geography, while theirs reflect a new process-orientation, more in line with current trends in geography as a whole. However, while the two pairs of texts have a useful complementarity, none incorporates comprehensively the full diversity of work undertaken or courses studied under the name of population geography around the world. As evidence, we may cite the recent contributions of the IGU Commission on Population Geography, which have been particularly policy-orientated and culture-orientated (Webb, Naukkarinen and Kosiński, 1981; *Population Geography*, 1981; Clarke and Kosiński, 1982; Clarke, Khogali and Kosiński, forthcoming), reflecting the immense variety of peoples, cultures and countries as well as of approaches, attitudes and policies to population phenomena.

This brief chapter will look at some of the many factors which have influenced the emergence, expansion and diversification of population geography. They may be grouped, somewhat arbitrarily, into four main categories: (i) population changes, both natural and migratory; (ii) changes in political structures and policies; (iii) the growing availability of data and the facility to handle them; and (iv) the academic evolution of geography, demography and population studies.

Population changes

Certainly the growth of population geography has coincided with the growing public awareness of the rapid increase in world population growth, brought about particularly by mortality decline preceding and greatly exceeding fertility decline in a large number of less developed countries (L.D.C.s). As the latter comprise the great majority of mankind, and the population growth of more developed countries (M.D.C.s) has dwindled fast, the absolute increase of population has been largely localized in the L.D.C.s, who are least able to cope. Their population growth came to be seen as a problem, especially for economic development, though curiously, in many parts of the world population growth is often seen as a problem, whatever the rate; and rates of population growth among countries have never been so diverse as since mid-century. So geographers came to realize that it was not enough to know about population numbers and their increase, but one should know about the process of demographic transition from high to low vital rates as well as the changes in population characteristics. The contrasts in age structure alone between M.D.C.s and L.D.C.s demonstrated the need for greater demographic understanding. Geographers interested in man-environment relationships had long known much more about the environment than about man. Now they wished to know more about man (and of course woman), his demographic characteristics and the processes affecting his numbers, not only in the present and past but also in the future, because it was apparent that they were crucial to an understanding of past, present and future geographies. In short, international concern about population growth, especially at the world level, has exercised an important, perhaps even excessive influence, and a recent elementary text on population geography by Peters and Larkin (1979) for the American public reflects markedly this fact.

Population geographers were also faced with the growing mobility of mankind, facilitated by improvements in all types of transportation, as well as growing diversity in the forms of mobility. In particular, there has been a considerable increase in circulatory movements:

(a) transient movements of a seasonal and periodic nature, such as the movements of migrant workers and military personnel, which do not involve a permanent change in location; and
(b) temporary movements of shorter duration, such as journeys to work, shop, worship and leisure, which to some extent express the inefficiencies of locations.

In M.D.C.s particularly, such movements have been augmented by the increased availability of motor cars, rapid rail and air transport, changes in retailing and the increased number of second homes, while telephones, transistors, freezers and refrigerators, for example, may have had the opposite effect. Many of these forms of mobility are inadequately enumerated by conventional censuses, yet they are vital in the functioning of society (Chapman and Prothero, 1983). Moreover, there is little doubt that there is a mobility transition over time in association with social and economic developments, and that it has some connections, even if feeble, with demographic transition. Growing awareness of the complexities of mobility transition (Zelinsky, 1971; 1979) and their implications upon population redistribution and growth has been an important influence upon the research of many population geographers, as recently summarized by Lewis (1982).

Another factor stimulating the growth of population geography has been the reduction in the land-boundedness of mankind, especially in the M.D.C.s (Clarke, 1973). Man-land relationships are less close because of transformations in agriculture, increased industrialization, improved transportation and trade, changes in forms of energy, massive urbanization and the rapid growth of the service sector. Population has assumed a more causal role, and is less responsive to environmental and economic dictates. Its distribution is becoming more concentrated, because in very many countries, especially L.D.C.s, urban growth rates far exceed population growth rates and urbanization is increasingly localized in huge cities. The growth processes of large cities and their manifold problems have become a compelling focus for research by population geographers, as indeed have the recent moves towards urban decentralization and deconcentration in M.D.C.s. The forces of concentration and dispersion are primary elements of population redistribution, a theme of growing significance during the 1970s and 1980s to population geographers and others (Gosling and Lim, 1979; U.N., 1981) concerned with policies trying to influence it.

Political changes

The period since mid-century has also seen the emergence of a large number of independent states, having the effect of nationalizing populations and to some extent stabilizing the overall world population distribution. State populations are separately administered and enumerated and have become the primary units of study by population geographers. Political boundaries act as demographic divides impeding free flows of people and separating populations with different demographic characteristics. Movements are still strongly divisible into internal and international, because the freedom of the former is usually much greater than of the latter, where checks, restrictions and quotas are frequently imposed in efforts to preserve national identities. Furthermore, as state populations are more closed than open, states feel responsible for their own population pressures and problems. All their policies have indirect effects upon demographic characteristics, but more and more governments are adopting direct policies to affect population growth and redistribution. So many governments are having an increasing influence upon demographic behaviour.

Countries vary enormously in population size and area, and during the 1970s population geographers became increasingly conscious of the effects of scale (Clarke, 1973; Kosiński and Webb, 1976). Micro-states are greatly affected by external migration, and are thus demographically more unstable than macro-states, which tend to be relatively more closed. The effects of scale may also be seen in the analysis of sub-national administrative units—also important units for population study—as, for example, the relative significance of natural change and migration tends to alter from one level of areal unit of analysis to another. As population geographers study populations ranging from enumeration areas to that of the whole world, the concept of scale has become an important theme, particularly for the I.G.U. Commission on Population Geography.

Although individual political units are the basic units of demographic consideration, continental regions have demographic as well as cultural distinctiveness which has attracted the attention of population geographers (Clarke, 1971; Trewartha, 1972 and 1978; Clarke and Fisher, 1972; Kosiński, 1970; Salt and Clout, 1976). The demographic characteristics of continental regions have probably become increasingly contrasted during recent decades, and consequently have become convenient units for syntheses and research projects, reflecting the geographer's awareness of the importance of socio-economic processes in relation to demographic phenomena.

Geographical studies have been facilitated by the work of the various United Nations regional organizations (e.g. E.C.W.A., E.C.A., E.S.C.A.P.), who have played an important role in elucidating regional trends and processes, training personnel and in publishing data. Of course, the many technical publications and the huge amounts of internationally comparable population data published by the U.N. Department of Social and Economic Affairs have proved invaluable, and these have been supplemented by the advice and expertise to governments, as well as the work of the United Nations Fund for Population Activities (U.N.F.P.A.), the largest single donor to population activities of all sorts. In addition, there are numerous other international organizations, like the Population Council (e.g. **Population and Development Review**), Population Reference Bureau (e.g. the annual World Population Data Sheet), the United Nations Committee for Coordination of National Research in Demography (C.I.C.R.E.D.) and the International Union for the Scientific Study of Population (I.U.S.S.P.), which have had major influences upon the availability of data, the development and publication of research, including population geography, and the attitudes and policies of governments. In many ways population study has become an international industry, and population geography has been stimulated by this.

Data availability and handling

Under the influence of these many agencies, censuses have become more ubiquitous internationally and better in quality and comprehensiveness. Vital registration is not nearly as comprehensive or accurate, and thus demographers have developed techniques of analyzing often defective census data for the estimation of rates. Nevertheless, the volume of population data available in most countries has augmented continuously, sometimes by means of sample surveys, which have frequently proved to be a more satisfactory means of elucidating population processes than unwieldy, expensive and sometimes politically affected censuses, whose snapshot technique is better as an inventory than for analyzing processes of change. Sample surveys are of course an indispensable tool of a geographer, and many geographers engage in surveys of a demographic nature, partly because census data provide only selected characteristics of populations and therefore only an imperfect picture of human behaviour.

Along with many other social scientists in M.D.C.s in particular, some population geographers have been much attracted by the burgeoning interdisciplinary field of historical demography, reconstructing past populations from deficient data, notably ecclesiastical registers of births, marriages and deaths. They have been used extensively in the analysis of both urban and rural populations, and a much brighter light has been shone on populations in the past to the extent of revising substantially our understanding of the emergence of industrial societies (Wrigley and Schofield, 1981).

As within geography as a whole, population geography has become more quantified, a much larger armoury of statistical and mathematical techniques being used than formerly, when the map was the principal form of analysis (James, 1954). The use of the data matrix for demonstrating numerical distribution within space has led to many studies of spatial association or covariation, described by correlation and regression analysis, but not without difficulties. Quantitative methods have gradually become more sophisticated, and their use has been aided by access to computers, which have been especially valuable in the handling of large data sets. Moreover, automated cartography has enabled the graphic representation of population data that could not otherwise be depicted, as for example the km square data of the 1971 census of Great Britain (C.R.U. and O.P.C.S., 1981), as well as more conventional mapping.

Quantification in population geography has also been associated with the building of models of the population system and the explanation of interactions (in the form of migrations) among regions. The model-building approach is largely confined to M.D.C.s, and does not have a large band of followers, but it is a definite research thrust and has important planning implications (Rees and Wilson, 1977). Rees (1979: 1–3) has explained that the main questions are: How do regional and local populations grow over time? How are they likely to grow? How do we study multi-dimensional populations? How can we predict the scale and direction of movement of people? What influence does migration have on the life expectancies of people living in regions or local areas? Such questions are particularly problematic in the fluctuating demographic, social, economic and political conditions of M.D.C.s.

Academic evolution

Not surprisingly, demography and population studies have flourished and expanded since mid-century. Formerly largely the prerogative of a number of M.D.C.s concerned about their slow population growth—France is the main example—they have been diffused extensively, especially to L.D.C.s which comprise an increasing proportion of the world's demographers. During the 1950s and 1960s demographers looked upon demography as the pure core science of population, essentially statistical and focusing primarily upon fertility and mortality, particularly the former partly because of the great concern shown about the lack of fertility decline in L.D.C.s. The broad and multi-disciplinary field of population studies, linking population with subjects like economics, law, sociology, anthropology, geography, political science, psychology, agriculture, genetics and medicine, was regarded by some demographers as somewhat peripheral. However, the 1970s saw an increased acceptance of population studies, as it was realized, by funding agencies in particular, that the population system cannot be easily dissociated from other systems such as the social, economic and political systems, and that it cannot be divided neatly into a series of discrete elements for separate analysis, as seen in the traditional textbooks of demography. In particular there was a growing realization that fertility control was far from being a universal remedy to the social and economic ills of mankind, and would not find immediate acceptance everywhere in the world. Different countries saw their population problems in different ways. So instead of concentrating upon reproduction, fertility and family planning, topics like population redistribution, women's role in population, the changing family, variations in marriage, differential mortality and government policies came to be seen as vital to our understanding of population processes (Hauser, 1979). In short, it was less a matter of core and periphery, and more a matter of an enlarged appreciation of the complexities of population systems and the diverse contributions of different disciplines to their understanding.

Population geography has been stimulated by this swing towards a more culture-specific orientation in population studies, for population geographers around the world tend to examine issues and problems of countries and regions. As we have mentioned already, these exhibit immense diversity. If one considers, for example, the contrasting cases of Australia, Netherlands, Venezuela, Sri Lanka, Nepal, Uganda and Czechoslovakia, all countries with roughly comparable population sizes but very different demographic characteristics, one recognizes the significance and relevance of the geographic approach. Indeed, much population geography is naturally 'relevant', in that it is of value to population planners and policy-makers, and this has been especially true in the planned economies (Udo, 1976) and in many Third World countries. Some population geographers have devoted their attentions to spatial inequalities such as ethnic and social segregation, regional disparities and movement and have taken an increasingly ideological approach to population problems. The radical or structural approach, which has developed strongly within geography as a whole is also seen within population geography, especially linked to developmental issues. Whatever ideological attitude is taken and no matter how relevant may be the research, population patterns and processes are not easily managed or controlled.

One other trend within population geography, which is seen within demography, population studies and geography in general, is the move from macro- to micro-approaches. Until the 1970s most population studies were macro-orientated, with the main emphasis upon countries, continental regions and the world as a whole, with explanations sought from aggregate data and with grand theories like that of demographic transition. Geography in the 1960s was also going through its phase of spatial analysis and positivism, and the search for universal laws for the human condition. Small wonder that population geography was particularly concerned with broad patterns, and that it profited from the evolution of social physics with such concepts as population potential, rank-size rule, nearest neighbour analysis and measures of concentration. During the 1970s demography, population studies, geography and population geography have all witnessed a swing away from the search for macro-generalizations derived from massive number-crunching towards a recognition of the immense complexity and diversity of processes influencing populations; consequently there have been far more studies based upon small area statistics and individual and household surveys of specific phenomena. The search for universal truths has been replaced or at least complemented by the search for more local understanding, a reflection of the rise of the behavioural approach in geography, evidenced by the work of Pryor (1979) and Chapman and Prothero (1983) on circulation. Population geographers are increasingly concerned with people.

Finally, it has been suggested that population geography is insufficiently based upon its own caucus of solid theory (Woods, 1979). This may well be the case, for population geography has borrowed heavily from population studies and demography. For example, in his volume *Theoretical Population Geography* Woods (1982) writes mostly about models and theories which originated outside of population geography rather than within it, but fails to mention some of the notable exceptions, such as Stewart's (1947) rules concerning the distribution and equilibrium of population, Jefferson's (1939) law of the primate city, Ackerman's (1959) population-resource regions and Zelinsky's (1971 and 1979) hypothesis of mobility transition, all of which have had a major influence upon population geography. Certainly, population geography has been more concerned with empiricism than theory, but over the last thirty years it has demonstrated considerable vitality which gives no indication of waning.

If one looks into a crystal ball, and tries to see how population geography will evolve in the future, one sees further diversification as population geographers look at the specific population problems of their countries and cultures. In Britain, they may be the phenomena of decentralization and de-urbanization of population or the remarkable growth in the proportions of very old (aged 75 and over); in Mozambique and Tanzania, the massive redistribution of population associated with the regrouping of settlement; in Saudi Arabia and many other oil-rich countries of the Middle East, the immense influx of migrant workers from other countries; in Bangladesh, high population pressure and growth in a deltaic environment; in Nepal, high mountain population pressure and out-migration from the mountains; in Mexico, the huge concentration of population in the capital, probably the largest city in the world; in Sudan, the impact of development projects upon population redistribution; in Mauritius, Fiji and many other islands in the Pacific and Indian Oceans and the Caribbean, the effects of pluralism and the rapidity of demographic transition; in Korea, the impact of growth pole policies upon population redistribution; in Indonesia, the effectiveness of transmigration policies; in Poland, the migration of the labour force. The list is endless. And naturally, while many of these problems are distinctive, there are many features of significance for international comparison and contrast: the role of women in population redistribution; the growing numbers of refugees in the less developed countries; the impacts of disasters, natural and human, upon population dislocation; the populations of small islands; the relationship of de-urbanization to low natural increase or decrease; the population problems of frontier colonization; those of regrouping of dispersed rural settlements into villages—in many of which population geographers have a great deal to offer, through their awareness of the relationships between population and the environment and of the spatial organization and behaviour of population.

As the multifarious links between the population system and other systems (social, economic, political, environmental, etc.) are seen to be so complex, it is inevitable that population geography will not stand still, but move in many different directions. We must avoid using Western-based techniques and theories for Eastern-based problems, and vice-versa. The search for general methods and laws has often obscured the complexities of reality.

References

Ackerman, E.A. (1959) Population and natural resources, in P.M. Hauser, and O. Duncan (eds.) *The Study of Population: An Inventory and Appraisal*, Univ. of Chicago Press, Chicago, 621–48.

Beaujeu-Garnier, J. (1956–58) *Géographie de la population*, 2 vols., P.U.F., Paris.

Beaujeu-Garnier, J. (1966) *Geography of Population*, Longman, London.

Chandna, R.C. and Sidhu, M.S. (1980) *Introduction to Population Geography*, Kalyani Publishers, New Delhi, Ludhiana.

Chapman, M. and Prothero, R.M. (eds.) (1983) *Circulation in Third World Countries*, RKP, London.

Clarke, J.I. (1965) *Population Geography*, Pergamon, Oxford.

Clarke, J.I. (1971) *Population Geography and the Developing Countries*, Pergamon, Oxford.

Clarke, J.I. (1973) Population in movement, in M. Chisholm and B. Rodgers (eds.) *Studies in Human Geography*, Heinemann, London, 85–124.

Clarke, J.I. and Fisher, W.B. (eds.) (1972) *Populations of the Middle East and North Africa: A Geographical Approach*, University of London Press, London.

Clarke, J.I., Khogali, M.M. and Kosiński, L.A. (eds.) (forthcoming) *Population and Development Projects in Africa.*

Clarke, J.I. and Kosiński, L.A. (eds.) (1982) *Redistribution of Population in Africa*, Heinemann, London.

C.R.U. and O.P.C.S. (Census Research Unit and Office of Population Censuses and Surveys) (1981) *People in Britain: A Census Atlas*, H.M.S.O., London.

Demko, G.J., Rose, H.M. and Schnell, G.A. (eds.) (1970) *Population Geography: A Reader*, McGraw Hill, New York.

George, P. (1951) *Introduction à l'etude géographique de la population du monde*, INED, Paris.

George, P. (1959) *Questions de la géographie de la population*, P.U.F., Paris.
Gosling, P. and Lim, L.Y.C. (eds.) (1979) *Population Redistribution: Patterns, Policies and Prospects*, UNFPA, Policy Development Studies No. 2, New York.
Griffin, P.F. (ed.) (1970) *Geography of Population: A Teacher's Guide*, Fearon, Palo Alto.
Hauser, P.M. (ed.) (1979) *World Population and Development: Challenges and Prospects*, Syracuse University Press, Syracuse.
James, P.E. (1954) The geographic study of population, in P.E. James and C. Jones (eds.) *American Geography: Inventory and Prospect*, Syracuse University Press, Syracuse, 106–22.
Jefferson, M. (1939) The law of the primate city, *Geographical Review*, **29,** 226–32.
Jones, H.R. (1981) *A Population Geography*, Harper and Row, London.
Kosiński, L.A. (ed.) (1977) *Demographic Developments in Eastern Europe*, Praeger, New York.
Kosiński, L.A. (1970) *The Population of Europe: A Geographical Perspective*, Longman, London.
Kosiński, L.A. and Webb, J.W. (eds.) (1976) *Population at Microscale*, IGU Commission on Population Geography and New Zealand Geographical Society, Christchurch.
Lewis, G.J. (1982) *Human Migration: A Geographical Perspective*, Croom Helm, London.
Noin, D. (1979) *Géographie de la population*, Masson, Paris.
Peters, G.L. and Larkin, R.P. (1979) *Population Geography: Problems, Concepts and Prospects*, Kendall/Hunt, Dubuque, Iowa.
Population Geography (1981), 3, nos. 1 and 2, I.G.U. Special issue on population redistribution in Asia and the Pacific Region.
Pryor, R.J. (ed.) (1979) *Residence History Analysis*, Demography Department, Australian National University, Canberra.
Rees, P.H. (1979) Population geography: a review of model building efforts, *School of Geography, University of Leeds, Working Paper 268.*
Rees, P.H. and Wilson, A.G. (1977) *Spatial Population Analysis*, Arnold, London.
Salt, J. and Clout, H. (eds.) (1976) *Migration in Post-War Europe: Geographical Essays*, Oxford University Press, London.
Trewartha, G.T. (1953) A case for population geography, *Annals of the Association of American Geographers*, **43,** 71–97.
Trewartha, G.T. (1969) *A Geography of Population: World Patterns*, Wiley, New York.
Trewartha, G.T. (1972) *The Less Developed Realm: A Geography of its Population*, John Wiley, New York.
Trewartha, G.T. (ed.) (1978) *The More Developed Realm: A Geography of its Population*, Pergamon, New York.
Udo, R. (1976) *Applied Population Geography: A Survey*, I.G.U. Commission on Population Geography, Edmonton.
U.N. (1981) *Population Distribution Policies in Development Planning*, Dept. of International Economic and Social Affairs, Population Studies, No. 75.
Webb, J.W., Naukkarinen, A. and Kosiński, L.A. (eds.) (1981) *Policies of Population Redistribution*, I.G.U. Commission on Population Geography and Geographical Society of Northern Finland, Oulu.
Wilson, M.G.A. (1968) *Population Geography*, Nelson, Melbourne.
Woods, R. (1979) *Population Analysis in Geography*, Longman, London and New York.
Woods, R. (1982) *Theoretical Population Geography*, Longman, London and New York.
Wrigley, E.A. and Schofield, R.S. (1981) *The Population History of England 1541–1871. A Reconstruction*, Arnold, London.
Zelinsky, W. (1966) *A Prologue to Population Geography*, Prentice-Hall, Englewood Cliffs.
Zelinsky, W. (1971) The hypothesis of the mobility transition, *Geographical Review*, **61,** 219–49.
Zelinsky, W. (1979) The demographic transition: changing patterns of migration, in Institute of Life and I.U.S.S.P., *Population Science in the Service of Mankind*, Conference on Science in the Service of Life, Vienna, 165–89.

2

The Roots of Population Geography

LESZEK A. KOSIŃSKI
(University of Alberta, Canada)

Population geography as a clearly distinguishable sub-discipline of geography appeared in the 1950s and the presidential address given by Trewartha (1953) to the Association of American Geographers is usually quoted as a benchmark in the development of this field of geography, at least in the English-speaking world.

It is the contention of this article that the roots of population geography go deeper into the past, that the antecedent developments can be traced in different countries and in different fields. The appearance of this sub-discipline after the second world war was not sudden, nor was it unexpected. Even the term was used earlier. And certainly it cannot be attributed to one man alone, no matter how distinguished and influential.

In preparing this review, the emphasis was placed upon developments in Germany, France, England, U.S.A. and Russia/U.S.S.R., although interesting and relevant work was being done also in other countries. An early bibliography compiled by Zelinsky (1962) and an even earlier one by Dörries (1940); brief comments on the history of the discipline made by Clarke (1966), Witthauer (1969), Pokshishevskii (1978), Noin (1979) and Kuls (1980); references to population cartography by Kant (1970); maps shown at an exhibition held in the British Museum in 1969 (Kosiński, 1970) are among heterogeneous sources used. Historical reviews by Freeman (1961), Bartels (1968), Buttimer (1971), Claval (1972), Schultz (1980) and of the International Geographical Congresses (I.G.U., 1972) as well as biographies of such influential personalities as F. Ratzel (Wanklyn, 1961), I. Bowman (Martin, 1980) and P.O. Semenov Tian-Shanskii (Lincoln, 1980) were also consulted.

In tracing antecedent developments, six interrelated factors can be considered: (a) population statistics; (b) population mapping; (c) human elements in geography; (d) development of related disciplines; (e) societal concerns and application of research; and (f) institutional framework. The present study concentrates on developments prior to 1953, but in many instances the discussion carries on into more recent years.

Population statistics

Improvements in cartographic standards and introduction of quantitative measures created the need for exact data. These were not readily available in the early part of the nineteenth century, and geographers/cartographers grouped around the leading centre—Geographische Anstalt Justhus Perthes in Gotha, Germany—were forced to engage in their own compilation and evaluation of disparate data sources. This work reached a particularly high level when A.H. Petermann (1822–78), already known for his work in Britain, joined this institution in 1854 (Witthauer, 1969:40). In addition to using these data in compiling maps (mainly to define the size of settlements), the Anstalt began publishing them in serial publications estalished then. Initially they were included in the *Geographisches Jahrbuch* (vols. 1–3, 1866, 1868, 1870), but soon the amount of material exceeded the space available and a new series was created especially for this purpose, although some statistical summaries were still provided by Fabricius and Nessmann in vols. 4–7 (1872–78) of the *Geographisches Jahrbuch.* Later data compiled by other authors were to be found only in the special volumes published in conjunction with an excellent periodical, established by Petermann and initially known as *Geographischen Mitteilungen.* E. Behm and H. Wagner were responsible for the first seven volumes (1872–1882), H. Wagner and A. Supan for volumes 8 and 9 (1891, 1893), A. Supan alone for the next four volumes (1899, 1901, 1904, 1909) and F. Tamss was the author of the fourteenth volume, the last to appear before the second world war (1931). All these volumes had the same title *Die Bevölkerung der Erde*, but not all of them covered the whole world. All appeared in the series *Ergänzungshefte zu Petermanns Mitteilungen.* The geographic and cartographic centre in Gotha survived the cataclysms of two world wars and continues its existence in the German Democratic Republic under the name V.E.B. Hermann Haack. The venerable quarterly *Petermanns Geographische Mitteilungen*, now in its 127th year (1983), still brings new statistical data which might be of interest to geographers and Witthauer was the author of two special volumes published in 1958 and 1969.

These early compilations were most likely the unique source of such data, but in later years as governmental and international agencies were making this kind of information available on a regular basis the need for private sources declined.

The international series included publications by the League of Nations and, after 1945, the United Nations. It was the U.N. Statistical Office which initiated in the 1940s global action aimed at the full world census coverage.

Principles and recommendations for census taking and processing were published and widely diffused, and expectations were quite high at that time. Even though this ambitious objective was not met in 1950 (nor, for that matter in subsequent census rounds), the U.N. agencies continued developing the methods and issuing instructions for censuses and for other demographic data sources, as well as published compilations of raw data in the annual *Demographic Yearbook* (1949–) and reports in the series *Population Studies* (1949–). U.N. Population Division remains an active and influential world centre of research and training and its regional affiliates perform similar roles in various parts of the globe.

Geographers have always been involved in gathering their own population data during field investigations, local and regional surveys, and expeditions of various kinds. In areas with existing government statistics such data only supply additional information; in countries without statistical data sources, the results of private investigations are the only ones available.

An interesting exceptional situation existed for over two decades in the Soviet Union from the 1930s. Although the first modern census was taken in 1897 and during the post-revolutionary period a number of censuses were conducted, this practice was abandoned when the 1939 census revealed the scale of losses caused by the collectivization campaign; the census bureau was purged, data were not available and the census results were published only twenty years later. The Soviet Union was the only European country which had no post-war census and gradual improvement began only in the late 1950s. This vacuum was partially filled in by geographers, who were involved in massive field investigations, called expeditions, which included all types of research representing both physical and human geography and involved population surveys. By necessity, the Soviet geographers were very much aware of the need for demographic data and were involved in activities pursued in other countries by statistical agencies.

It appears that in various parts of the world the early post-war years brought an increasing demand for demographic data and reasonable expectation that these would be made available. This expectation was met and the flow of data has been growing enormously to reach later the present staggering size. If the limitations in the basic demographic information were allegedly an important factor inhibiting the development of both population geography and demography (Zelinsky, 1962: vii), the situation has changed most dramatically since mid-century.

Population mapping

Population mapping is often narrowly conceived as mapping of population distribution only. It is true that the early population maps were mostly concerned with distribution and density—the first atlas of world population was limited to dot maps only (Burgdörfer, 1954) and the world map of population was a focal point for population geographers in the 1950s—but population cartography has had a much broader scope for quite some time (Preuss, 1937; Grothe, 1940).

In fact, among the early maps displayed in the British Museum at a memorable exhibition held in 1969 there were interesting examples of maps portraying various population characteristics such as literacy in France in 1827 by Charles Dupin, crimes in France in 1830 by Adolphe Quetelet, 'improvident marriages' in England and Wales in 1844 by James Fletcher and crimes in England in 1864 by A.M. Guerry. At the same exhibition, references were made to the earlier statistical maps by A.F.W. Crome in the 1780s and A.M. Guerry in 1833 (Kosiński, 1970).

Nevertheless, maps of population distribution and density have occupied an important position in geographical inquiry since the early part of the nineteenth century. In historical overviews one can find references to such landmarks of population geography as the first map of population distribution of France by Frère de Montizon in 1830 (Kant, 1970:8), maps of population density in Ireland in 1837 by H.D. Harness, an Irish census map of 1841, British population maps based on the 1841 and 1851 censuses made by A. Petermann (Freeman, 1966:230–2), the first world map of population distribution by P. Scrope, 1833 (Andrews, 1966) or the early map of population distribution included in the 1842 *Berghaus Physikalischer Atlas* (Witthauer, 1969:62).

In the second half of the previous century, a number of population maps have been published and it is not surprising to find at the turn of the century Hettner's (1900) appeal that a population base map should be treated as a point of departure in any geographical inquiry.

During the inter-war years European geographers were very much preoccupied with such maps and during several International Geographical Congresses, particularly those held in Paris, 1931, in Warsaw, 1934, and Amsterdam, 1938, very lively debates, led mostly by the Swedes Sten de Geer and A. Söderlund and the Britons C.B. Fawcett and H.S. Winterbotham, were later reflected in the terms of reference for the I.G.U. Commission on Population and Rural Settlements, not very active because of war, and indirectly resulted in the creation of the I.G.U. Commission on a World Population Map (Kosiński, 1980). In fact, the theme of population mapping was probably the most important one for geographers interested in population well into the 1960s and a large number of maps, based on the 1950 and 1960 census rounds and following the recommendations of the I.G.U. Commission on a World Population Map, was the outcome of this interest (William-Olsson, 1963; Prothero, 1965; Radó and Zombay, 1971).

Changes of the political map of Europe following the first world war increased interest in ethnic statistics and maps, since the national factor assumed such an importance at that time. Large numbers of maps were produced particularly in those countries which were involved in territorial disputes: Germany, Poland (Gawryszewski, 1969), Hungary and Romania. Balkan ethnic complexities became a subject of a major British study (Wilkinson, 1961). German ethnic maps were numerous and not limited to Germany alone (Kosack, 1937). In some cases, a single map which allegedly played a significant role in political decisions could become a subject of long and acrimonious debate continuing for years. Ethnic mapping was one of the main tasks of secret cartographic centres of Nazi Germany (Kosiński, 1976).

In the post-war years the complexities of multinational societies encouraged Soviet scholars to focus their attentions on ethnic mapping (Bruk and Kozlov, 1961), resulting in the production of a unique global atlas of nationalities (Bruk and Apenchenko, 1974) and a series of more detailed maps.

There is no doubt that a geographic interest in population maps, particularly of population distribution and ethnic characteristics, has a long history. It was certainly well established in the early 1950s and, even if it seems to have abated later, it continues to attract the attention of both geographers and cartographers.

The production of the population atlas of the world initiated by the U.N. in connection with the World Population Year 1974 was abandoned, but another major project of this type begun in the Institute of Ethnography, Soviet Academy of Sciences in the early 1960s might still come to fruition (Bruk, 1970). And nowadays various global, national and regional atlases contain many more population maps than in the past.

Human elements in geography

Carried away by enthusiasm for scientism, geography turned away in the second half of the nineteenth century from human concerns and focused on physical aspects of the discipline. This was particularly true in Germany but also in other countries (Bartels, 1968: 123). But by the end of the nineteenth century the foundations for what was to become a distinct branch of geography were already laid. Friedrich Ratzel (1844–1904) is usually credited with establishing a new sub-discipline, for which he adopted the term *Anthropogeographie*, apparently first used in 1842. His monumental work appeared in two volumes (1882 and 1891, several editions) and was quite influential in attracting attention of scholars to population and its characteristics, but also became a symbol of certain interpretation of the relationship between man and environment. Ratzel is usually depicted as founder of the deterministic school, and if extreme determinism is perhaps clearly identifiable in works of his followers he himself 'apparently saw man and the earth evolving together as a result of reciprocal influences' (Freeman, 1961:76). Through his teaching and his publications he became one of the towering figures in the history of geography (Steinmetzler, 1956; Wanklyn, 1961). Anthropogeography flourished in Germany in the inter-war years and there is a long list of notable scholars representing this geographic discipline, including Schlüter (1919) and Hassinger (1938). Ratzel's concepts were popularized in North America by his enthusiastic pupil Semple (1911).

The other school of thought was the French *géographie humaine*, known for a more moderate approach in interpretation of man-earth relationships (Buttimer, 1971). P. Vidal de la Blache (1845–1918) was a very influential founder of this school and in his posthumously published work a summary of his earlier writings can be found (Vidal de la Blache, 1922). The French school of human geography became well known not only through the works of its principals (Brunhes, 1910; Sorre, 1943–53) and their translations, but also by the works of their followers.

Although they were instrumental in redirecting the attention of fellow geographers to human activities, their critics pointed out later that their emphasis was so much focused on the impact of man on the cultural landscape that population itself was neglected (Trewartha, 1953). Nevertheless, one should remember that even in the late nineteenth century and certainly at the beginning of the present century there were studies dealing specifically with population: in France (Lavasseur, 1889; Vidal de la Blache, 1917), Germany (Ratzel, 1892), U.S.A. (Whitney, 1894), Russia (Voieikov, 1906, 1909; Semenov-Tian-Shanskii, 1910) and various other countries. It is true, however, that on the whole population was neglected and even the term population geography hardly appeared in various major and influential works, the fact much complained about by Trewartha (1953).

A notable exception was Hettner (1927) who recognized *Bevölkerungsgeographie* as a major subdivision of human geography termed *Geographie der Menschen*, and this approach found later expression in the bibliographic review by Dörries (1940).

In Poland the term *demogeografia*, used in reference to a sub-field of human geography, became quite accepted in the inter-war years (Ormicki, 1933) but the international impact of Polish anthropogeographers was negligible. Later the term became reasonably popular in France (Beaujeu-Garnier, 1965).

After the second world war, the earliest, if unsuccessful, attempt to gain acceptance for social geography of population as a separate discipline was made in the 1940s (Kabo, 1947). But it was only the early work of George (1951) and the later very influential statement of Trewartha (1953) which made a major impact upon the emergence and recognition of a new field within geographical studies.

Developments in related disciplines

Population geography is a part of geography but is also closely associated with demography (George, 1950; Beaujeu-Garnier, 1956–58; Ackermann, 1959). There is no doubt that a considerable overlap between the two disciplines exists. Hence, one would expect that the development of demography or lack of it could influence the parallel changes in the population-related field of geography.

Although population studies had a sound theoretical and organizational base during the inter-war years and, as a result of growing interest among scholars, the International Union for the Scientific Study of Population (created in 1928) sponsored a number of international population congresses, it was only after the second world war that interest in demography increased very markedly and the Union became a massive, relatively affluent and influential organization (Lorimer, 1959). The first major post-war population congress was held in Rome in 1954 and some geographers played an important role in this event as well as in subsequent congresses sponsored by this organization.

The mutually supportive relationship existed not only at an international level, but also at a national level. The example of France is particularly instructive, for concern about population issues both before and after the second world war was keenly felt and resulted in special policy measures and funding for research. The Institut National d'Etudes Démographiques (INED) was established in 1945 and the first important book of George (1951) was published in the INED series. He himself was associated with INED and later headed the demographic institute of Paris University (I.D.U.P.).

Germany offers an opposite example. Serious difficulties were experienced after the war by demography, which previously had been uncomfortably closely related to Nazi doctrines and policies (Schubnell, 1959:207). Very likely these problems were also instrumental in the marked decline of population studies undertaken by geographers; the first textbooks in population geography appeared here much later than in other European countries and this applies to both East (Weber and Benthien, 1976) and West Germany (Kuls, 1978). It is fair to say, however, that in West Germany geography of population was earlier defined by Schöller (1968) or, as part of social geography, by Ruppert and Schaffer (1969). Much earlier, Nellner (1953) dealt with the terminology of the discipline.

The Soviet Union provides an example of still another relationship. An early and impressive growth of population geography in that country was undoubtedly related to the non-existence of demography, which recovered from the purges of the 1930s only some thirty years later (Besemeres, 1980:5). Even today, however, population geographers who managed to occupy the empty niche, are probably in the strongest position among the students of population.

Societal needs

Collections and rather rudimentary interpretations of population data at a local or regional scale, for the use of emerging state administration, were made from the late eighteenth century. These can hardly be defined as works in population geography, but they certainly reflected a need felt by politicians and administrators to have a better base for their decisions and day-to-day actions.

In the inter-war years different practical applications of population studies were also attempted. Above all, ethnic maps and the knowledge of ethnic patterns were essential at a time when European boundaries were changed (Bowman, 1921). They are usually classified as part of political geography, although one could claim that they did represent spatial analyses of population patterns which are a recognized domain of population geography.

The situation changed substantially when regional and urban planning were introduced and the need for data and basic research increased. Post-war reconstruction and acceptance of planning created an atmosphere conducive for the development of an academic discipline which could expect to contribute to the solution of practical problems.

Not surprisingly, many geographers went into planning, and others cooperated with planning agencies by engaging in applied research on various aspects of the physical and social environment, including population. It was precisely in the early 1950s when this interaction between academia and government was growing, and it is not unreasonable to suggest that it has contributed to the emergence of a specialized sub-discipline with clear applied potential.

Institutional framework

One of the indicators, or perhaps even causal factors, in the development of an academic discipline, is the creation of an institutional framework. There seems to be little doubt that it was true when development of modern geography was taking place. The situation is somewhat different when one looks at a sub-discipline. After all, it would be unreasonable to expect the emergence of major research or teaching units devoted exclusively to population geography. Some institutional framework has been created, however, and undoubtedly its emergence was indicative of growing interest and increasing vitality of the area of study.

These developments were taking place at both international and national levels and could be observed in two areas at least–professional associations and teaching institutions.

The activities of the International Geographical Union in relation to population geography have been recently described elsewhere (Kosiński,

1980) so they are only briefly summarized here. It appears that international commissions dealing with various population issues were established in 1891 (emigration), 1928 (settlement), 1931 (overpopulation) and 1934 (population and rural settlement). They were responsible for generating interest among geographers and provided fora for discussions during and between the congresses, but their effectiveness varied and the second world war interrupted their activities. The first post-war congress held in Lisbon, 1949 accepted recommendations of the secretary of the previous commission, P. Gourou (France), and the proposals made at the congress by A.G. Ogilvie (U.K.), and set up a Commission for the Study of Population Problems chaired initially by C.B. Fawcett (U.K.) and later by A.G. Ogilvie. The initiative of the Commission, among whose members was G.T. Trewartha (U.S.A.), met with limited response, and in fact the Washington Congress, 1952 did not renew the mandate of the Commission despite great hopes that close cooperation could be established with the United Nations and the expertise of geographers used in population mapping projects (Ogilvie, 1952). It was four years later in Rio de Janeiro that a new special commission under W. William-Olsson was appointed to investigate the questions of a world population map in conjunction with the approaching 1960 round of censuses. The commission adopted the dot method, first developed by Sten de Geer at the beginning of the present century. All subsequent congresses recognized the need for population-orientated commissions and they became an ever present feature of the international geographical life, chaired in turn by a Swede (W. William-Olsson, 1956–64), a Briton (R.M. Prothero, 1964–72), a Canadian (L.A. Kosiński, 1972–80) and another Briton (J.I. Clarke, 1980–). The names of the commissions, their terms of reference, orientation and level of activity changed over time, but their impact on growth of the discipline was undoubtedly quite considerable, as can be seen in the role played by various individuals associated over the years with the commissions, and the number and quality of publications resulting from various projects sponsored by these commissions.

At a national level one should note the emergence of working groups and interest groups, usually existing within national geographic associations. Probably the earliest was the Commission for Population and Urban Geography attached to the Moscow branch of the Geographical Association of the U.S.S.R., established in 1945 and existing ever since (Khorev, 1959, 1962). As Melezin (1963) pointed out, although the commission initially focused its attention on urban geography, from the very beginning it became a forum for discussing both theoretical and empirical papers and sponsored a number of volumes which were appearing in the series *Voprosy Geografii*. The growing interest in this area of study was reflected in national conferences on population geography, the first taking place in 1962, when a bibliography of Soviet population geography for the years 1955–1961 was compiled by

Khorev (1962). Even earlier, an extensive discussion of the Russian and Soviet population geography appeared in Polish (Kosiński, 1958).

The idea of creating similar interest groups was later adopted in other countries, including the Population Geography Study Group of the Institute of British Geographers (1963–), the Population Geography Interest Group of the Association of American Geographers (1980–), and the Commission de Géographie de la Population du Comité National de Géographie de la France.

Reference should also be made to various population-related courses or research projects, gradually introduced during recent decades. A survey taken in the early 1970s showed that although in many universities population geography courses were routinely offered, in others population was incorporated into different courses but no specialized courses were listed in the curriculum (Hansen and Kosiński, 1973). This survey was made, however, at a stage when population geography was fairly well established. The situation was quite different in the early post-war years. At that time, courses in human or cultural geography were quite frequent, but population geography was hardly ever taught as a separate subject.

Here the credit must be given to Soviet geographers who introduced population geography courses as early as 1947 at Moscow University (Kovalev, 1952). The man responsible for this innovation was Kabo, who not only tried to evoke interest in similar courses elsewhere (Kabo, 1947), but at the same time argued for the need to recognize this field of inquiry as a separate sub-discipline of geography. This was not accepted, although population geography enjoys a very special status within the all-embracing 'economic geography' (Pokshishevskii, 1978:33).

The first textbooks on population geography appeared in the Soviet Union in 1946 (Lyalikov, 1946), in France in 1951 (George, 1951), in Britain and the U.S.A. in 1966 (Clarke, 1966; Zelinsky, 1966). Major specialized bibliographies were published in Germany (Dörries, 1940), U.S.A. (Zelinsky, 1962) and U.S.S.R. (Khorev, 1962).

It seems that during the first post-war decade there was a considerable interest in creating an international forum which could accommodate interests of population geographers. At a national level they were in turn creating an infrastructure for the emergence of a new specialized sub-discipline by introducing courses, preparing or publishing textbooks and arguing for the need to give greater recognition to this area of geographical inquiry.

Conclusion

Various developments described above were increasing the awareness of and the need for a specialized sub-discipline within geography. Combinations of factors were admittedly different, and the situation was not the same in various countries.

Germany had an early start and impressive tradition but the events of the Nazi era created a deep shock felt also by the academia, and as a result the post-war developments, now in two separate German states, were considerably delayed as compared to other countries. Nevertheless, there is a new vitality and further developments can be expected (Schöller, 1968; Kuls, 1980).

In France the development was perhaps the most organic, from the early beginnings of *géographie humaine* to relatively early formulations of population geography in the 1950s, with impressive and continuous literature on the subject (George, 1951, 1959; Beaujeu-Garnier, 1956–58, 1965; Noin, 1979). Emergence and growth of population geography was parallel to and closely associated with that of demography.

British traditions were of a different kind. There was considerable experience in population mapping and there was a close relationship with urban and regional planning in that country. In the early post-war years British teaching had a strong impact upon development of population geography in former colonial countries, and British geographers continued to play an important role in the international geographical life; most recently, the largest number of new textbooks have appeared here.

The United States were in the early years very much influenced by European tendencies (James, 1954: 110), but even in the 1920s new concepts were appearing which were later incorporated in the body of geographical theory (Aurousseau, 1923). The enormous upsurge in post-war American geography was felt by various sub-disciplines and new directions of research originated here during the last three decades. Not surprisingly, it was in the U.S.A. that an appeal for a new population geography was launched by Trewartha (1953), an appeal which is now considered a milestone in the development of this area of studies not only in the English-speaking countries but also elsewhere.

Soviet scholarship was isolated from developments in other parts of the world for quite some time. Although the early beginnings in population studies were promising, the domination of extremists in academic geography during the inter-war years was only gradually overcome after the second world war (Melezin, 1963). This restricted the chances for the development of human geography but, on the other hand, the weakness of demography provided the niche which Soviet population geographers were able to exploit. As a result the post-war years witnessed an impressive growth of an area of study, which is, however, denied the position of independent discipline, although in terms of the output, number of practitioners and the early start, it compares favourably with other countries (Pokshishevskii, 1978).

Population geography as a clearly separate field of geographical inquiry seems to have withstood the proof of time since the first attempts in the nineteenth century, the seminal study of Ratzel and the early post-war appeals by Kabo, George and Trewartha.

References

Ackermann, E.A. (1959) Geography and demography, in P.M. Hauser and O.D. Duncan (eds.) *The Study of Population: An Inventory and Appraisal*, Univ. of Chicago Press, Chicago, 717–27.
Andrews, J.H. (1966) An early world population map, *Geographical Review*, **41,** 447–8.
Aurousseau, M. (1923) The geographic study of population groups, *Geographical Review*, **13,** 266–82.
Bartels, D. (1968) *Zur wissenschaftstheoretischen Grundlegung einer Geographie des Menschen*, Geographische Zeitschrift Beihefte, Steiner, Wiesbaden.
Beaujeu-Garnier, J. (1956–58) *Géographie de la population*, Librairie de Médicis, Paris, 2 vols. English abridged translation *Geography of Population*, Longman, London.
Beaujeu-Garnier, J. (1965) *Trois milliards d'hommes, traité de démogéographie*, Hachette, Paris. Second edition 1969.
Besemeres, J.F. (1980) *Socialist Population Politics*, M.E. Sharpe, White Plains.
Bowman, I. (1921) *The New World: Problems in Political Geography*, World Book Company, New York. Subsequent editions in 1923, 1924, 1928.
Bruk, S.I. (1970) Atlas naselenya mira [Atlas of world population], *Sovietskaia Etnografia*, no. 1, 111–22.
Bruk, S.I. and Apenchenko, V.S. (eds.) (1974) *Atlas Narodov Mira* [Atlas of the nations], GUGK, Moskva.
Bruk, S.I. and Kozlov, V.I. (1961) Osnovnyie problemi etnicheskoi kartografii [Basic issues in ethnic cartography], *Sovietskaia Kartografia*, no. 5, 9–26.
Brunhes, J. (1910) *La géographie humaine: Essai de classification positive*, Alcan, Paris. Second revised edition in 1912, several later editions. The English translation of the second edition ed. by I. Bowman and R.E. Dodge in 1920. The abridged version by Mme M. Jean-Brunhes Delamarre and P. Deffontaines in Paris 1947, English translation in London, 1952.
Burgdörfer, F. (1954) *Welt-Bevölkerung Atlas: Verteilung der Bevölkerung der Erde um das Jahr 1950*, Falk, Hamburg.
Buttimer, A. (1971) *Society and Milieu in the French Geographic Tradition*, Rand McNally, Chicago.
Claval, P. (1972) *La pensée géographique: Introduction à son histoire*, Société d'Edition d'Enseignement Supérieur, Paris.
Clarke, J.I. (1966) *Population Geography*, Pergamon, Oxford, Several reprints. Second edition 1972.
Dōrries, H. (1940) Siedlungs- und Bevölkerungsgeographie (1908–1938), *Geographisches Jahrbuch*, **55,** 3–380.
Freeman, T.W. (1961) *A Hundred Years of Geography*, London, Duckworth. American edition by Aldine, Chicago in 1962. Several printings.
Gawryszewski, A. (1969) *Polskie Mapy Narodowościowe, Wyznaniowe i Językowe: Bibliografia 1827–1967*, [Polish ethnic, religious and linguistic Maps: Bibliography 1827–1967], Dokumentacja Geograficzna No. 4, Warszawa.
George, P. (1950) Géographie de la population et démographie, *Population*, **5,** 291–300.
George, P. (1951) *Introduction à l'étude géographique de la population du monde*, Presses Universitaires de France, Paris.
George, P. (1959) *Questions de géographie de la population*, Presses Universitaires de France, Paris.
Grothe, H. (1940) Die Möglichkeiten kartographischer Darstellung der Wanderungsbewegung, *Archiv für Wanderungswesen*, **17,** 85–8.
Hansen, J. Chr. and Kosiński, L.A. (1973) *Population Geography 1973*, I.G.U. Commission on Population Geography, Edmonton.
Hassinger, H. (1938) *Die Geographie der Menschen (Anthropogeographie)*, Handbuch der Geographischen Wissenschaft, vol. 2, Potsdam.
Hettner, A. (1900) Über bevölkerungs-statistischen Grundkarten, *Geographische Zeitschrift*, **6,** 185–93 (enclosed is a map by C. Uhlig with his text, Fig. 3, 192–3).
Hettner, A. (1927) *Die Geographie, ihre Geschichte, ihr Wesen und ihre Methoden*, Ferdinand Hirt, Breslau. New revised edition by H. Schmitthenner 1947.

IGU (1972) *Geography through a Century of International Congresses*, International Geographical Union, Commission on History of Geographic Thought, Caen.

James, P.E. (1954) The geographic study of population, in P.E. James and C.F. Jones (eds.) *American Geography: Inventory and Prospects*, Syracuse University Press, Syracuse, 106–22.

Kabo, R.M. (1947) Prioroda i chelovek v ikh vzaimnykh otnosheniakh kak predmet sotsialno-kulturnoi geografii [Nature and man in their inter-relationship as an object of socio-cultural geography], *Voprosy Geografii*, **5**, 1–28.

Kant, E. (1970) *Über die ersten absoluten Punktkarten der Bevölkerungsverteilung*, Lund Studies in Geography B, 36.

Khorev, B.S. (1959) Obzor raboty Komisii Geografii Naselenia i Gorodov Moskovskogo Filiala Geograficheskogo Obshchestva Soiuza SSSR, 1945–1957 [Work of the Commission on Population and Urban Geography of the Moscow Branch, Geographical Association of USSR, 1945–1957] *Voprosy Geografii*, **45**, 227–45.

Khorev, B.S. (1962) Sovietskaia literatura po geografii naselenia i smezhnym disciplinam (1951–1961) [Soviet literature on geography of population and related disciplines], *Materialy I Mezhduvedomstvennogo Soveshchania po Geografii Naselenia* (Ianvar-Fevral 1962), vol. 6, Moskva-Leningrad, 28–114.

Kosack, H.P. (1937) Ein Beitrag zur Metodik der Bevölkerungskarte. Nationalitätenkarte von Bulgarien, *Zeitschrift der Gesellschaft für Erdkunde zu Berlin*, **36**, 348–72.

Kosiński, L.A. (1958) Radziecka geografia zaludnienia i osadnictwa [Soviet geography of population and settlements], *Przegląd Zagranicznej Literatury Zagranicznej*, **1**, 1–76.

Kosiński, L.A. (1970) Exhibit of early distribution maps in the British Museum, *Geographical Review*, **60**, 267–69.

Kosiński, L.A. (1976) Secret German war sources for population study of East-Central Europe and Soviet Union, *East European Quarterly*, **10**, 21–34.

Kosiński, L.A. (1980) Population geography and the International Geographical Union, *Population Geography*, **2**, 1–20.

Kovalev, S.A. (1952) *Geografia Naselenia v Moskovskom Universitie tie* [Population geography in Moscow University], Moskovskii Gosudarstviennyi Universitiet, Moskva.

Kuls, W. (1978) *Probleme der Bevölkerungsgeographie*, Wege der Forschung 468, Darmstadt.

Kuls, W. (1980) *Bevölkerungsgeographie: eine Einfuhrung*, B.G. Teubner, Stuttgart.

Levasseur, E. (1889) *La population française*, Rousseau, Paris.

Lincoln, W.B. (1980) *Petr Petrovich Semenov-Tien-Shanskii: The Life of a Russian Geographer*, Oriental Research Partners, Newtonville.

Lorimer, F. (1959) The development of demography, in P.M. Hauser and O.D. Duncan (eds.) *The Study of Population: An Inventory and Appraisal*, Univ. of Chicago Press, Chicago, 124–79.

Lyalikov, N.I. (1946) *Geografia Naselenia SSSR* [Population geography in USSR], Zaochnyi Kreditno-Ekonomicheskii Institut, Moskva.

Martin, G.J. (1980) *The Life and Thought of Isaiah Bowman*, Archon Books, Hamden.

Melezin, A. (1963) Trends and issues in the Soviet geography of population, *Annals of the Association of American Geographers*, **53**, 144–60.

Nellner, W. (1953) Bevölkerungsgeographische und bevölkerungsstatistische Grundbegriffe, *Geographisches Taschenbuch*, 459–70.

Noin, D. (1979) *Géographie de la population*, Masson, Paris.

Ogilvie, A.G. (1952) *Report of the Commission for the Study of Population Problems*, prepared for the International Geographical Congress 1952, Constable, Edinburgh.

Ormicki, W. (1933) Regionalizm demogeograficzny Polski [Demogeographic regionalism of Poland], *Wiadomości Geograficzne*, 3/5.

Pokshishevskii, V.V. (1978) *Naselenie i Geografia* [Population and Geography], Mysl, Moskva.

Preuss, W. (1937) Über Bevölkerungskarten: Darstellung und Verteilung, Dichte, Entwicklung und Bevegung, *Allgemeine Vermessungsnachrichten*, 453–63 and 479–83.

Prothero, R.M. (1965) *Catalogue of an Exhibition of Maps Presented by the IGU Commission on Population Geography and Cartography of World Population*, World Population Congress, Belgrade.

Radó, S. and Zombay P. (1971) *Bibliography of Maps Showing Distribution by Dotting Method*, National Office of Lands and Mapping of the Hungarian People's Republic, Budapest.

Ratzel, F. (1882–1892) *Anthropo-Geographie oder Grundzüge der Anwendung der Erdkunde auf die*

Geschichte, Engelhorn, Stuttgart. First edition 1882, several subsequent editions in 1899, 1909, 1921 etc. *Anthropogeographie. 2. Teil. Die geographische Verbreitung der Menschen*, Engelhorn, Stuttgart. First edition 1891, second edition 1912.

Ruppert, K. und Schaffer, F. (1969) Zur Konzeption der Sozialgeographie, *Geographische Rundschau*, **21**, 205–14.

Schlüter, O. (1919) *Die Stellung der Geographie des Menschen in der Erdkundlichen Wissenschaft*, Berlin.

Schöller, P. (1968) Leitbegriffe zur Charakterisierung von Sozialräumen, in K. Ruppert (ed.) *Zum Standort der Sozialgeographie*, Münchner Studien zur Sozial- und Wirtschaftsgeographie, **4**, 177–84.

Schubnell, H. (1959) Demography in Germany, in P.M. Hauser and O.D. Duncan (eds.) *The Study of Population: An Inventory and Appraisal*, Univ. of Chicago Press, Chicago, 203–16.

Schultz, H.-D. (1980) *Die deutschsprachige Geographie von 1800 bis 1970: ein Beitrag zur Geschichte ihrer Methodologie*, Abhandlungen des Geographischen Instituts, Anthropogeographie Bd. 29, Berlin.

Semenov-Tian-Shanskii, P.P. (1910) *Gorod i Derevnia v Europeiskoi Rosii* [Town and country in European Russia], Zapiski Russkogo Geograficheskogo Obshchestva vol. 10, Petersburg.

Semple, E.C. (1911) *Influences of Geographic Environment (on the Basis of Ratzel's System of Anthropology)*, New York.

Sorre, M. (1943–53) *Les fondements de la géographie humaine*, Armand Colin, Paris, 3 vols., 1943, 1948, 1953.

Steinmetzler, J. (1956) *Die Anthropogeographie Friedrich Ratzels und ihre ideengeschichtliche Wurzeln*, Bonner Geographische Abhandlungen 19, Bonn.

Trewartha, G.T. (1953) The case for population geography, *Annals of the Association of American Geographers*, **43**, 71–97.

Vidal de la Blache, P. (1917) La répartition des hommes sur le globe, *Annales de Géographie*, **26**, 81–9 and 241–54.

Vidal de la Blache, P. (1922) *Principes de géographie humaine*, Armand Colin, Paris. English translation *Principles of Human Geography* ed. by E. de Martonne, Holt, New York, 1926.

Voieikov, A.I. (1906) Razpredelenie naselenia zemli v zavisimosti ot prirodnykh uslovii i deiatelnosti cheloveka [Distribution of world population in relation to natural environment and human activity], *Izvestia Russkogo Geograficheskogo Obshchestva*, **42**, 649–782.

Voieikov, A.I. (1909) Lindnost selenii Ievropeiskoi Rosii i Zapadnoi Sibiri [Population of settlements in European Russia and Western Siberia], *Izvestia Russkogo Geograficheskogo Obshchestva*, **45**, 21–7.

Wanklyn, H. (1961) *Friedrich Ratzel: A Biographic Memoir and Bibliography*, University Press, Cambridge.

Weber, E. and Benthien, B. (1976) *Einführung in die Bevölkerungs-und Siedlungsgeographie*, VEB Hermann Haack, Gotha-Leipzig.

Whitney, J.D. (1894) *The United States, Supplement 1, Population: Immigration*, Boston.

Wilkinson, H.R. (1951) *Maps and Politics: A Review of the Ethnographic Cartography of Macedonia*, Liverpool University Press, Liverpool.

William-Olsson, W. (1963) The commission on a world population map: history, activities and recommendations, *Geografiska Annaler*, **45**, 243–50.

Witthauer, K. (1958) *Die Bevölkerung der Erde: Verteilung und Dynamik*, VEB H. Haack, Gotha.

Witthauer, K. (1969) *Verteilung und Dynamik der Erdebevölkerung*, VEB H. Haack, Gotha.

Zelinsky, W. (1962) *A Bibliographic Guide to Population Geography*, Univ. of Chicago, Department of Geography, Research Paper No. 80, Chicago.

Zekinsky, W. (1966) *A Prologue to Population Geography*, Prentice-Hall, Englewood Cliffs.

3

Methodological Problems in Population Geography

ROBIN J. PRYOR
(Numurkah, Victoria, Australia)

Introduction

This chapter provides an overview of some of the methodological problems of population geography, but it is important to note at the outset that theory and methodology cannot be separated completely: differing philosophies or theories have differing methodological consequences. Similarly, the prevailing definition and scope of this branch of social science has implications for methodology. It is assumed here that population geography deals with the analysis and explanation of interrelationships between population phenomena and the geographic character of places as both vary through time and space. Population phenomena include the dynamics of population distribution, urban/rural location, density and growth (or decline); mortality, fertility, and migration; and structural characteristics including age, sex, ethnicity, marital status, economic composition, nationality, and religion.

These foci, and problems and policy issues related to them, not the availability of census or other statistical data, should define the methodology of research in population as in other sub-fields of human geography. This needs to be stressed, because the accumulation of data and the availability of 'number-crunching' computer hardware and software have far outstripped our ability to explain underlying social processes and develop even culture-specific theories (let alone more general hypotheses, laws and paradigms). Finally, it is necessary to recognize the differing ways geographers have been 'socialized' to look at the world. The logical positivist scientific view dominated the social sciences in the 1950s and 1960s, emphasizing quantification, model building, hypothesis testing, pattern seeking and scientific method. Appropriate methodology stressed statistical techniques and sophisticated cartographic presentation. The 1970s and 1980s have seen a questioning of economic models of human behaviour and scientific geography, and the emergence of humanistic and hermeneutic schools of thought: here the emphasis is on 'letting the data speak for themselves' (Gould, 1981), on interpretation and empathy with the subjects of causal explanation (see the objects of descriptive analysis). Rather than primarily seeking patterns of regularity and system-wide analyses, the view that meaning derives from individual consciousness has led to emphasis on differences, phenomenology and intuitive perceptions of places; this distinction has become apparent even in Soviet population geography (Gol'ts, 1981). It may be argued that these are complementary rather than mutually exclusive views of reality, but methodological concerns necessarily have become 'softer', as suggested by the five aspects discussed below.

Data availability and quality

Inaccuracy, non-comparability and high rates of response refusals are greater problems than total data gaps in the 1980s. In the past, population research was sometimes confined to topics on which data were readily available; now, at least some researchers have the luxury of seeking the most appropriate data on particular problems and to test hypotheses, but the added problem of integrating diverse types of data. In a study of internal migration in Malaysia, the writer was able to analyze the volume and patterns of population movements using census data, sample surveys designed for other purposes but incorporating mobility characteristics, a specially devised mobility survey, and national registration data on changes of address on the electoral roll and the national identity card system (Pryor, 1974). Despite the plethora of data, however, only the mobility survey was designed and executed to accord with the researcher's own theoretical orientation. Financial limitations confined the survey to one state, precluding the analysis of national patterns and comparisons with other migration data; and there are no methods available for integrating such diverse data sets.

Some countries still have very limited statistics but the situation has changed rapidly through the last decade as United Nations funding and expertise have been made available to developing countries. Skilled personnel and data processing systems are now widely available, but small Pacific Island countries and the Peoples Republic of China provide examples of inadequate data availability at the opposite extremes of demographic size. The main problem facing small island countries is the shortage of skilled manpower for census-taking, tabulation, analysis and report-writing; there is also concern about the use of inappropriate theoretical models, survey schedules and tabulation procedures imported from other (usually Western industrial) cultures.

China, despite its present population of over 1,000 million and its rich cultural history, was until very recently isolated from the international demographic community: very limited census data have been collected and published this century (hopefully to be rectified by the 1982 census). Little has been released for primary let alone secondary analysis; data sources are scattered, series incomplete, and sources are often informal, anonymous and virtually unverifiable. Central censorship is extensive, and varies by region as well as over time; and vital registration data range from non-random to haphazard. The political climate of the Leap Forward, Cultural Revolution and food crisis eras combined major demographic impact (e.g. famines and massive relocations) with halts in data collection or dissemination, and manipulation of the limited data for ideological purposes (Aird, 1982). These problems of availability and quality of population data are still typical of a number of developing countries and a few others in the East European bloc.

There are data collection problems in small, poor and geographically fragmented populations, as among the Indonesian islands, and in regions broken by fiords, swamps, mountain or jungle terrain. Different research strategies are needed in small isolated communities and in large urban centres (Burnley *et al.*, 1980). In some sparsely settled shires and townships of the state of Victoria (Australia), very small numbers of women in the reproductive years and/or children under five years of age, mean that calculated fertility rates may be less meaningful than those based on much larger populations in metropolitan Melbourne.

Some inadequacies in population data are due to sampling error, and some to non-sampling error—the latter is usually more substantial and more difficult to correct by weighting procedures; others are due to the high costs of ensuring complete census enumeration or constantly monitoring vital registration systems. The main sources of inaccuracy in population data include (a) difficulties of physical access to some regions; (b) the mobility of some aboriginal or nomadic groups and seasonal workers; (c) security problems and religious or other taboos restricting access to some areas or population sub-groups; (d) ignorance of the purpose and value of census and registration systems, or conversely the desire to avoid documentation at some point (e.g. illegal immigrants); (e) resentment of the supposed invasion of privacy and civil liberties, and suspicion that the data will not remain confidential but can be accessed by other government departments such as the taxation office; (f) intentional or accidental false statements of age, occupation or location at a previous census date; (g) language problems in immigrant districts and areas with low functional literacy; and (h) the timing of census enumeration or surveys in areas affected by natural disaster, seasonality of labour or the influx of holiday makers, pilgrims, or short-term guest workers.

Because of these problems, census under-enumeration of 4–5 per cent is typical, and even higher in some developing countries or lagging regions (Casley and Lury, 1981). The Australian census has redefined aboriginal persons (or allowed them to define themselves) several times over recent censuses, creating almost insurmountable problems of non-comparability; and the *de jure/de facto* bases of census and survey enumeration cause problems of inter-regional and intercensal comparison where no consistency has been accepted in the definition of residential location.

Areal units and scale problems

The standardization of population terms, statistical techniques, and the definition of areal units is important for research both within and between countries. Changing definitions of urban/rural, the growth or decline of populations across size or density thresholds, and alterations in local, regional or national political boundaries all cause major difficulties for the comparison of areas over time. Areas defined for purposes of government administration are rarely the most appropriate for the analysis of functional regions in terms of population characteristics and interrelationships. Standardization of areal units has improved in recent years, but international comparative studies still require many exceptions and qualifications to be noted (U.N., E.C.E., 1979: 50ff, 175ff). Towns (and rural districts) vary considerably in social and economic character from one culture to another, and from one period to another. It is thus understandable but somewhat frustrating in comparative research that countries in the Asia-Pacific region have been free to accept an ESCAP recommendation 'that each country should define urban and rural in accordance with the country's planning and administrative needs' (U.N., ESCAP, 1982:9).

This problem of urban/rural definition has relevance also on the fringes of a rapidly growing city where urban residence and function have spilled far beyond the political and administrative bounds of the metropolitan area; various remedies in data collection and 'flexible' or moving-boundary area definitions have been attempted. This is a specific example of the general problems of (i) choosing areas for use in the analysis of population (e.g. the choice between homogeneous and nodal regions); (ii) the implied immobility of population at some arbitrary time of data collection (Clarke and Rhind, 1976); and (iii) the fact that development processes differentially reflect and affect smaller/larger, rural/urban, and growing/declining populations and regions. Kosiński (1976) has discussed the impact of administrative divisions, and of changes in these areal units, on the availability and content of population data for eight countries of East-Central Europe.

The territorial size of statistical units is a major constraint in geographical analyses. Inferences as to processes derived from pattern analysis are not independent of the scale of analysis, because a given process is relevant only at a certain scale. Hence the need for appropriate areal units in the analysis of international migration, inter-province migration, intra-urban mobility, and rural-urban circulation; and if the focus of attention is the spatial behaviour of an individual or family, census data collection areas may be irrelevant. Further, conclusions and explanations derived from studies at one scale should not be expected to apply equally to studies at another scale: demographic transition has been studied at the national level but is unlikely to be analyzed effectively at the county level due to the intervention of many local and idiosyncratic variations at this scale.

In terms of the differing theoretical perspectives mentioned in the introduction to this chapter, it is interesting to note that at the macro-level, population geographers tend to work from a logical positivist viewpoint, stressing statistical analysis, and search for generalizations across large areal units; it is now becoming apparent that such generalizations can at best be only culture-specific, and that local variations are not aberrations but a reflection of the scale of enquiry. Those working from a humanistic perspective do so on the meso- (group) or micro- (individual) levels of analysis, not just because of the complexity and weight of numbers, but because the theoretical and hence the methodological focus is different. The problem remains as to how to integrate various scales of enquiry. Jones (1980:256) has stressed 'how significant indeterminacy is at the micro-level, and that it is no more than hidden statistically at the macro-level. If we wish to raise the level of explanation of the latter it can only be done by understanding the former'. One implication is a different approach to data collection, analysis and interpretation, with a movement away from dependence on censuses and vital registration; population geographers are learning from the methods of sociologists and anthropologists, pursuing participant-observer research styles, life history analysis, family reconstitution, tracer surveys of out-migrants, and the continuous monitoring of demographic behaviour; high accuracy is needed in small and highly mobile populations (Pryor, 1979a).

It does not follow, of course, that the 'most useful' results or the 'best explanations' are found only at the finest scale—much depends on problem definition, the validity and reliability of data collection, and further development of scale-appropriate and scale-integrating research procedures.

Structural description versus causal interpretation

Both the description of population structural characteristics and the interpretation of demographic behaviour across space and over time have their place in population geography; the problem is to link satisfactorily the two approaches at a given scale and according to one's theoretical perspective and research focus.

Migration matrix analysis has undergone considerable development in the past decade; Rogers (1980) has developed migration rates and schedules along the lines of those long available for mortality and fertility. Age- and sex-specific migration probabilities are now being built into model multiregional life tables, and policy intervention elements are also being introduced. This signals a significant shift in emphasis even in strongly quantitative approaches, as regional population accounting becomes more sensitive to variations in population structure and policy decisions. There is still a long way to go, however, before progress in understanding locational decision-making and the full range of mobility behaviour is adequately reflected in descriptive and projective models. Similarly, the analysis of fertility, mortality and natural change is underdeveloped from a spatial perspective. The diffusion of demographically innovative behaviour, such as the spread of effective modern contraception, could be pursued simultaneously in terms of spatial and social filtering processes if these were included in research designs.

The demographic transition theory epitomizes some of the methodological problems of concern here: in intention it is heuristic rather than mechanistic, and culture-specific rather than universal, but it has apparently too often been seen as a description (even justification) of 'the ways things are'. The concept was originally based on the lowering and convergence of fertility and mortality rates of European countries late in the nineteenth century. By contrast, countries of South-East Asia, among others, do not replicate European experience at similar levels of urbanization and economic development (Pryor, 1979b: 329). The theory cannot account for some unitary, universal process, but it can provide helpful insights in time- and culture-specific processes of demographic change if its limitations are recognized.

Similar criticisms have been levelled at the mobility transition theory proposed by Zelinsky (1971). Various patterns of population movement supposedly accompany phases of urbanization and demographic transition, but again research indicates a wide diversity of patterns within one region at a point of time. In the Asia-Pacific context, the theory doesn't allow for the typical temporary and circular migrations; the processes of involution by which un- and under-employed migrants are absorbed into urban areas; the roles of the modern/traditional sectors of origin and destination in migratory processes; and it underrates metropolitanization and overstresses international migration (Pryor, 1979b: 329). Again, the answer seems to be a greater attention to the culture-specificity and space-time context of the transition as process.

Causal interpretation in all aspects of population geography requires a new emphasis on processes and behavioural variations, rather than on patterns and 'laws' of spatial interaction. This is in line with the behavioural counter-revolution of the 1970s which seeks understanding and explanation rather than description and generalization: 'data manipulation is an aid to, rather than a part of, explanation' (Johnston, 1982: 125). The challenge in our analyses of population is to move beyond mathematically describing complex spatial patterns, to comprehending the processes involved in their creation; it is relevant to note that this implies a belief in absolute truth in the sense that explanations are assumed to exist even if they are not yet available. One implication is that population model-building should focus on behaviour rather than static structure; another is that population research needs to identify the interrelations between societal processes and individual values, perceptions and preferences; finally, concepts such as distance decay, intervening opportunities and hierarchical filtering, while attempting to honour broad regularities in population patterns, must be seen as secondary to the identification of specific causes of demographic change.

Adequate contextualization is a requirement of population analyses and geographic interpretation (Berdoulay, 1981). This was discussed above in relation to the demographic and mobility transitions. Haggett (1965) developed an analytical framework for the study of regional systems, based on five spatial concepts—movements, networks, nodes, hierarchies, and surfaces. These logical and interesting concepts were never adequately anchored in a specific historical and cultural context, and did not produce any substantial explanation of underlying processes which might give these spatial forms their meaning and value. Much geographical enquiry suffers from this failure to recognize, let alone to call into question, the Western capitalist value system behind many of the patterns and processes analyzed by Anglo-American geographers (and many of their Third World counterparts). We have to learn not only to see the world through the eyes and minds of specific groups of people (Jones, 1980:255), but also consciously to identify their spatial-political-cultural-temporal context, and where necessary to contrast these with alternative views of the world. This contextual emphasis is the key to the concerns of much 'radical geography' (Peet, 1977), and to the growing methodological links between geography and sociology.

Analysis versus synthesis

Both theory formulation and empirical research are dependent on the availability of accurate data, but judging by much of the population geography literature, there is a need for greater methodological emphasis on the relationship of population trends to social and economic change. This relates to the contextualization issue above, but more importantly to the inductive/deductive nature of research models and the appropriateness of multi-factorial methods. Among modern quantitative methods, the statistical approach is broadly inductive, resulting in the culling of generalities from the data, while the mathematical approach is broadly deductive in the sense of producing mathematical statements of population theories or hypotheses, then testing these.

Another way of expressing the analysis/synthesis dichotomy is in terms of causal as against correlational approaches. For example, population growth over the past 200 years may have been too readily correlated with medical improvements. Analysis has been important in identifying one or more associated factors, but a wider ranging, historical approach as well as improved multivariate techniques are necessary to synthesize the many contributing elements and to sort out their relative importance. Even then, it has to be remembered that data manipulation even by the most sophisticated techniques cannot provide explanations but only help define the object of study and discourage premature generalizations. Factor and principal components analysis are techniques widely used in the search for regional synthesis, but like any multivariate techniques they require a number of subjective methodological decisions, and interpretation of results in terms of one's theoretical orientation (for case studies of Malaysian and Philippines development, see Pryor, 1979b, chaps. 9 and 21).

Johnston (1982:124) suggests that explanation requires two levels of analysis which are interlocking and complementary: (i) the configurational, which seeks to discover 'why people did what they did'; and (ii) the immanent, which investigates the dynamic processes that 'produce the environment within which decisions are made'. The cultural and historical contexts (the 'why' and the 'why *here*') are as important as the geographer's traditional emphasis on the spatial manifestations (the 'what' and the 'where') of population phenomena; and the particularities and peculiarities of a local case are as important as the traditional preoccupation with seeking 'laws' of population. To put it another way, the particular and the general have to be held in tension, rather than allowing the pendulum of research to swing to one extreme or the other—'there are no simple formulas to explain the geography of the world's population' (Zelinsky, 1966:24).

Knowledge versus policy orientation

It has already been argued that population dynamics need to replace static, net descriptions; and that there should be closer attention to the relationship of population trends to other pervasive social, economic and political changes. It is a corollary to these viewpoints that population geography should not confine itself to a gazetter approach, to the accumulation of ever more information, nor even to the better comprehension of why things are the way they are in the demographic world. Geographers have never been unaware of the implications and social relevance of their work, but the past decade has seen a welcome sharpening of the debate about international economic disparities, intra-national social inequalities, and the conflicting demands of energy generation and environmental conservation. There is a new concern about the relevance of population research to issues of public interest, and hence a new interest in policies as well as problems. To some extent the debate has been forced on geography and sociology by Marxist thinkers (Peet, 1977). It is also fair to say that other researchers have become more aware of the role of direct policies and the more subtle impact of indirect policies at all levels of government and private business, on the geographic redistribution and social and economic behaviour of people. Part of the contextualization of research in population geography must involve an explicit questioning of the part played by policy makers. The matrix below suggests some relevant areas of investigation:

	Attributes of policies		
Population-related concerns	Intention, direct or indirect	Target or susceptible population	Impact
Fertility			
Mortality			
Migration			
Development			

Studies, for example, of urbanization in Australia, population control in Singapore, the immigration of Filipinos to the U.S.A., ethnic segregation in London and the ageing of the population of the U.K., would each benefit from an investigation of the intention and relative impact of a range of international, national, regional and local policies (for elaboration of the possibilities of policy analysis in migration and development planning see Pryor, 1976, 1979b, and U.N., D.I.E.S.A., 1981). Administrative, social planning, investment, and party political goals and programs, as well as overtly locational policy decisions, have a diverse impact on population patterns and processes at all areal scales; research in population geography requires attention to past, current, and projected policies if our comprehension and explanations are to have improved social relevance.

Conclusion

This chapter could have been written as a 'cook-book' on scientific method as applied to geography, or statistical and mathematical techniques of relevance to spatial-demographic research. But it is the author's conviction that methodology is a function of philosophy as well as of 'data-massaging' technology; of theoretical orientation as well as of data collection; of decisions regarding style of research as well as the selection of specific analytic tools. Our choices of methodology must serve, not replace, our drive to understand and explain human spatial behaviour. Our research techniques have to acknowledge that people occupy a subjective as well as a rational world; that people are not uniformly predictable; that differences between individuals, groups and nations may be small but significant, and generalizations sometimes too abstract to be culturally and temporally valid; and that while our comprehension of population changes will never be complete, holistic and intuitive approaches to spatial behaviour may contribute as much to theory formation and research relevance as exercises in 'number-crunching'—all are needed for one purpose or another.

References

Aird, J. (1982) Population studies and population policy in China, *Population and Development Review*, **8**, 267–98.

Berdoulay, V. (1981) The contextual approach, in D.R. Stoddart (ed.), *Geography, Ideology and Social Concern*, Blackwell, London, 8–16.

Burnley, I.H., Pryor, R.J. and Rowland, D.T. (1980) *Mobility and Community Change in Australia*, University of Queensland Press, St. Lucia.

Casley, D.J. and Lury, D.A. (1981) *Data Collection in Developing Countries*, Clarendon Press, London.

Clarke, J.I. and Rhind, D.W. (1976) The relationship between the size of areal units and the characteristics of population structure, in L.A. Kosiński and J.W. Webb (eds.), *Population at Microscale*, Hamilton, New Zealand, New Zealand Geographical Society, 55–64.

Gol'ts, G.A. (1981) An approach to perfecting models of population movements, *Soviet Geography*, **22**, 81–91.

Gould, P. (1981) Letting the data speak for themselves, *Annals, Association of American Geographers*, **71**, 166–76.

Haggett, P. (1965) *Locational Analysis in Human Geography*, Methuen, London.

Johnston, R.J. (1982) On the nature of Human Geography, *Transactions, Institute of British Geographers*, **7**, 123–5.

Jones, E. (1980) Social Geography, in E.H. Brown (ed.), *Geography Yesterday and Tomorrow*, London, Oxford University Press, 251–62.

Kosiński, L.A. (1976) Impact of administrative divisions upon availability of demographic data: East-Central Europe, in L.A. Kosiński and J.W. Webb (eds.), *Population at Microscale*, New Zealand Geographical Society, Hamilton, New Zealand, 47–54.

Peet, R. (ed.) (1977) *Radical Geography: Alternative Viewpoints on Contemporary Social Issues*, Methuen, London.

Pryor, R.J. (1974) *Spatial Analysis of Internal Migration: West Malaysia*, Geography Department, James Cook University, Townsville.

Pryor, R.J. (ed.) (1976) *Population Redistribution: Policy Research*, Demography Department, Australian National University, Canberra.

Pryor, R.J. (ed.) (1979a) *Residence History Analysis*, Demography Department, Australian National University, Canberra.

Pryor, R.J. (ed.) (1979b) *Migration and Development in South-East Asia: A Demographic Perspective*, Oxford University Press, Kuala Lumpur.

Rogers, A. (1980) *Migration Patterns and Population Redistribution*, International Institute for Applied Systems Analysis, Laxenburg, Austria.

United Nations, Economic Commission for Europe (E.C.E.) (1979) *Labour Supply and Migration in Europe: Demographic Dimensions 1950–1975 and Prospects*, United Nations, New York.

United Nations, Department of International Economic and Social Affairs (D.I.E.S.A.) (1981) *Population Distribution Policies in Development Planning*, United Nations, New York.

United Nations, Economic and Social Commission for Asia and the Pacific (ESCAP) (1982) *Migration, Urbanization and Development in Malaysia*, United Nations, New York.

Zelinsky, W. (1966) *A Prologue to Population Geography*, Prentice-Hall, Englewood Cliffs, N.J.

Zelinsky, W. (1971) The hypothesis of the mobility transition, *Geographical Review*, **61**, 219–49.

4

Space and Population

ROSA ESTER ROSSINI
(University of São Paulo, Brazil)

In almost all fields of knowledge the study of population has been an extremely important element. Although in texts of human geography there is always a chapter concerning population, the way to approach it has changed very much in time and space.

We consider geographical space as an historical product which suffered and still suffers a process of technical and cultural accumulation, and as a consequence presents at each moment the characteristics of the society producing it. It must in no way be seen as a hindrance to human action, as the scenery where men live, for the idea of space as a product cannot be related to the idea of a container, a passive and inert element.

> 'Space as a social product is a process of real production, born from labour, which in turn is nothing else than man's answer to a series of necessities that he must satisfy in order to survive. Thus, the genesis of space is human existence, an essential condition for man to "make history", produce and transform his own space. It is conscious human action that transforms the natural milieu into geographical space' (Carlos, 1979: 27–31).

Geographical space has an eminently social character. Above all it represents a relation between environment and the members of society. Seen as a social product, whose production is continuous and uninterrupted, space is not something ready and finished, but is in perpetual evolution. It is the result of physical matter worked in its totality. It is exclusively dynamic, for evolution never ends, especially because space production is considered a result of human existence, i.e. of human work.

There is a dynamic that is inherent to the general process of production in which population is the agent, the producing element. Population, in this sense, is not a mere abstraction, but a synonym of *society*, of an historical society, in which the elements participate in a differentiated way by

> 'the place they occupy inside the historically determined system of production, by the relations they establish towards the means of production, by the role they play in the organization of work and by the mode and proportion in which they get the part of social wealth available' (Cueva, 1974: 3, 87).

This means a society divided into social classes and not only human groups. Man does not live merely in groups, he is a social being who lives and reproduces himself in society.

Marx sees the process of man's universalization, the becoming human as the transition from the particular to the general, i.e. the constitution of the individual made by the exchange (not as a relation of equality but a social relation) of products for the satisfaction of human necessities. Human production is an uninterrupted process, where the transformation of society derives from concrete social relations and not from ideal ones. Man becomes historical through concrete relations created by himself in and through society. Thus population cannot be treated as an abstraction.

In the same way the causes of spatial distribution, instead of being searched for in natural factors associated to historical ones, as some authors affirm, must be looked for in history and in the social relations that produce it. The physical environment has an ever decreasing role owing to the present level of productive forces. The unequal distribution of population is linked with the unequal process of production deriving from the division of labour that separates city and country. This will define the role of each part of space in general production of men as well as of geographical space.

Geographical space is a humanized space precisely because society produces it and appropriates it, and not because of being inhabited.

We rely on the basic statement that space is a human production and its process of creation and transformation is determined by the mode men produce their existence, i.e. by the actual mode of production and thus

> 'in fact every historical concrete mode of production has its own laws of population, laws that govern it in a historically concrete way. Abstract laws of population exist only for animals and plants as long as men don't intervene historically in these domains' (Marx, 1973:534–5).

Hence each mode of production has its own law of population.

> "This seems quite obvious in what refers to mortality and migrations, whose relations with economy, i.e. with production and distribution of goods and services (values of use), are clear. In what refers to fertility, however, there are other conditions with a social and psychological character that seem to predominate in today's societies. Apparently, the productive activity 'strictu sensu', that is, the production of new human beings is subject to individual choice, influenced only in part by material circumstances. It happens, nevertheless, that the material consequences (economic, social and political) of the level of population reproduction are very significant. Thus, it is necessary not to abandon the hypothesis that the social conditioning of individual choice (mainly in modern societies) follows class interests and so far derives straightly from the global mode of production (and reproduction) of society. In the final analysis, when one verifies that a given population entirety has the same mode of producing and reproducing itself *as a society* (and that is what mode of production means) it necessarily presents a corresponding mode of reproducing itself *as a population*. In a more concrete way, a population entirety integrating a capitalist mode of production establishes relations of producing with given characteristics between the social groups into which it is divided.
>
> Nothing is more likely then that this same population entirety will also establish

characteristical relations of reproduction of itself and that these relations of reproduction (marriage and procreation are among the most important of them) will be linked in a quite complex way and with many mediations, to the relations of production' (Singer, 1982:237).

The mode of production being only one element of the determining totality and determined by it, the process of space production must be analyzed from this totality, that is, the most general category: the economic formation of society.

Hence, if the act of producing is at the same time the act of space production, it is in this direction that the geographer will analyze the process of production: as a social and historical process, producer of geographical space. This doesn't mean that he must abstain from actual and concrete relations which determine and create the laws and the objectives of this mode of production—and this happens at the level of the superstructure (political, ideological, juridical and religious) of the economic formation of the society to which this mode of production belongs.

If the process of production of existence and at the same time the process of production of space are historically determined, the geographical space today, in the case of capitalist countries, has its production determined by the economic formation of the capitalistic society, which is different from, for example, the feudal and the socialist ones.

In this sense, it is necessary to reflect about the way by which the process of production of existence and the process of production of space come about from the point of view of population, which is the agent of the process.

Birth and death are, first of all, biological facts, but they are social facts too. In the case of the capitalistic society, mortality is directly linked with a class conception, conditioned to a great extent by income distribution. Even population movement in space corresponds in general with group movements in social structure.

> 'Now, these group movements are subject to determined laws derived from (a) the mode by which productive activities are distributed (and redistributed) in space; (b) the volume of labour force required by each activity especially localized (something which depends, in its turn from the applied technique, upon the natural resources, etc.); (c) the performance in space of special structure' (Singer, 1982:236).

Thus, population is first seen in the perspective of a class society, and otherwise in the perspective of space production, which it does through the work relation.

Here one must underline however that

> 'labour force is not population, but the working capacity of a given population. This working capacity may have a lowest limit, equal to man's muscular strength, but its highest limit is totally elastic in relation to population reserve: this elasticity is given by capital, by the process of consumption of living labour force, potentiated by dead labour or by accumulated capital' (Oliveira, 1976:16).

At the same time as being a producing population, it is a consumer population to the extent it appropriates this space to provide its necessities.

The consumption of labour's products, however, will be determined by production: private consumption made through dwelling and collective consumption, recreation, transport, sanitation, etc. The access to this consumption is highly unequal, for while the process of production is a collective task, the product of labour process is a private one. This private and unequal appropriation of geographical space produced by the work of society can be seen in the urban scenery with slums and low standard apartments and houses side-by-side with mansions and high standard apartments.

The appropriation of geographical space is made formally by the appropriation of land, but in fact when a capitalist buys a given space he appropriates everything it contains, for example the transportation system, sanitation, education and health facilities, because this portion is inserted in a global space.

From the point of view of the process of production one must consider that the capitalistic production presupposes the expropriation of people, who have only their labour force to sell. Thus, it presupposes a labour market. On the other hand, merchandises produced in the productive process must be purchased, that is, sold and consumed so that production becomes viable. For the full agility of the cycle of capital it is necessary that the capitalist does not leave the process of production to sell his merchandise, and so the process of production creates a whole serial of activities (circulation, distribution and exchange) that links the process of production to that of consumption.

In the capitalist mode of production, industry has the leading role in economy, subordinating, creating and redefining other activities, changing agriculture into just one of its branches. Industry is the basic cell of the productive process. The development of the industrialization process tends to eliminate the fragmented artisan production and to transform the productive process into a serial production, done by machines. Machinery is the material base that makes the utilization of women's and children's work possible.

The capitalist process of production, whose aim is the production of surplus value, presupposes 'continuity' and 'scale production' for its reproduction. Production at a greater scale is necessary to the economy in the conditions of production. Capitalism aims at increasing the productivity of labour, diminishing the cost of the products and the part of the workday dedicated to necessary labour. The question of continuity in the productive process is the characteristic of capitalist production determined by the technical base, and it implies the transformation of the whole cyclic process in its unity, without the interruption of the process (Carlos, 1979:80–1).

These two characteristics tend to increase spatial concentration as they force the integration and deepen the division of labour between the branches of economy, and this deepens the dependency of spatial units uniting them in the general productive process, through spatial division of labour. The concentration of capital and the subsequent spatial concentration of activities in the capitalist mode of production, have a common link. Since the concentration of capital tends to surpass the limits imposed by the industrial technology, spatial concentration also tends to be much greater than that deriving from the technical needs of the productive process.

It is necessary to notice that the tendency to urban overconcentration, understood as concentration of activities and population in one or few units, by harming the rest of the 'urban net', above the requirements of technology, is a contradiction presented by capitalism in developed countries (Britain, France, Italy) as well as in underdeveloped countries (like Brazil).

> 'Urbanization is a phenomenon that cannot be examined in itself, or just in its links with the process of industrialization. In fact, the process comes about in the measure of the emergence and expansion of capital through the process of accumulation. Today's pattern of urbanization is a purely capitalist phenomenon. Urbanization and accumulation are processes derived from the more and more enlarged evolution of the productive process.
>
> The formation of great metropolitan centres derives from the concentration of the productive process and, as a consequence, from the process of accumulation in strategical points of the territory, which commands the process of production through the division of labour between spaces of territory organized in a hierarchy and the expropriation of the surplus produced in these spaces.
>
> Thus, the processes of reproduction of capitalist relations engenders an articulated and dependent system, inherent to the reproduction of the system of production itself' (Carlos, 1979:87–8).

We can make a separation between that part of population objectively building the produced space, which is the living social labour force necessarily embodying the part of accumulation, and that part of population which does not produce space directly.

In the first case, it is necessary to reassert what we have already said: labour that provides (in the process of production) the products necessary to the production of human existence, is at the same time producing space; therefore, it is necessary to think about this production from the point of view of productive forces and their development.

From the point of view of population, the process of development of capitalistic production demands first the expropriation of the means of production of a great part of the population. This majority forms a class which has as its only condition of survival the sale of its labour, i.e. a contingent of 'free men', deprived of their means of production, ready to sell their labour to the capitalist, as the only way to assure their existence.

With the accumulation and the subsequent development of labour's productive forces, grows the force of expansion of capital beyond the technical conditions that the process of production itself allows, rapidly transforming the surplus product into new means of production. However, the absolute variations of capital accumulation express themselves as relative variations of the mass of labour force that can be exploited, what brings about oscillations.

The development of productive forces caused by industrial capitalism has as a result a deep and marked reduction of mortality. In almost all countries, the mortality level today is a third or even less of what was the case before the Industrial Revolution.

> 'In such conditions, reproductive activity—fertility—becomes side by side with migration, the main element in the law of population of any group of population' (Singer, 1982:241–2).

In what concerns the class of proletarians, what happens is that capital and its subsequent enlarged reproduction constantly reproduces two phenomena:

—the active population, that works for the production of capital;

—an available population that is not absorbed by capital and that forms the industrial reserve army.

The system needs great masses of available men so that they can be used at decisive moments without the scale of production being broken (it is necessary to have full agility and viability of the cycle of capital with no interruption). Reproduction of men exists as these are to be used as merchandise by capital, and the cycle of capital is determined through its organic composition, which in its turn is determined by the degree of accumulation of capital. The level of reproduction will be determined by salary, which derives from status in his class, and, as a consequence, in the process of production with the respective remuneration deriving from it.

The reproduction of men, in general, is linked to the peculiar form of the capitalist system—to create value by the appropriation of unpaid labour. This means that reproduction of men in the capitalist mode of production takes over historical specificity different from that of precedent periods, creating a specific law of population, i.e. capital, according to its necessities, will strive to increase the working population, at the same time that it constantly diminishes the time of necessary labour. Here is one of the great contradictions of capitalism, for at the same time that it creates surplus labour, it abolishes the necessary labour, and the first one can exist only departing from the second. On the other hand, the notion of overpopulation is directly linked to the privation of the individual from the conditions of reproduction of his own existence. Thus, in a given moment of the development of social production, there can or cannot exist overpopulation.

Another inner contradiction of capitalism is in the fact that the amount of commodities produced increases in an uninterrupted way and the system absorbs a smaller labour force. At the same time that the system needs a surplus working population, it needs an outlet for its production. This outlet needs the presence of consumers, that is people with purchasing power, besides the salaried workers that the system tends to reduce relatively in a systematic way.

The limits of population depend on the elasticity of the given form of production. They vary, contracting and expanding according to its conditions. The absolute growth rate of population changes; as a consequence the same happens to overpopulation. It is the productive base that at each time determines overpopulation, as it determines the optimal production.

The total population is then the necessary population and the surplus population that a determined productive base has the conditions to create. History shows that population develops in very different ways and that the necessary population as well as the surplus population are historical relations. Thus, population cannot be determined by numbers, nor by an absolute limit of food productivity, but, on the contrary, it is determined and has its limits fixed by the conditions of production. The movement of total population (necessary and surplus population) is given by employment's historical laws, which make the individual to be a part of the necessary population or of the surplus one, which will determine the degree of human reproduction of the salaried worker (Marx, 1968: 167–79).

But the effectively 'active' or working population as well as the surplus population are created at the same time and articulated by the mode of production based on capital and as a function of its necessities. This production needs not only a mass of workers working and cooperating, but also presupposes an overpopulation or surplus population. The degree of integration of this overpopulation in the productive process will depend on the additional capital that will permit the level of enlarged reproduction at a given moment of production. Thus, its creation may imply the necessity of a growing population able to be put into the labour market following the creation of additional capital.

If there is a part of the population which effectively and directly produces the space through a given pattern of work (in agriculture or industry), there is also a part of the population that participates in an indirect way in the measure that its work does not directly produce the space (trade, services) but it makes viable the former part. And we still have a part of population that is out of the labour market because it does not definitely participate in the social process of production or because it has been expelled from the labour market, or still because it is part of the industrial reserve army.

All parts of the population, in one way or another, are unequal and differentiated, and finally appropriate one portion of this socially produced space. This happens to the extent that all individuals in one way or another live in this space, move in it, use the collective social equipment, consume recreation space, etc. The process of appropriation of space will thus be established by an individual's social status and, subsequently by the place of his social class in society, in the actual mode of production*.

Furthermore, we must underline that this work has aimed to present our way of thinking about geography of population, and that the great merit of going from the traditional up to the modern in geography belongs especially

* Many of the ideas of this chapter were extracted from the works of Ana Fany Alessandri Carlos, whom I thank.

to Pierre George who, together with J. Beaujeu-Garnier, guided us to this field of geography and to whom we dedicate this short essay.

References

Carlos, A.F.A. (1979) *Reflexões sobre o espaco geográfico*, Masters dissertation, University of São Paulo.

Lenin, V.I. (1974) *Obras escogidas*, vol. 3, Ed. Progresso, Moscow, 232, cited in Cueva, A. *La concepción marxista de las clases sociales*, in Debate e Critica no. 3, Hucitec, São Paulo.

Marx, K. (1968) *Fondements de la critique de l'économie politique*, ebouche 1857–1858, Edition Anthropus, Paris, vols. 2–3.

Marx, K. (1973) *El Capital*, Mexico Fondo de Cultura Economica 8th printing.

Oliveira, F. (1976) *A produção dos homens: notas sobre a reprodução da população sob o capital*, in Estudos CEBRAP no. 16, Edições CEBRAP, São Paulo.

Singer, P. (1982) *Leis de População e Pesquisa de Fertilidade*, in *Reproducción de la población y desarrolle*, no. 2, Conse jo Latinoamericano de Ciencias Sociales, São Paulo.

5

Spatial Demography

ROBERT WOODS
(University of Sheffield, U.K.)

Definitions

To know that 'demography' is the study of population and that 'geography' involves the study of the earth's surface is in itself not particularly helpful. One also needs to understand precisely what the subject matter comprises, what particular methodologies are employed, and what questions are deemed to be relevant for enquiry. As far as demography is concerned, its practitioners have tended to concentrate their activities on a rather limited part of the broad field of population studies. Their main aim has been to analyze population structure and in so doing they have preferred to concentrate on mortality and fertility, together with the interaction between them. The life table and the stable population model provide two of their most sophisticated analytical devices. Demographers have only rarely concerned themselves with migration as an end in itself; they have also largely avoided such issues as the problems of urbanization and the redistribution of population. Their methodologies are generally of the statistical-inductive variety with a strong empirical orientation. The precise measurement and description of population structures has been their goal, to the extent that explanation and theory have often been forced into second or third place, behind data analysis and pattern identification (Bourgeois-Pichat, 1973).

Spatial demography is, therefore, demography viewed from the spatial perspective. It has all the preoccupations of demography, but migration now takes up equal importance with fertility and mortality. Spatial, together with temporal, variations in mortality, fertility and migration are studied as preliminaries to the investigation of population structure in its entirety. The methodology of demography may be supplemented by a greater emphasis on modelling, theory construction and, ultimately, explanation. There is no one epistemology; positivism, behavouralism and structuralism can all make their contribution once the empirical scene has been set.

How does spatial demography differ from population geography? In principle there is no reason why there should be any difference, but in practice geographers of population have by tradition occupied themselves with matters of distribution, with identifying population types, and especially with migration, but Noin (1979) and particularly Jones (1981) have shown how the demographic approach can be used by geographers. Apart from the map, their analytical tools have been surprisingly unsophisticated when compared with those of demographers, many of whom have been trained as social statisticians. For the geographer population distribution is the dependent variable to be associated with environmental, economic, social and political variables. 'Who lives where, how and why?' are the relevant questions. The demographer is more likely to ask 'how many children will an average female have borne on reaching 50?' and 'what is the life expectation at birth of a population?' By this means fertility and mortality become dependent variables in their own right occupying for demographers the position taken by population distribution amongst geographers.

Spatial demography, whilst not being exactly a no-man's-land, has certainly been sparsely populated. But it is now possible to distinguish several waves of colonists whose work in the new area is bearing some fruit. The origins and aims of these temporary migrants will be discussed in the next section.

The work of spatial demographers

Of the many important issues that face the modern student of population three will be singled out here to illustrate the spatial demographic approach. They are: the demographic transition; the links between population and development; and the problems posed by estimation and modelling.

The demographic transition

The origins of the demographic transition concept as a model and a theory can be traced to the work of Thompson (1929) and especially that of Notestein (1945). The theory itself is not a strong one, relying for its motivating force on the rather vague process of modernization, but the model which depicts three stages in the move from high to low birth and death rates still retains a strong hold on the imagination. Studies by historical demographers of the first stage in the transition have been hampered by the poor statistical coverage that exists for the West before the nineteenth century. In spite of this, several studies have dealt with the role of demographic crises in the maintenance of high mortality levels (Del Panta and Livi Bacci, 1977; Wrigley and Schofield, 1981), whilst in France Dupâquier (1979) has used a plethora of village studies to examine spatial variations in the population structure of the Paris Basin in the period 1671–1720. In Sweden, where long runs of vital statistics exist,

Hofsten and Lundström (1976) were able to reconstruct the changing regional patterns of mortality and fertility from 1750 onwards. Although none of these studies is conclusive, they do serve to remind us of the variability of the demography of pre-industrial Europe, both over time and through space (Flinn, 1981).

Some of the most important studies illustrating the spatial demographic approach have been concerned with the decline of mortality and the control of fertility, that is the second stage of the transition. Coale (1969) has used specially designed fertility indices to chart the changing fertility pattern in Europe, and by so doing he has been able to confirm the importance of nuptiality in depressing overall fertility before the decline of marital fertility in North-West Europe. Several other researchers associated with the Office of Population Research, Princeton University, have used the same indices to trace spatio-temporal patterns of fertility decline in individual European countries. Knodel (1974) for Germany, Livi Bacci (1977) for Italy, van de Walle (1974) for France, and Lesthaeghe (1977) for Belgium provide the best examples. The last-mentioned has also constructed and tested a multivariate model of the fertility decline process which suggests that the urbanization, industrialization and secularization of society are all correlated with the decline of marital fertility, but that the two linguistic and cultural areas in Belgium must be treated separately since the timing of decline varied substantially. Woods (1982a and b) takes a similar line in his study of variation in mortality and fertility decline in nineteenth-century England and Wales.

During the last stage of the demographic transition there has been considerable spatial convergence in terms of the regional mortality and fertility patterns of the developed countries. Variations in population growth rates are now largely attributable to local and inter-regional migration streams. Coward's (1978, 1982) studies of the fertility decline in Ireland provide good examples of a geographer's attempts to come to grips with the problems of analyzing changing regional demographies (Hobcraft and Rees, 1980). However, relatively little work has been done on contemporary regional fertility cycles (Eversley and Köllmann, 1982). Research on inter-regional migration has been advanced by the use of the economists' concept of 'human capital' (Sjaastad, 1962), which has been taken up by geographers, demographers and economists alike and employed within the framework provided by the multiple regression model (Masser and Gould, 1975; Greenwood, 1969, 1981; Remple and Todaro, 1972). Although some of these studies are disappointing in terms of their ability to account for variation in migration flows, they nonetheless represent a substantial advance when compared with earlier contributions which appear to have E.G. Ravenstein as their intellectual mentor (see Grigg, 1977).

Spatial demography has made several important contributions to the empirical examination of the demographic transition model, but the theory itself remains as insecure as ever because of the problems of relating it to modern conditions in Asia, Africa and Latin America.

Population and development

The relationship between the rate of population growth, together with the structure of population, and economic development is a persistently troublesome one (Cassen, 1976; Coale and Hoover, 1958). Whilst it is clear that economic development can be retarded by rapid population growth, it is equally obvious that economic growth may be restricted when a population is stationary (Simon, 1977). On the other side of the coin, there is a large number of studies that show the extent to which advances in economic development and social modernization are capable of increasing life expectation, reducing marital fertility and stimulating migration, especially that of the rural-urban variety. It is with this form of this relationship that the spatial demographers have been most concerned. At the national scale, Preston (1975) has identified a curvilinear association between life expectation at birth and level of economic development while Mauldin and Berelson (1978; United Nations, 1977) have reviewed the pattern of fertility decline and its associated variables. The approach has probably been most effective at the regional level, however. In Latin America alone there have been numerous studies of the spatial impact of economic development on, for example, migration in Colombia (Fields, 1979; Schultz, 1971), on demographic patterns and migration in Brazil (Merrick and Graham, 1979), and on fertility in Mexico (Hicks, 1974; Seiver, 1975).

The importance of these kinds of studies for the population and development debate is considerable since they provide means of directly investigating issues which would probably be tackled differently in the statistically advanced countries. In the less developed world the supply of social, economic and demographic data for local administrative units provides the basis for ecological analyses which, despite their drawbacks, are superior to the often rudimentary information that is available on individuals from social surveys.

Estimation and modelling

Most of the examples cited above rely on the availability of population census and vital statistics, but in many developing countries the system of collecting vital data is either non-existent or it yields statistics that are riddled with inaccuracies. In consequence, the development of highly sophisticated techniques for demographic estimation has been an important preliminary to the study of spatial variations in demographic patterns. Many of these techniques rely on stable population theory (Coale, 1972; Coale and Demeny,

1966) which can be used to estimate the vital rates of a population for which only the age structure is known (Woods, 1979:202–15). Although the results so derived are dependent upon the validity of the assumptions it is necessary to make in order to operate the techniques, they are nonetheless substantial improvements on what would otherwise be available. Carvalho (1974) has used these methods with considerable success in his investigation of the changing regional demography of Brazil.

In their *The Demography of Tropical Africa*, Brass *et al.* (1968) provide perhaps one of the best illustrations of what can be accomplished when only limited data are available, but it also serves as a warning against over-optimism since their approach has, of necessity, to be descriptive; their aim is to identify patterns as objectively as possible using corrected data. They have provided preliminary statements upon which others can elaborate and to which explanations may be added (Adegbola, 1977; Page and Lesthaeghe, 1981).

The considerable potential of estimation techniques is beginning to be explored in historical demography where similar or even more intractable problems remain. Through the efforts of Lee (1978) and Wrigley and Schofield (1981), we now have pictures of temporal variations in the demography of pre-industrial England; these methods can also be applied to local and regional populations. For the nineteenth century, Teitelbaum (1974) has used stable population models to estimate birth under-registration among the English and Welsh counties in order to better approximate the changing level of fertility. These methods do not solve the problems to which they are addressed, but they do help to clear the ground and even lay foundations.

The techniques of demographic modelling and what has become known as spatial demographic accounting have been advanced considerably over the last twenty years (Rogers, 1975; Rees and Wilson, 1977; see Chapter 6). Here one of the primary objectives is to provide a means of forecasting future regional population structures by combining age- and area-specific estimates of mortality, fertility and migration. First results have been encouraging in two ways. Firstly, the forecasts themselves have proved useful if for no other reason than that they demonstrate what will happen 'if present trends continue', so that direct action can be planned to avert the otherwise inevitable (Rees, 1979). Secondly, the modelling techniques themselves have important implication for the work of demographers in general, since they deal with the entire demographic system in an explicitly spatial fashion. Here the geographers have made their most significant contributions so far to spatial demography.

What is to be done?

It is the case with every 'new approach' that while some old questions may be answered others will remain to be complemented by yet more unsolved problems. To the demographer, the spatial perspective offers the prospect of gaining new insights, of identifying new patterns and relationships, and of utilizing population data more efficiently. To the geographer, spatial demography represents both an approach which is technically more sophisticated than has been common in population geography and a change of emphasis in the subject matter for enquiry. There are of course disadvantages for both groups. For geographers there appears to be unwarranted restriction on the range of topics that are relevant and the methodologies appropriate for their study. Demographers may feel that the spatial viewpoint merely raises more problems than it solves, that it clouds the issues because it not only complicates measurement, but also reveals a new dimension of demographic disorder. Although these fears are justified spatial demography nonetheless provides a focus for geographers and demographers to work together in an area that is partly familiar to both groups. This coincidence of interests and approaches can thus provide a melting-pot for the creation of a single unified 'population studies'—a true demography—in which sectional interests would be removed. The way forward lies in this direction.

References

Adegbola, O. (1977) New estimates of fertility and child mortality, south of the Sahara, *Population Studies*, **31**, 467–86.

Bourgeois-Pichat, J. (1973) *Main Trends in Demography*, Allen and Unwin, London.

Brass, W. *et al.* (1968) *The Demography of Tropical Africa*, Princeton University Press, Princeton.

Carvalho, J.A.M. (1974) Regional trends in fertility and mortality in Brazil, *Population Studies*, **28**, 401–21.

Cassen, R.H. (1976) Population and development: a survey, *World Development*, **4**, 785–830.

Coale, A.J. (1969) The decline of fertility in Europe from the French Revolution to World War II, in S.J. Behrman, L. Corsa and R. Freedman (eds.), *Fertility and Family Planning: A World View*, Michigan University Press, Ann Arbor, 3–24.

Coale, A.J. (1972) *The Growth and Structure of Human Populations: A Mathematical Investigation*, Princeton University Press, Princeton.

Coale, A.J. and Demeny, P. (1966) *Regional Model Life Tables and Stable Populations*, Princeton University Press, Princeton.

Coale, A.J. and Hoover, E.M. (1958) *Population Growth and Economic Development in Low-Income Countries: A Case Study of India's Prospects*, Princeton University Press, Princeton.

Coward, J. (1978) Changes in the pattern of fertility in the Republic of Ireland, *Tijdschrift voor Economische en Sociale Geografie*, **69**, 353–61.

Coward, J. (1982) Fertility changes in the Republic of Ireland during the 1970s, *Area*, **14**, 109–17.

Del Panta, L. and Livi Bacci, M. (1977) Chronologie, intensité et diffusion des crises de mortalité en Italie: 1600–1850, *Population*, **32** (Numéro Spécial), 401–46.

Dupâquier, J. (1979) *La population rurale du Bassin Parisien à l'époque de Louis XIV*, Éditions de l'E.H.E.S.S., Paris.

Eversley, D. and Köllmann, W. (eds.) (1982) *Population Change and Social Planning*, Arnold, London.

Fields, G.S. (1979) Lifetime migration in Colombia: tests of the expected income hypothesis, *Population and Development Review*, **5**, 247–65.

Flinn, M.W. (1981) *The European Demographic System, 1500–1820*, Harvester Press, Brighton.

Greenwood, M.J. (1969) An analysis of the determinants of geographic labour mobility in the United States, *Review of Economics and Statistics*, **51**, 189–94.

Greenwood, M.J. (1981) *Migration and Economic Growth in the United States*, Academic Press, New York.

Grigg, D.B. (1977) E.G. Ravenstein and the 'laws of migration', *Journal of Historical Geography*, **3**, 41–54.

Hicks, W.W. (1974) Economic development and fertility change in Mexico, 1950–1970, *Demography*, **11**, 407–21.

Hobcraft, J. and Rees, P.H. (eds.) (1980) *Regional Demographic Development*, Croom Helm, London.

Hofsten, E. and Lundström, H. (1976) *Swedish Population History: Main Trends from 1750 to 1970*, Urval: Skriftserie Utgiven av Statistika Centralbyrån No. 8, Statistika Centralbyrån, Stockholm.

Jones, H.R. (1981) *A Population Geography*, Harper and Row, London.

Knodel, J.E. (1974) *The Decline of Fertility in Germany, 1871–1939*, Princeton University Press, Princeton.

Lee, R.D. (1978) Models of preindustrial population dynamics with application to England, in C. Tilly (ed.) *Historical Studies of Changing Fertility*, Princeton University Press, Princeton, 155–207.

Lesthaeghe, R.J. (1977) *The Decline of Belgian Fertility, 1800–1970*, Princeton University Press, Princeton.

Livi Bacci, M. (1977) *A History of Italian Fertility during the last Two Centuries*, Princeton University Press, Princeton.

Masser, I. and Gould, W.T.S. (1975) *Inter-Regional Migration in Tropical Africa*, Institute of British Geographers, Special Publication No. 8, London.

Merrick, T.W. and Graham, D.H. (1979) *Population and Economic Development in Brazil: 1800 to the Present*, Johns Hopkins University Press, Baltimore.

Mauldin W.P. and Berelson, B. (1978) Conditions of fertility decline in developing countries, 1965–75, *Studies in Family Planning*, **9** (5), 89–147.

Noin, D. (1979) *Géographie de la population*, Masson, Paris.

Notestein, F.W. (1945) Population: the long view, in T.W. Schultz (ed.), *Food for the World*, Chicago University Press, Chicago, 36–57.

Page, H.J. and Lesthaeghe, R.J. (eds.) (1981) *Child-Spacing in Tropical Africa*, Academic Press, London.

Preston, S.H. (1975) The changing relation between mortality and level of economic development, *Population Studies*, **29**, 231–48.

Rees, P.H. (1979) *Migration and Settlement: 1. United Kingdom*, International Institute for Applied Systems Analysis, Laxenburg, Austria.

Rees, P.H. and Wilson, A.G. (1977) *Spatial Population Analysis*, Arnold, London.

Remple, H. and Todaro, M.P. (1972) Rural to urban labour migration in Kenya, in S.H. Ominde and C.N. Ejiogu (eds.), *Population Growth and Economic Development in Africa*, Heinemann, London, 214–31.

Rogers, A. (1975) *Introduction to Multiregional Mathematical Demography*, Wiley, New York.

Schultz, T.P. (1971) Rural-urban migration in Colombia, *Review of Economics and Statistics*, **53**, 157–63.

Seiver, D.A. (1975) Recent fertility in Mexico: measurement and interpretation, *Population Studies*, **29**, 341–54 and **31**, 175–7.

Simon, J.L. (1977) *The Economics of Population Growth*, Princeton University Press, Princeton.

Sjaastad, L.A. (1962) The costs and returns of human migration, *Journal of Political Economy*, **70** (Supplement), 80–93.

Teitelbaum, M.S. (1974) Birth under-registration in the constituent counties of England, 1841–1910, *Population Studies*, **28**, 329–43.

Thompson, W.S. (1929) Population, *American Journal of Sociology*, **34**, 959–75.

United Nations (1977) *Levels and Trends of Fertility Throughout the World, 1950–70*, Department of Economic and Social Affairs, Bureau of Social Affairs, Population Studies No. 59, United Nations, New York.

Van de Walle, E. (1974) *The Female Population of France in the Nineteenth Century*, Princeton University Press, Princeton.

Woods, R.I. (1979) *Population Analysis in Geography*, Longman, London.

Woods, R.I. (1982a) *Theoretical Population Geography*, Longman, London.

Woods, R.I. (1982b) The structure of mortality in mid-nineteenth century England and Wales, *Journal of Historical Geography*, **8**, 373–94.

Wrigley, E.A. and Schofield, R.S. (1981) *The Population History of England, 1541–1871: A Reconstruction*, Arnold, London.

6

Spatial Population Accounting

PHILIP H. REES
(University of Leeds, U.K.)
and ANDREW L. CONVEY
(Trinity and All Saints College, Leeds, U.K.)

Principles

The nature of population accounts

Population accounts are devices for organizing information about population stocks and flows in a consistent way, from which the rates for a variety of useful population models can be generated. They are particularly applicable in investigating spatial population change; they force the reseacher to estimate all the flows—births, deaths, internal migration, external migration—that alter a population, and thus avoid the partial nature of much demographic analysis.

What do population accounts look like? To make the concepts involved clear, we will work through an annotated numerical example. Figure 6.1 displays an accounts table for a French three-region system over the period 1968–75 between the last-but-one and last-but-two French censuses. The entries in the table are the numbers of people making transitions over the seven-year period between initial states (the rows of the table) and final states (the columns of the table). The initial states in this simple example are either existence at the start of the period (that is, at census date in 1968) or birth during the 1968–75 period. Each starting life state can be classified as to region of origin: either the department of the Gard in the Languedoc-Roussillon region or the rest of France or the rest of the world. The final states are either survival at census date 1975 in one of the three regions or death during the intercensal period in one of the locations.

Each of the entries in the table is a particular and familiar demographic flow or stock. These components of the accounts are numbered in Figure 6.1 in order of their usual entry into the model used to estimate the full accounts

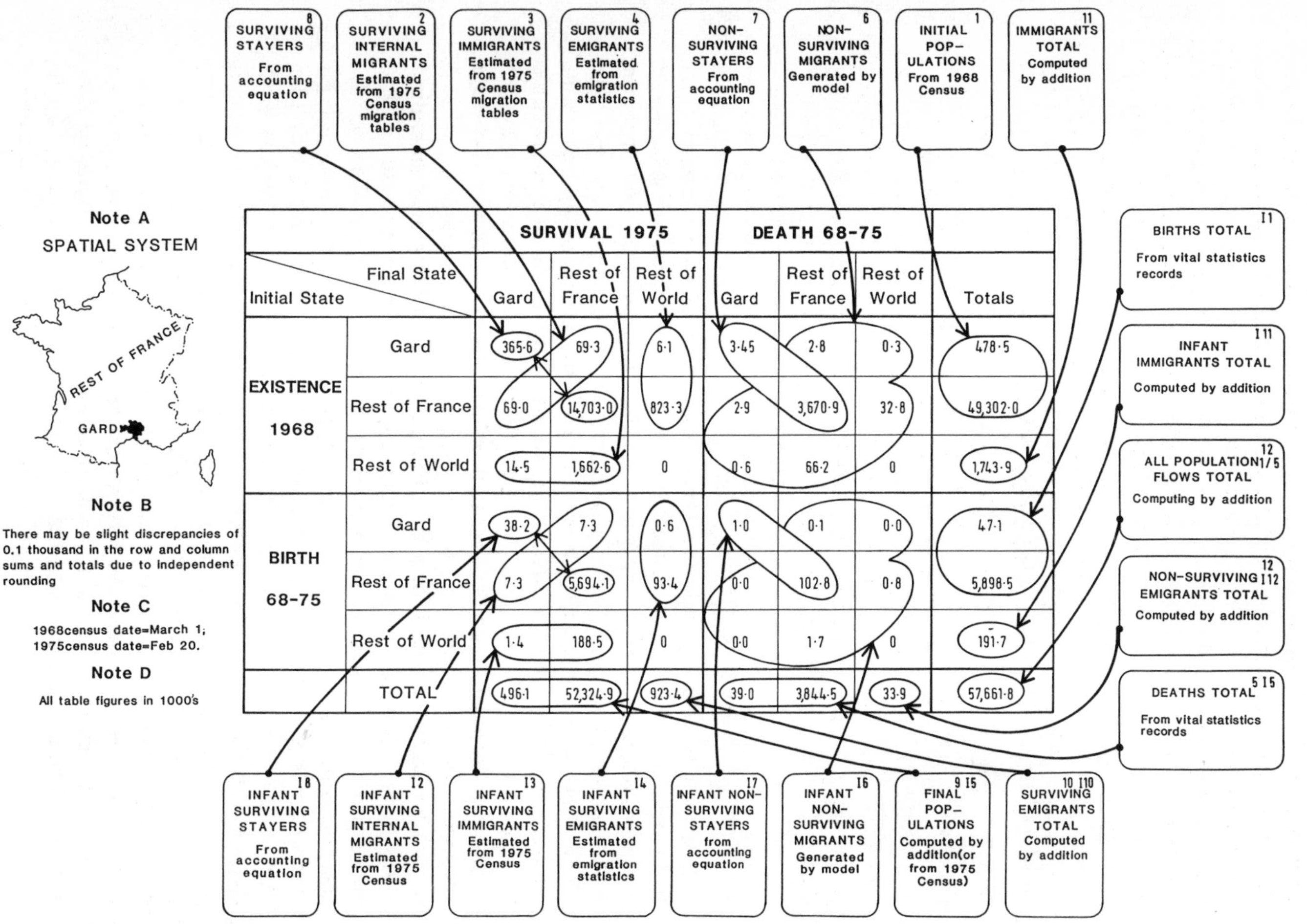

Initial State \ Final State		SURVIVAL 1975 Gard	SURVIVAL 1975 Rest of France	SURVIVAL 1975 Rest of World	DEATH 68-75 Gard	DEATH 68-75 Rest of France	DEATH 68-75 Rest of World	Totals
EXISTENCE 1968	Gard	365·6	69·3	6·1	3·45	2·8	0·3	478·5
	Rest of France	69·0	14,703·0	823·3	2·9	3,670·9	32·8	49,302·0
	Rest of World	14·5	1,662·6	0	0·6	66·2	0	1,743·9
BIRTH 68-75	Gard	38·2	7·3	0·6	1·0	0·1	0·0	47·1
	Rest of France	7·3	5,694·1	93·4	0·0	102·8	0·8	5,898·5
	Rest of World	1·4	188·5	0	0·0	1·7	0	191·7
	TOTAL	496·1	52,324·9	923·4	39·0	3,844·5	33·9	57,661·8

FIGURE 6.1. *The structure of a population accounts table for a French Département*

matrix and table. *Initial populations*, component 1, are the row totals for the first two rows in the tables, and for the Gard and the rest of France derive from the 1968 French census. The 'populations sans doubles comptes' were used. The third row sum, *Immigrants total*, component 11, is the aggregate of immigrants who enter France during 1968–75 and either survive there at census 1975 or die there; because flows within the rest of the world are ignored (set to zero) this row sum is not the population of the rest of the world.

The existence-survival quadrant of the table is made up of sets of *surviving migrants internal* to France, component 2, *surviving immigrants* from outside France, component 3, *surviving emigrants* from France to the rest of the world, component 4, which are all estimated externally and input to the estimation model, and the set of *surviving stayers*, component 8, which is estimated with the model. There are two elements in each set, one for the Gard and one for the rest of France. These four components are repeated in the birth-survival quadrant of the table where they are labelled *infant surviving migrants* and so on. The term infant, in this context, means a person born in the 1968–1975 period. In the survival in 1975 columns these were persons aged under seven in the 1975 census. There are equivalent terms to these under and over seven years of age components in the right-hand half of the table, though all of the terms must be estimated in the accounts building model. Fortunately, this estimation can be closely tied to the *totals for deaths* in the regions (by ages under and over seven) which appear in the totals rows at the bottom of the table.

The *birth totals* for the regions appear as totals for the regional rows in the bottom half of the table. The *final populations* at the end of the accounting period appear as totals for the first two columns of the accounts. These may be a product of estimating the accounts (as in Fig. 6.1) or may be input independently.

The population accounts defined in Figure 6.1 are multiregional generalizations of the closed demographic accounts invented by Stone (1971). The generalization involves dividing Stone's amorphous 'Outside World' state into 'Rest of World', birth and death states as well as the disaggregation of his national unit into regions (see Rees and Wilson, 1977, chap. 13 for full details). The major gain from the generalization is that the accounts terms can be more explicitly and correctly linked to data available from national demographic information systems. The fuzziness of the data-model link is removed. Population accounts are also generalizations of the widely used components-of-change tables that divide population change into natural increase and net migration terms. If the reader has understood the nature of Figure 6.1 thoroughly, he or she should be able to draw up a components-of-change table for the Gard and the rest of France.

Transition rates in accounts

Since population accounts show how people make transitions from intial to final states, it is of interest to measure the rate at which they take place. In the first, second, fourth and fifth rows of Figure 6.2 the transition rates are computed by dividing each element of the accounts table by its row total. These have a very simple interpretation: they allocate an initial state population to final states. Thus, 76.4 per cent of the population of the Gard department in 1968 survive there seven years later; 14.5 per cent have migrated

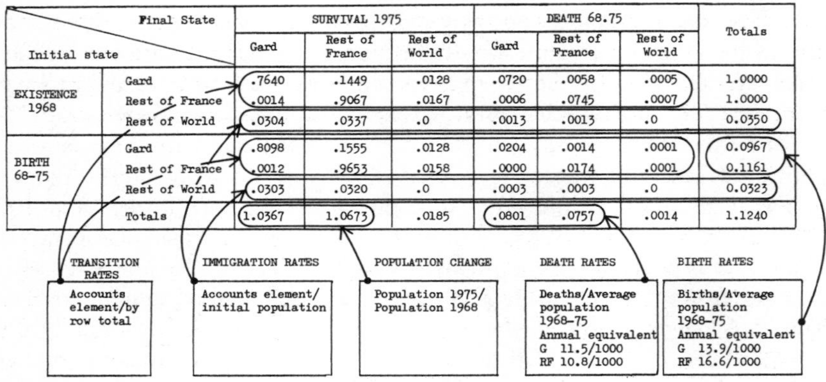

Initial state \ Final State		SURVIVAL 1975 Gard	SURVIVAL 1975 Rest of France	SURVIVAL 1975 Rest of World	DEATH 68.75 Gard	DEATH 68.75 Rest of France	DEATH 68.75 Rest of World	Totals
EXISTENCE 1968	Gard	.7640	.1449	.0128	.0720	.0058	.0005	1.0000
	Rest of France	.0014	.9067	.0167	.0006	.0745	.0007	1.0000
	Rest of World	.0304	.0337	.0	.0013	.0013	.0	0.0350
BIRTH 68-75	Gard	.8098	.1555	.0128	.0204	.0014	.0001	0.0967
	Rest of France	.0012	.9653	.0158	.0000	.0174	.0001	0.1161
	Rest of World	.0303	.0320	.0	.0003	.0003	.0	0.0323
	Totals	1.0367	1.0673	.0185	.0801	.0757	.0014	1.1240

FIGURE 6.2 *Rates generated from the 1968–75 accounts*

to and live in 1975 in the rest of France; 1.3 per cent have emigrated; 7.8 per cent of the population died in the period, 7.2 per cent in the Gard and 0.6 per cent after migration elsewhere. Rates of other kinds can also be computed and Figure 6.2 displays immigration rates, birth and death rates and population change rates. The population of the Gard grew by 3.7 per cent, while that of the rest of France grew by 6.1 per cent.

These rates apply to a period just nine days short of seven years. Annual equivalent rates can be calculated by dividing by the period length for births and deaths. However, although we can do this also for the transition rates in the body of the table, the resulting rates would not be the same as the average of transition rates computed from seven annual accounts. The reasons for this are complex (Ledent, 1980; Ledent and Rees, 1980), but shed important light on our understanding of migration behaviour.

Transition accounts and movement accounts

Migration can be measured in one of three ways (Courgeau, 1980): by a question in a census that asks respondents where they were living at some fixed point in the past (at the time of the previous census), by a question in a census that asks where respondents last lived and when they last moved, and by questions in a registration system at time of the migration about where a person is moving from and to. Only data from the first question which generate information on *transitions* have so far been built into accounts. Thus, the Figure 6.1 accounts are transition accounts. Migration data generated from the second question (place of last residence migration) have not yet been employed in accounts. However, the principles (if not the practice) of building population accounts using movement data have recently been worked out (Rees and Willekens, 1981).

Movement data are generated in countries where citizens are required to register their usual residences and any changes in those residences. Births and deaths data can also be regarded as movements. Movement data can be put together in rather simpler accounts tables than transition data, as can be seen from Figure 6.3. In this table we have taken the figures from the 1968–75

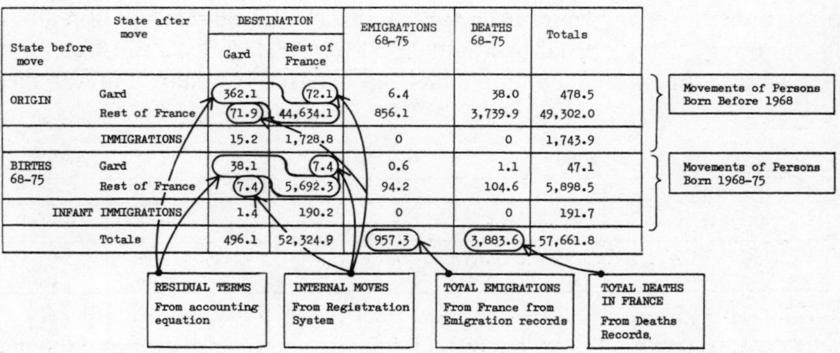

State before move	State after move	DESTINATION Gard	DESTINATION Rest of France	EMIGRATIONS 68–75	DEATHS 68–75	Totals
ORIGIN	Gard	362.1	72.1	6.4	38.0	478.5
	Rest of France	71.9	44,634.1	856.1	3,739.9	49,302.0
	IMMIGRATIONS	15.2	1,728.8	0	0	1,743.9
BIRTHS 68–75	Gard	38.1	7.4	0.6	1.1	47.1
	Rest of France	7.4	5,692.3	94.2	104.6	5,898.5
	INFANT IMMIGRATIONS	1.4	190.2	0	0	191.7
	Totals	496.1	52,324.9	957.3	3,883.6	57,661.8

FIGURE 6.3 *A hypothetical movement accounts table for a French Départment*

transition accounts, assumed that only one move per transition has taken place (although 1.5 to 2 moves are more likely), aggregated terms where necessary and constructed movement accounts for a French department. Note that the final populations of the Gard and the rest of France are the same as in the transition accounts. Assuming that the census migration tables and registration migration tables were of the same accuracy, transition and movement accounts should, in theory, yield the same final populations because all moves surplus to transitions, when summed for each region, cancel out.

Models and applications

Unconstrained and constrained population accounts

There are many ways of building population accounts. Just some of the alternatives are described here. A full review of the alternative models is given in Rees (1981) along with details of a computer program, ABM (Accounts Based Models), that implements those models. The program is available on magnetic tape from the author.

The first point to note is that in constructing population accounts for a period in the past there may well be further information that we have not included. For example, in the French accounts of Figure 6.1 we derived the surviving migrant figures from the 1975 census, but did not use the 1975 population figures, preferring instead to add up the terms in the columns of the accounts. Such accounts are said to be unconstrained. We could use the additional information on 1975 populations in a variety of ways, but one of the most useful is to employ them as constraints to which the unconstrained accounts matrix is adjusted using iterative balancing factor or biproportional matrix techniques (Rees, 1979). The Figure 6.4.1 accounts matrix (interior part of the table) is adjusted so that rows and columns add up to external sums. The external column sums which we needed were end-of-period census populations, surviving emigrant totals, deaths in the regions, and non-surviving emigrants. The external row sums used were the same as those in Figure 6.1. The total of external column sums and external row sums did not agree.

4.1 HISTORICAL ACCOUNTS: CONSTRAINED

CONSTRAINED		SURVIVAL 1975			DEATH 68-75			HISTORICAL
Initial State	Final State	Gard	Rest of France	Abroad	Gard	Rest of France	Abroad	Totals
EXISTENCE 1968,	Gard	367.5	67.0	6.7	34.4	2.7	0.3	478.5
	Rest of France	71.6	44,583.0	936.3	3.0	3,670.9	37.3	49,302.0
	Abroad	15.1	1,661.8	0	0.6	66.4	0	1,743.9
BIRTH 68-75	Gard	34.7	9.6	1.7	1.0	0.1	0.0	47.1
	Rest of France	5.0	5,594.7	194.2	0.0	102.8	1.7	5,898.5
	Abroad	1.0	188.9	0	0.0	1.7	0	191.7
	Totals	494.9	52,105.1	1,138.9	39.0	3,844.5	39.3	57,661.8

4.2 ESTIMATED ACCOUNTS: CONSTRAINED

CONSTRAINED		SURVIVAL 1982			DEATH 75-82			HISTORICAL EST
Initial State	Final State	Gard	Rest of France	Abroad	Gard	Rest of France	Abroad	Totals
EXISTENCE 1975	Gard	387.2	69.7	2.5	32.9	2.6	0.1	494.9
	Rest of France	77.1	48,011.0	320.7	2.9	3,681.3	12.1	52,105.1
	Abroad	1.2	350.5	0	0.0	13.0	0	364.8
BIRTH 75-82	Gard	30.5	8.3	0.3	0.9	0.1	0.0	40.1
	Rest of France	4.5	5,067.5	39.3	0.1	102.9	0.4	5,214.6
	Abroad	0.1	39.7	0	0.0	0.4	0	40.2
	Totals	500.5	53,546.6	362.8	36.9	3,800.3	12.6	58,259.7

4.3 PROJECTED ACCOUNTS: UNCONSTRAINED

UNCONSTRAINED		SURVIVAL 1989			DEATH 82-89			PROJECTED
Initial State	Final State	Gard	Rest of France	Abroad	Gard	Rest of France	Abroad	Totals
EXISTENCE 1982	Gard	391.5	70.5	2.5	33.3	2.6	0.1	500.5
	Rest of France	79.2	49,348.3	320.7	3.0	3,783.4	12.0	53,546.6
	Abroad	1.2	350.5	0	0.0	13.1	0	364.8
BIRTH 89-89	Gard	29.9	8.4	0.3	1.9	0.1	00.0	40.6
	Rest of France	4.6	5,104.5	39.3	0.1	209.9	0.4	5,358.7
	Abroad	0.1	39.7	0	0.0	0.4	0	40.2
	Totals	506.5	54,921.8	362.8	38.4	4,009.5	12.5	59,851.5

FIGURE 6.4. *A sequence of population accounts*

They were reconciled by adjusting upwards our estimate of the emigration figures somewhat, since these were held to be the least reliable of the totals.

The resulting constrained accounts are shown in the first accounts table in Figure 6.4. The major changes are in the third columns, and lesser changes have occurred in the first and second columns. Currently, the method employed allows all elements of the accounts matrix to be adjusted; it might be better to allow certain elements within the matrix to remain fixed as well. However, the changes that occur in internal migrant figures, for example, are well within the confidence bands of those figures, based as they often are on a sample of questionnaires from the census.

Historical, estimated and projected accounts

All the terms in the 1968–75 accounts input externally to accounts estimation model are input as flows or stocks, that is, as actual numbers of people. Such accounts are labelled *historical.* In the next period, 1975–82, at the time of construction (1981) only some of the stocks and flows were known, others had to be estimated. This meant 'forecasting' birth and death rates in 1981 and 1982 when the figures for those years had not been published, though the events themselves had already happened. No internal migration information was yet available from the 1982 census so that migrant flows between the Gard and the rest of France were estimated by multiplying the corresponding transition rates from the previous period by the 1975 populations. Both emigration and immigration were estimated from national movements data for the 1975–82 period, whereas previously only emigration had been so estimated. The accounts were constrained to estimated 1982 populations for the two regions. Such tentative accounts are labelled *estimated*, and could, in fact, now be improved using preliminary counts from the 1982 census.

The third set of accounts in Figure 6.4 are for a period still mainly in the future. They are thus labelled *projected.* The projection is carried out using what Alexander (1981) calls a mixed migration model. The internal migrant flows are forecast using the 1975–82 transition rates, whereas the external migrant terms are input as flows. The projected accounts are not quite a constant extrapolation of 1975–82 behaviour, however, as the birth and death rates are extrapolated from those available in 1979 and 1980 rather than for the whole 1975–82 period. The birth rates in 1979 and 1980 were marginally higher than in 1975–78. No constraints were placed on the projected accounts. If they had been, the purpose of accounts building would have shifted from forecasting to exploration of the implication of population targets.

Figure 6.5 shows what happens if we project the populations of the Gard and the rest of France forward using the 1982–89 model and appropriate rates and flows. Before 1996 France will have overtaken the U.K. in population (assuming the latter remains stationary at just below 56 million). The Gard

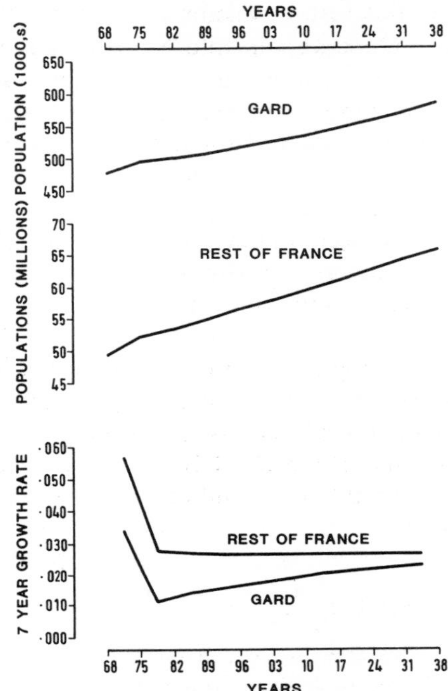

FIGURE 6.5. *Projections of the populations and growth rates of the Gard and the Rest of France*

grows more slowly than the rest of France, but their growth rates converge because of the increasing numbers of migrants from the latter to the former region. However, given the dramatic changes in fertility levels and external migration that a careful comparison of the Figures 6.4.1 and 6.4.2 tables reveal, it would be unwise to expect such a smooth population development to 2038.

Conclusions

A full discussion of spatial population accounting would encompass a wide range of other topics. For example, population accounts need to be disaggregated by sex and by age because of the profound differences between the sex and age groups in their demographic behaviour or experience. All the principles and models outlined above apply to such disaggregated populations so long as the age disaggregation is by 'cohort-in-a-time period': this is the scheme adopted by Stone (1971) and Rees (1981). Adoption of an 'age group-in-a-period' scheme leads to unnecessary complications (as in Rees and Wilson, 1977).

Spatial population accounts have close links to other, independently developed, multiregional models—the multiregional cohort survival model and the multiregional life table model (Rogers and Willekens, 1978)—and these links are made explicit in two pieces of cross-national collaboration (Ledent and Rees, 1980; Rees and Willekens, 1981).

Do accounting principles apply outside the field of regional population development, with which we have illustrated them in this chapter? Further disaggregation of the population by a large variety of socio-economic characteristics can lead to rather 'empty' and unuseful accounts matrices, and other techniques such as micro-simulation may be more useful. However, as an interface between data and population model, accounts have a key role to play in many fields. A knowledge of accounting principles in general is an important aid to disciplined thinking about population processes.

References

Alexander, S. (1981) A model of population change and return migration. *Working Paper 318, School of Geography, University of Leeds.*

Courgeau, D. (1980) *L'analyse quantitative des migrations humaines*, Masson, Paris.

Ledent, J. (1980) Multistate life tables: movement versus transition perspectives, *Environment and Planning A*, **12**, 533–62.

Ledent, J. and Rees, P.H. (1980) Choices in the construction of multiregional life tables, *Working Paper 289, School of Geography, University of Leeds, Leeds, U.K./Working Paper WP-80-173, International Institute for Applied Systems Analysis, Laxenburg, Austria.*

Rees, P.H. (1979) Regional population projection models and accounting methods, *Journal of the Royal Statistical Society, Series A*, **142**, 223–55.

Rees, P.H. (1981) Accounts based models for multiregional population analysis: methods, program and users' manual, *Working Paper 295/Computer Manual 13, School of Geography, University of Leeds, Leeds U.K.*

Rees, P.H. and Willekens, F. (1981) Data bases and accounting frameworks for IIASA's comparative migration and settlement study, *Collaborative Paper CP-81-39, International Institute for Applied Systems Analysis, Laxenburg, Austria.*

Rees, P.H. and Wilson, A.G. (1977) *Spatial Population Analysis*, Arnold, London.

Rogers, A. and Willekens, F. (1978) *Spatial Population Analysis: Methods and Computer Programs*, Research Report RR-78-18, International Institute for Applied Systems Analysis, Laxenburg, Austria.

Stone, R. (1971) *Demographic Accounting and Model Building*, O.E.C.D., Paris.

Note

Space precludes a detailed account of sources for each item in the accounts. The main sources were:—

Croze, M. (1976) *Tableaux démographiques et sociaux (reliefs géographiques et historiques)*, INSEE-INED, Paris.

Croze, M. (1979) Supplement to Croze (1976).

Chi, D.Q. and Labat, J.C. (1979) Projection de population totale pour la France 1975–2000, *Les Collections de l'INSEE*, Séries D. (Démographie et Emploi) No 63, Paris.

7

Historical Population Geography

PHILIP E. OGDEN
(Queen Mary College, University of London, U.K.)

There has been something of a renaissance over the last decade in the contribution of geographers to the study of the past. Historical geography had emerged relatively unscathed by the worst excesses of the quantitative revolution of the 1960s and has seemed very receptive to new ideas and new approaches. Equally, and to a large extent coincidentally, historical demography has emerged as a major field of intellectual enquiry over the last thirty years, developing a distinctive approach and methodology (Willigan and Lynch, 1982). It is from this latter, markedly interdisciplinary, field that a flood of publications has emerged on the evolution and structure of populations in the past in the developed and, increasingly, in the less developed countries; a flood which has begun to reveal how exciting and significant may be the findings of historical demography and which may yet seem a trickle compared to the research tasks which lie ahead. There is as yet no textbook, or even collection of essays, entitled 'historical population geography' which marries these two strands of research activity. It may indeed be to some extent unhelpful semantics to suggest that such a field exists. Yet it is of interest to realize both that geographers have already played a significant part in the study of the populations of the past and that, in the future development of historical demography, the aptitude of the geographer for analyzing demographic patterns and their causes at a variety of scales may be highly relevant. There is no denying that distinct spatial patterns of demographic structure and behaviour existed in the past and that where someone lived affected the chances of survival, the size of family or household of which he was a part, and his likeliness to migrate.

Historical demography

The development of historical demography has been linked to wider changes in approaches to the study of history in general. Not least, historical demography has benefited from the so-called 'Annales' school of history (Stoianovitch, 1976) which grew in France and which emphasized an interdisciplinary approach to the study of 'total history'. Thus, while much activity in historical demography has necessarily been devoted to the pursuit of sources and of appropriate techniques (Hollingsworth, 1969), the fascination with figures has not on the whole blinded researchers to the much wider issues which may be illuminated by the painstaking minutiae of data gathering. The main concerns of historical demography—the measurement of population growth, fertility, mortality, marriage, family size and structure, and migration—are clearly of an interdisciplinary nature and are intimately concerned with the broader themes of social and economic history. Thus, whilst one of the most significant landmarks has been the development in France of the process of family reconstitution as a technique for identifying and tracing people in the past, and while the computer has allowed major progress in the handling of data (Marcilio and Charbonneau, 1979; Guillaume and Poussou, 1970) others have sought to bring imaginative and sensitive interpretation to the understanding of past 'mentalités', of experience and behaviour (e.g. Flandrin, 1979; Chambers, 1972; Stone, 1977; Laslett, 1972). An important point is that much of the impetus of historical demography came not from demographers gazing into the past but from historians looking at their field with a fresh and expansive vision. Not surprisingly, and in part at least because so little was known before, distinct directions have developed in research, leaving evident gaps.

One illustration of this is, indeed, in the progress made in constructing geographies of past populations. There has been an inevitable concentration of research in Europe and North America (see, for example the range of material in Glass and Eversley, 1965; Glass and Revelle, 1972 or Lee, 1977). In addition, there is a polarization in the geographical scale of enquiry between strictly local studies, using a very carefully handled source, and national trends. Thus in the study of mortality, for instance, there is a gap in regional coverage within countries which would relate national experiences of changing life expectancies to the wide range of experience of individual groups and areas. Equally, in the study of fertility there have been many highly localized studies through family reconstitution, but fewer attempts—because of the mass and complexity of material required—at analyzing regional patterns for whole countries. Historical demographers, however, whether trained as geographers or not, have not been unaware of the geographical dimension and have sketched variations at the broadest of scales, for example Hajnal's (1965, 1982) influential studies of marriage and household patterns. The distinguished series from Princeton on the decline of European fertility is analyzing data from more than seven hundred provinces with diverse cultures and economic conditions (e.g. Knodel, 1974; Livi-Bacci, 1977; Lesthaeghe,

1977). Such work on earlier periods and on other continents is in its infancy. Yet pessimism would be misplaced: great strides have been made in recent years in the study of pre-industrial populations by the ingenious use of sources, for example in England by the Cambridge Group for the History of Population and Social Structure.

The role of geographers

The role of geographers in the study of population patterns in the past, although closely tied to the general development of historical demography, is worthy of note in three respects. First, geographers have made distinguished contributions to historical demography *per se*, without necessarily developing a distinctively 'geographical' approach; second, some of the main advances alluded to above have been made by scholars unaided by a geographical training; third, as is broadly the case with contemporary studies of population geography, geographers have been rather more active in the field of migration than in studies of fertility, mortality or the family. This is particularly so in the development of theoretical innovation. An illustration of the current activities of historical geographers interested in population may be drawn from an analysis of the contents of the *Journal of Historical Geography* from its inception in 1975 to 1982 (Table 7.1). Whilst only a partial indication of research achieved, and in particular biased towards British and American authors, it does provide general evidence of the liveliness of geographers' interest in topics as diverse as labour migration in pre-industrial Japan (Vol. 4, 1978, No. 2), the demography of Ecuador in the eighteenth and nineteenth

TABLE 7.1. *Papers relating to population studies published in the Journal of Historical Geography 1975–82 (vols. 1–8 inclusive)*

Total papers published		133
Relating to population studies		26
By country	Britain and Ireland	11
	North America	10
	Latin America and Caribbean	2
	Rest of Europe	1
	Other	1
By topic	Migration	10
	Mortality and morbidity	6
	Urban social structure	5
	Fertility	1
	Other	4
By period	19th and 20th centuries	18
	18th and 17th centuries	3
	before 1600	4
	no period	1

centuries (Vol. 5, 1979, No. 3), marsh fever and malaria in England from the sixteenth to the nineteenth centuries (Vol. 6, 1980, No. 4) or pronatalism in France (Vol. 8, 1982, No. 3). Of 133 major papers published over the eight years, about one-fifth dealt with population topics. Heavy bias was apparent both in topic and in time period. More than half the papers dealt with migration or with urban social structure, a handful with morbidity and mortality and only one with fertility. In addition, the great majority of papers dealt with the nineteenth or early twentieth centuries. This last point reflects research by British historical geographers generally (Wild, 1980) who are less keen to delve into the pre-1800 mists than they are to deal in the more familiar and more certain events of the nineteenth century.

Availability of sources

A principal limitation on demographic research on the past is indeed the availability of sources and we may use this as an illustration of the ingeniousness of the field. For even in developed European countries, a degree of recorded certainty—and then usually far from total—is introduced only from the beginning of the nineteenth century. Thus, something as fundamental as establishing world population totals, individual populations by country and series of vital events, particularly for the currently less developed world, over a long historical time-span is still more often a matter for speculation than exactitude. Historical demography has been notably inquisitive in finding new sources—for example using, however unreliably, Roman tombstones to establish age structures (Durand, 1960) or in developing demographic archaeology (Hassan, 1981)—and technically expert in their analysis and interpretation. Researchers may often proceed from named individuals and their families, relating a variety of records to piece together the jigsaw puzzle of birth, marriage, death and mobility. In most cases, three main problems apply: unreliability and omissions in the source; relating highly local studies to conclusions of regional or national significance; and, especially important for the study of geographical patterns, gathering sufficient data to provide reliable regional comparisons. These problems have proved considerable for Europe and North America, and are the more so for the populations of Latin America, Asia or Africa.

Two sources stand out as having provoked most progress in historical demography: ecclesiastical or parish registers recording vital events, and the census. Rather paradoxically, both provide so much potential information that computerized techniques have become indispensable and, indeed, where records are good it is sometimes possible to reconstruct populations of the past more easily or completely than those of the present. In the first case, the use of parish registers, available quite widely and over long periods, for example from 1538 in England (Finlay, 1981), has given rise to major methodological innovation, first in France and later in Britain and elsewhere. The major work of Wrigley and Schofield (1981) provides eloquent evidence of the range of material available, the care needed in its analysis and the exciting and fundamental questions the pursuit of aggregate totals may raise and, at least partly, solve. The process of family reconstitution has produced a mass of studies, principally at the village level. As Wrigley (1973:2) himself noted, the general approach afforded by nominal record linkage—that is, the process by which items of information about a particular named individual are associated with each other into a coherent whole—'is a means of discovering things about the lives of ordinary men which would otherwise remain obscure'. At that stage, Wrigley listed ten countries throughout the world where such work was under way; and Flinn (1981) was able to use data from well over 600 parish-level analyses concerning periods between 1500 and 1820. How far we may now draw conclusions about the historical geography of English population, for example, has been carefully sketched for the period 1500–1730 by Smith (1978) while Levine (1977) or Macfarlane (1977) provide a flavour of research possibilities.

The second source—the census—because it becomes effective for most European countries only during the nineteenth century explains the bias noted above, not least amongst geographers interested in migration. The census begins to provide detailed coverage of individuals within a city, region or country and therefore to provide comparable data (Lawton, 1978a), although not without gaps and complexities. The census enumerators books in England, and their equivalent in many other countries, have provided much material; for example, birthplace data have been extensively used in the study of migration by recent researchers (Lawton, 1978b) just as Ravenstein relied upon them almost a century ago (Grigg, 1977). The nineteenth century is also enriched by the availability of civil registers of vital events—for example, from 1806 in France, 1837 in England and Wales and 1855 in Scotland. This has to some extent allowed historical geographers (e.g. Pooley, 1977) to ask similar questions about cities in the past as their colleagues ask about the cities of today. Beyond the civil and parish registers, and the census, lie a large number of sources an account of which may be found in Hollingsworth (1969). The availability of these sources allied of course to the growing importance of the phenomenon itself, has stimulated a large number of studies into internal and international migration or the fate of the migrant in the city (Ward, 1971).

Population geography of the past

A recent general observation on progress in the field has been that 'European historical demographers are catching their breath on a cloudy ledge' (Tilly, 1981:706) where, after a quarter century scrambling up a steep slope, the results of parish-level, family reconstitution studies are showing how complex was the European experience and how inadequate old theories may be in coping with such diverse research results. One of the difficulties is precisely related to the problem of geography: not only how to measure geographical variations accurately and consistently, but above all how to explain them and relate them to the wider social and economic environment. We have seen that geographers, and geography, have been intimately concerned with the study of past populations. In addition, just as population geographers may add a valuable dimension to the work of demographers of contemporary populations, four distinct aspects of the geographical approach to the past are worth emphasizing here. First, there is much still to be learnt about the relationship between population growth and resources, to add to the Malthus-Marx debate, about the controls of the geographical environment which influence for example the process of agricultural change and population fluctuations (Grigg, 1980), and about the whole relationship between different demographic regimes and long-term geography of economic change. Second, the search to discover detailed regional variations in the components of demographic change—why it was for example that where an individual lived in one country rather than another, in countryside or town, in one part of a city rather than another influenced his chances of survival—must continue and be further extended beyond Europe and North America. Third, the adaptation of existing models and theories and the development of new ideas are required to cope specifically with geographical variations (Woods, 1982), from the concept of demographic transition (Noin, 1983) to the diffusion of fertility behaviour or disease. Lastly, the study of migration and mobility in the past is likely to remain, and be developed as, a distinctly geographical approach to the past. This may encompass not only the study of migration for its own sake, and applying the models and theories developed for contemporary populations to the past, but also looking more closely at the relationships between movement and demographic behaviour.

References

Chambers, J.D. (1972) *Population, Economy and Society in Pre-industrial England*, Oxford University Press, Oxford.

Durand, J. (1960) Mortality estimates from Roman tombstone inscriptions, *American Journal of Sociology*, **65**, 365–73.

Finlay, R. (1981) *Parish Registers: an Introduction*, Historical Geography Research Series, No. 7.

Flandrin, J.L. (1979) *Families in Former Times: Kinship, Household and Sexuality*, Cambridge University Press, Cambridge.

Flinn, M.W. (1981) *The European Demographic System 1500–1820*, Johns Hopkins University Press, Baltimore.

Glass, D.V. and Eversley D.E.C. (eds.) (1965) *Population in History, Essays in Historical Demography*, Arnold, London.

Glass, D.V. and Revelle, R. (eds.) (1972) *Population and Social Change*, Arnold, London.

Grigg, D.B. (1977) E.G. Ravenstein and the 'laws of migration', *Journal of Historical Geography*, **3**, 41–54.

Grigg, D.B. (1980) *Population Growth and Agrarian Change*, Cambridge University Press, Cambridge.

Guillaume, P. and Poussou, J-P. (1970) *Démographie historique*, Armand Colin, Paris.

Hajnal, J. (1965) European marriage patterns in perspective, in D.V. Glass and D.E.C. Eversley (eds.) *Population in History*, Arnold, London, 101–43.

Hajnal, J. (1982) Household formation patterns in historical perspective, *Population and Development Review*, **8**, 449–94.

Hassan, F.A. (1981) *Demographic Archaeology*, Academic Press, London.

Hollingsworth, T.H. (1969) *Historical Demography*, Cornell University Press, Ithaca, New York.

Knodel, J.E. (1974) *The Decline of Fertility in Germany, 1871–1939*, Princeton University Press, Princeton N.J.

Laslett, P. (1972) *Household and Family in Past Time*, Cambridge University Press, Cambridge.

Lawton, R. (ed.) (1978a) *The Census and Social Structure: an Interpretative Guide to Nineteenth Century Censuses for England and Wales*, Cass, London.

Lawton, R. (1978b) Population and society 1730–1900, in R.A. Dodgshon and R.A. Butlin (eds.) *An Historical Geography of England and Wales*, Academic Press, London, 313–66.

Lee, R.D. (ed.) (1977) *Population Patterns in the Past*, Academic Press, London.

Lesthaeghe, R.J. (1977) *The Decline of Belgian Fertility 1800–1970*, Princeton University Press, Princeton N.J.

Levine, D. (1977) *Family Formation in an Age of Nascent Capitalism*, Academic Press, New York.

Livi-Bacci, M. (1977) *A History of Italian Fertility During the Last Two Centuries*, Princeton University Press, Princeton, N.J.

Macfarlane, A. in collaboration with Harrison, S. and Jardine, C. (1977) *Reconstructing Historical Communities*, Cambridge University Press, Cambridge.

Marcilio, M.L. and Charbonneau, H. (1979) *Démographie historique*, Presses Universitaires de France, Paris.

Noin, D. (1983) *La transition démographique dans le monde*, Presses Universitaires de France, Paris.

Pooley, C.G. (1977) The residential segregation of migrant communities in mid-Victorian Liverpool, *Transactions, Institute of British Geographers*, New Series, **2**, 364–82.

Smith, R.M. (1978) Population and its geography in England 1500–1730, in R.A. Dodgshon and R.A. Butlin (eds.) *An Historical Geography of England and Wales*, Academic Press, London, 199–237.

Stoianovitch, T. (1976) *French Historical Method: the Annales Paradigm*, Cornell University Press, Ithaca, New York.

Stone, L. (1977) *The Family, Sex and Marriage in England 1500–1800*, Weidenfeld and Nicolson, London.

Tilly, C. (1981) Review of M.W. Flinn (1981), *Population and Development Review*, **7**, 706–8.

Ward, D. (1971) *Cities and Immigrants. A Geography of Change in Nineteenth Century America*, Oxford University Press, London.

Wild, M.T. (ed.) (1980) *Register of Research in Historical Geography*, Historical Geography Research Series, No. 4.

Willigan, J.D. and Lynch, K.A. (1982) *Sources and Methods of Historical Demography*, Academic Press, London.

Woods, R.I. (1982) *Theoretical Population Geography*, Longman, London.

Wrigley, E.A. (ed.) (1966) *An Introduction to English Historical Demography*, Weidenfeld and Nicolson, London.

Wrigley, E.A. (ed.) (1973) *Identifying People in the Past*, Arnold, London.

Wrigley, E.A. and R.S. Schofield (1981) *The Population History of England 1541–1871, A Reconstruction*, Arnold, London.

8

Special Problems in the Population Geography of Small Populations

A. C. WALSH
(Massey University, New Zealand)

Much of my work has been in the Pacific Islands and if a working definition of 'small' is needed the Pacific Islands are my measure. They are small but discrete populations and not part-populations (such as minority groups or socio-economic classes in urban places) which are often also small and of concern to population geographers. The comments which follow derive from my Pacific experience but it is likely that some study problems will be shared by students of part-populations and that not all the problems mentioned will be 'special' to small populations. This is because population geographers share broadly similar problems, irrespective of their scale of operation.

One of the popular misconceptions about small population studies is that they are easy because small numbers are involved. It is often difficult to explain that small does not mean simple, as opposed to complex, and that both small and large population studies require similar numbers of calculations. In these days of the pocket calculator and the computer, small number calculations are only fractionally quicker than calculations involving large numbers. Small is also often associated with isolated, dependent and undeveloped. Where this is the case, it is often more difficult to obtain data and be confident about its reliability than it is in large places. Yet the smaller the data set, the more important that it is accurate, for smallness frequently produces variability and distortions of 'normal' population distributions, even without inaccuracy.

A good way to understand a problem is to be confronted by it yourself. Let us look at some problems of scale and definition in the Pacific Islands context, as illustrated by Table 8.1. If you were given—as I recently was—the task of preparing a United Nations monograph on the ten countries listed in Table

TABLE 8.1. *Some Characteristics of Small Populations in the Pacific Islands*

Country	Population (000) 1978 est.	Land Area sq. km.	Crude density p sq. km.	Annual Population Change (a)	Largest Urban Place (000)	% Urban	Census Edit (b)	Internal Migration (c) 1	2	3	External Migration
Cook Islands	18.5	240	77	−3.2	4.5	25.0	M	3	24.2	6	High
Fiji	607.0	18 272	33	2.1	117.8	37.2	C	6	30.9	98	Low
Kiribati	56.0	712	79	1.6	18.1	32.0	M	4	45.9	14	High
Nauru	7.0	21	333	1.7	—	100.0	M	—	n.a.	—	High in
Niue	3.7	259	14	−5.1	1.0	26.8	MC	—	n.a.	—	High
Western Samoa	153.0	2 935	52	0.7	32.1	21.1	C	4	25.7	38	High
Solomons	214.0	28 538	8	3.4	18.6	9.4	MC	8	18.0	25	Low
Tokelau	1.6	10	160	−0.3	n.a.	n.a.	MC	—	n.a.	—	High
Tonga	93.0	699	133	1.5	18.3	30.1	C	5	18.6	18	High
Tuvalu	7.4	26	285	4.6	2.2	29.8	M	2	32.1	3	High in and out

(a) Percentage change, last two censuses.
(b) Manual, Computer.
(c) Migration: lifetime migrants aged 15 years and over except Cook Islands and Tonga where population all ages.
1. Number of regional units used in author's study (United Nations, 1982)
2. Percentage of population defined as migrants.
3. Mean population size of regions in thousands.

n.a. Not applicable, Nauru and Niue; not available, Tokelau. Nauru and Niue are single islands. Migration was defined to always involve inter-island movement in the smaller islands or major movements in the larger islands.

Source: United Nations ESCAP (1982) *Migration, Urbanization and Development in South Pacific Countries*, Comparative Studies on Migration, Urbanization and Development in the ESCAP Region, Country Report VI, New York.

8.1, and if this study was to be in a series with volumes from much larger Asian countries:

1. Would you accept all ten countries as equally worthy of study?
2. What degree of detail would you adopt so that your work was of use to local administrators yet not cause your Asian colleagues to yawn or, worse still, to laugh at the pettiness of your scale?
3. To study migration we need boundaries. How many would you have in territories so different in size? An equal, or proportionate, or an arbitrary number? Remember, your number will determine the number of people defined as migrants and the level of migration in each territory.
4. How would you define 'urban'? Can Alofi, the capital of Niue, with a population of about 1,000 really be considered urban, and compared with Suva (117,800)?
5. To what extent can you study internal migration without also considering emigration? Note how the level and type of external migration differs between the countries.
6. In short, what definitions and measures would you accept to permit internal, Pacific and perhaps world comparability? Or would you treat each island as unique and thumb your nose at theory and the search for generality?
7. Finally, how would you arrive at all these decisions? In your office? Very dangerous.

Local knowledge is essential in studying small populations. Write to the islands for advice? You're joking. Countries with small populations are often short of skilled administrators. They are likely to be too busy to write to you, or they may be on an overseas course or have been transferred since you last met. So you must go to the islands. The cost is astronomical due to the airline's barely profitable load-distance ratio. The countries noted in Table 8.1, for example, extend over 13 million sq km, yet their total land area is only 52,000 sq km and their total population is less than one million. Perhaps this begins to give you some idea of the problems—and the challenges—of small population studies in the Pacific, and I suspect they are not too different elsewhere.

Most problems confronting the population geographer derive from:

1. the smallness of the society to be studied;
2. the small data set that it generates; and
3. the effect that small societies often have on researchers.

Problem one: the small society

Small societies react quickly to some (and exceedingly slowly to other) situations precisely because they are small. This poses special problems for the researcher.

Physical smallness

Not all societies small in number are also small in areal extent. However, where societal and areal smallness coincide, as in the Pacific islands, chance events and the impact of change can produce considerable demographic distortions. The introduction of European diseases such as influenza and measles, for example, periodically decimated some populations in the Pacific as late as the 1920s. Hurricanes, like diseases, rarely affect all people and places alike. Frequently they hit one side of an island and not another, and where and when they hit is unpredictable. Island-to-metropolitan country migration, which tends to be age and sex selective, is influenced by chance events such as hurricanes, and present-day patterns may be influenced by such events which occurred many years ago. Smallness and isolation also lead to highly-localized genetic differences, some of which have demographic implications.

Small societies tend to be rather conservative but when a new idea is accepted its influence is likely to be pervasive. In terms of the classical S-curve of acceptance, saturation point is often quickly reached. They are, however, also very parochial, and sometimes when an idea such as family planning is quickly adopted by people of most villages, it may not be accepted at all by others. Acceptance or non-acceptance in this case could perhaps be traced back to village rivalries, leading one village to accept a religious denomination which today is sympathetic to family planning and the other to accept another denomination which is totally opposed to it. Similarly, a village's over-representation in some highly paid jobs or in certain migration streams today may be due to earlier acceptance of a mission school which gave that village educational advantages over others in seeking employment on the island itself and overseas. A population geographer needs to be something of an anthropologist and an historian in studying small populations.

Shortage of local expertise

Small societies are frequently dependent on outside expertise because they are short of skilled labour. This is especially evident at census time. Reliance on outside skills, however, does not always have desirable results, for a change in experts can also result in changes in basic census questions and definitions, making intercensal comparisons difficult. One recent Pacific island census, for example, changed to *de jure* enumeration hoping to disclose the extent of internal and short-term external migration which was thought to be considerable. It was not very successful in achieving its aim and many comparisons with the previous *de facto* census were just not possible, especially at local levels. In another country the expatriate census commissioner decided that town populations had been under-enumerated. He therefore introduced raising factors, different for each town, which he assumed would give more realistic figures for urban growth. Unfortunately, he left the country with no-one knowing the raising factors. Ten years later researchers and planners are still having problems due to this man's work.

Lack of local expertise often also leads to problems with the recording and processing of data. Few small societies have their own computer, and much census and survey data are sent overseas for programming and analysis. Something of the uneven situation in the Pacific is shown in Table 8.1. Even where there are local computers, the tapes are used so infrequently that they quickly deteriorate with sometimes rather bizarre results. In Fiji, for example, the 1966 census tape (replayed in 1975 for the first time!) showed some villages to have no males and other, supposedly Fijian, villages to be entirely inhabited by Indians! Manual processing, however, often causes bigger problems as, for example, in the island where the whole census (over 50,000 people) was recorded on cards in a massive pigeonhole filing system the top of which could only be reached by a stepladder. Such were the lengths to which the commissioner was prepared to go, rather than let the census be processed overseas! A somewhat more advanced manual system was the punch-hole card system used in another island, but in both cases even simple cross-tabulations represented a herculean task. Researchers in small societies are more likely than their 'bigger' brothers to have to do much of the processing of data themselves. It will also probably require much more cross-checking.

In populous, developed countries reliable vital statistics are available at local and national levels. In small, underdeveloped countries local records, on which national vital rates statistics are based, are often not very reliable. An overworked local nurse in a remote rural area, for example, is not likely to send very reliable birth and death information to the regional hospital where it is needed for the compilation of records to send on to the national capital. A change in clerical staff at this level can also produce changes in vital statistics. The frequent 'doctoring' of vital statistics, from local through to national levels, produces unreliable data which cannot be used to check the validity of census data. This makes it even more important that census data are reliable, for the census then becomes the *only* base for reasonable estimations of vital rates, life expectancy and age-specific migration.

Outside influences

Size is no guarantee of independence, but much of the economy, life style and the demography of small countries are shaped by larger countries, and students of small countries should be aware of these influences. Relatively small injections of aid, the re-routing of a shipping or an airline service, or the decision to build a hotel here or a secondary school there can produce significant changes in the structure and distribution of population. A change in the world economy and the international job market can lead to strict or generous immigration regulations in larger countries which prompt the movement or otherwise of people whose number on the international scene is few, but whose absence in an island village distorts local age and sex structures, leaves the labour force depleted, and may even produce a non-viable village economy.

Improved contact with the bigger world has heightened this dependence for small societies as a whole, but it has also heightened societal and areal differences within them. Thus, in most Pacific islands there are today often significant income differences between individual households, villages and regions, which cannot be ignored by the geographer.

Finally, much in the recording systems of small countries is determined for them. As a consequence, some statistics collected at the request of larger nations or international agencies are not always very appropriate to the local scene, but often they are the only statistics available.

Problem two: the small data set

The problems of working with a small data set are both conceptual and operational; the former deriving from the societal causes of variability, the latter from the considerable inaccuracies often encountered in studying small populations.

In one way the study of small populations can be compared with the problems of sampling around a normal curve. How confident can we be that the study we are conducting at this particular time is typical of longer time periods (for time depth is often lacking in small population statistical records)? How far can we accept the national average as typical? Should we not try to include a longer time period and perhaps disaggregate the data into smaller, and even more variable, units so that we can see if the sum truly represents the whole? If we are concerned about the 'meaningless mean' at national level, should we also not ask: 'How low can you go' in disaggregation? Further, since variability is a characteristic of small populations, should it not be exposed in statistical ranges rather than be hidden in means? Just how useful is a mean without a standard deviation? Is this chance event typical and to be included in our calculations, or should it be excluded? Can a chance event ever be typical? These are the sorts of *conceptual* questions that pose much difficulty for students of small populations.

The *operational* problems of small data sets derive from the likelihood that even small errors and inaccuracies can have quite major effects. The problem is one of quality of data and the absence of other data against which one's own material can be checked. It is often necessary to check and counter-check each boundary, definition and record back as far as the raw statistic and beyond that to what we might expect as a reasonable figure. The need to think about and to check data in this very detailed manner in small population studies is a useful reminder that we accept much too readily figures provided by others.

The answers to both types of problems require that the student be fully familiar with the substance and the form of his data. In answering conceptual questions he must constantly remind himself of his research purposes. It is so easy in small population studies to wander off into the glades of micro-analysis, to become immersed and even parochial oneself, and to lose sight completely of the useful generality once searched for. Studies of small populations, besides being useful to small country administrators, should also add, no less than studies of larger countries, to our knowledge of population dynamics. Indeed, some population problems are often best studied in small populations. One thinks, for example, of motivational factors in migration, of individual and socio-cultural factors influencing age of marriage and preferred family size, and of the vast labyrinth of interconnections between individual behaviour and the social and physical environment which we still but barely understand.

Problem three: the researcher

Small population studies also require something special from the researcher. A person is drawn into small societies in ways that are not possible in larger societies. During field research one is almost a member of the society, and the participant-observer role is not always easy. Inclusion in the society is essential for the success of the study but it has its responsibilities and dangers. Obviously, one must be especially wary of protecting local confidences; less obviously, one must not be seen to be too attached to any particular household or village or faction. Attachment leads to some sources of information drying up and to partiality creeping into one's work with adverse effects on its quality and use. A poor impression left by a researcher makes the work of researchers who follow him most difficult. People in small communities have long memories.

Really, I suppose, what is most needed of the student of small populations is balance, in the field and in preparing and writing up the work. Research imbalance produces its own distortions to add to those of the small population and data base. Personal bias or favour in the field is one form of imbalance. Too narrow a focus on the area of study is another. Small societies need to be seen against a fairly wide backdrop but their distinctive characteristics should not be submerged to conform to preconceptions based on other societies. Finally, societal elements are so inextricably interwoven in small societies that disciplinary balance—or rather, interdisciplinary balance—is much needed. In this, at least, the population geographer should have no special problems. Whether it is from training, inclination or sheer cussedness that the geographer so often rebels against disciplinary restriction, I do not know, but the resultant eclecticism is an asset in small population studies.

References

Bakker, M.L. (1977) *Demographic Data in the Pacific: Reliability, Improvement, Application*, University of the South Pacific, Suva.

Benedict, B. (ed.) (1967) *Problems of Smaller Territories*, Athlone, London.

Economic and Social Commission for Asia and the Pacific (ECSAP) (1982) *Migration, Urbanization and Development in South Pacific Countries*, Comparative Study on Migration, Urbanization and Development in the ECSAP Region, Country Report VI, United Nations, New York (written by author).

Kosiński, L.A. and Webb, J.W. (eds.) (1976) *Population at Microscale*, I.G.U. and N.Z. Geographical Society, Palmerston North.

Ward, R.G. and Proctor, A. (1980) *South Pacific Agriculture: Choices and Constraints*, Asian Development Bank and Australian National University, Canberra, 3–72, 484–7.

9

Population Geography at Micro-scale: Residential Mobility and Public Policy

W. A. V. CLARK
(University of California, Los Angeles, U.S.A.)

Introduction

Research on residential mobility (intra-urban migration) has proliferated in the past dozen years, but much of this research until very recently has focused on analytic models of the residential mobility process and the attempt to develop generalizations of the way in which people choose houses and neighbourhoods. Up-to-date reviews of this analytic research can be found in Quigley and Weinberg (1977), Short (1978) and Clark (1982). The reviews analyze and evaluate the contributions of this analytic stream of research to understanding residential mobility. It is clear that there has been a significant increase in our understanding of the mobility process. In addition to (a) micro-studies of mobility decision making, there are (b) substantial studies of small area population change and the role of residential relocation in those areal changes, (c) aggregate accounting models of population movements in metropolitan areas, especially the relationship between central city and suburban rings, and (d) detailed studies of neighbourhood change and the role of economic, social and spatial variables in generating those neighbourhood changes over time. There are now several plausible models of the relocation process itself. Elsewhere, I have surveyed this analytic research, and suggested some broad classifications of the research that has been conducted in the past half dozen years (Clark, 1982).

Beginning in the mid-1970s, and increasing in emphasis, there have been a number of critiques of the explicit analytic studies of residential mobility. Short (1978) and Moore and Harris (1979) have emphasized the need to bring policy issues directly into studies of residential mobility. Short, who has been the most critical of the analytic mobility work, has argued from a Marxist perspective that studies of residential mobility serve little purpose unless they are part of the larger societal analyses of population distributions, housing markets and labour markets. Moore and Harris are critical of the analytic studies which merely add policy implications as an afterthought, and suggest that the lack of any contribution of mobility studies to policy issues has been the unwillingness of social scientists in general, and geographers and economists particularly, to address specific questions framed by practitioners in local and federal government. It is these practitioners who are often required to make decisions with respect to political intervention in the housing and labour markets.

The concern with the links between policy and mobility has come somewhat more slowly for studies of residential mobility than for studies of migration in general. In particular, studies of international migration have long had a concern with the political issues related to population redistributions across national boundaries, and increasingly, as reflected in a recent progress report by Clarke (1979), there has been a concern amongst population geographers to address population redistribution policies in developed and developing countries and a number of conferences and conference volumes have examined that specific issue.

It seems probable that the analytic research on residential mobility will continue, but that research can no longer ignore the interconnection of the analytic models and the wider societal structures.

Mobility and policy—a framework for analysis

Establishing links between policy and mobility is complicated (especially in the United States, and to a lesser extent in Europe) because policy is in essence the sum of many different specific public programs. Thus, in addressing the issue of links between mobility and policy, and attempting to understand residential mobility and public policy, it is critical to analyze specific public programs which either have direct or indirect effects on mobility, or are influenced by mobility. It is the thrust of this chapter to focus on specific programs and their relationship to mobility. In this way, it will be possible to develop research which is informative with respect to the outcomes and impact of mobility on policy, and policy on mobility.

However, even though I will concentrate on approaches which have, either analytically or conceptually, linked programs and mobility, there is a considerable body of mobility research which has general policy overtones (Moore and Clark, 1980). Some of this research provides examples of indirect interactions between mobility and government policies. There are notable studies of the migration of the elderly and the potential impacts of changing regional concentrations of the elderly (Wiseman, 1979); the impacts on public services of changing metropolitan concentrations of the elderly (Golant, 1980); the differential impacts of information availability and use on housing search by black and white households (Lake, 1981); the role of real estate agents in providing information for buyers (Palm, 1976); the tendency of rent control to decrease rates of mobility (Clark and Heskin, 1982); and the changing impacts of household size and life cycle structures on the propensity to move (Kobrin, 1976; Stapleton, 1980). At an aggregate level, studies of the ongoing demographic processes and the changing social composition of the central city have shown that much of the differentiation between black central cities and white suburbs is largely independent of specific single policies (Frey, 1979, 1980).

The remainder of this short paper is designed to examine the recent research which attempts to provide a more specific link between analytic models and public policy and to comment in detail on the geographic contributions to the links between studies of residential mobility and public policy.

Mobility and policy: emerging themes

In a recent review of the relationship between residential mobility and public programs, Clark and Moore (1982) suggested three ways (one direct and two indirect) in which mobility relates to public programs. First, there are the relationships, particularly in the housing area, where the programs themselves depend on the mobility of the individuals to produce the desired program effects. Thus, rent subsidies to individuals were designed to improve the quality of housing consumed by low and moderate income households. These are direct relationships. Second, there are public programs which by changing the attributes of local environments, introduce new patterns of mobility. The indirect effects of public funds for major new highways and for neighbourhood facilities have influenced the attractiveness of neighbourhoods, and therefore, relocation patterns. Third, there are programs which are indirectly influenced by population distributions. Many programs are designed to deliver certain services, and the magnitude of the services clearly depends on the size of the population in a receiving area—services for education, or for the elderly are all sensitive to changing population distributions. To clarify the nature of the relationship between policy (programs) and mobility, examples will be reviewed of direct and indirect relationships between mobility and public programs.

Direct intervention—mobility and public programs

Much of the present concern with the relationship between policy and mobility in the United States was directly stimulated by the Experimental Housing Allowance Program (EHAP), which was a Housing and Urban

Development (HUD)-funded experiment involving housing allowances to induce families to consume better housing and to lower the degree of economic, racial and ethnic residential segregation (Rossi, 1979). Clearly, mobility is a central and important element of any experiment which involves payments for housing, because as Rossi notes, the acquisition of better housing means either upgrading the present housing or moving to better accommodation. Thus, intervention in the mobility process is an essential part of the program.

Several analytic investigations of the impact of the EHAP subsidies were conducted by economists and sociologists. Unfortunately, there are a number of measurement problems in the EHAP studies, and the different funding plans that were used further complicated the potential to measure the relationship between the programs themselves and their impacts on residential mobility. However, when the evidence is analyzed, there were experimental effects. In one of the sites (Phoenix, Arizona) households with subsidies were more likely to move than households without subsidies, but this experimental effect was not discovered in the other site (Pittsburgh, Pennsylvania). And, even in Phoenix, where there was an effect of housing subsidies, the experimental effect was very small in terms of the general probabilities of moving amongst low-income renters. The general patterns of mobility tend to be far more pervasive than even modestly large interventions in the system by a particular program. It is clear that the general patterns and behaviours related to mobility are more important than temporary payments, and that there are substantial local effects in terms of residential mobility behaviour, although these local effects have not yet been fully analyzed (Moore, 1981).

Indirect intervention—mobility and government impacts on environments

There are many public programs which indirectly have an impact on household location and relocation, but most of these have not been examined for their specific influences on residential mobility. It is clear that mortgage deductions and the construction of freeways, to mention only two programs (policies) in the United States, have had important impacts on broad patterns of household relocation in North American urban areas. But it is difficult, if not impossible, to untangle the specific effects of these programs from the myriad of other policy impacts that are ongoing in urban areas at the same time.

A recent attempt to untangle the effects of specific programs (versus general demographic processes) and their potential impacts on mobility rates utilized data from a study of the Dutch housing market (Clark and Everaers, 1981). Data on 40 medium-sized Dutch cities were used to examine the variations in mobility rates across cities against variations in demographic variables, housing measures and government policies (programs).

To assess the extent to which policy variables are important influences on mobility outcomes, demographic (age and family composition) and housing (renter/owner ratios, single/multi-family ratios, and age of housing stock) variables were introduced as measures of context (which are known to influence mobility rates at an individual level). Policy measures included the extent to which the national government distributed subsidized housing and offered renewal subsidies to cities.

In order to test the relative contribution of policy measures to variations in mobility rates across cities, the regression model was constructed in a hierarchical manner in which demographic and housing variables were entered first and the policy measures were entered last. In this manner, in which the initial variables are 'forced' into the regression equation, we are able to assess the added contribution to each set of variables. As expected, demographic variables account for a little more than one-third of the variation in mobility rates. Cities with significant populations of younger persons (defined in the study as the proportion of the population between 20 and 35 years) have higher mobility rates and the cities with more families have lower rates. The added explanation by the three measures of housing stock is quite small, 5 per cent, and most of it can be attributed to the variable-'housing stock built prior to 1930'. This association reflects both cheaper housing, often more easily rented, and the interaction of young single persons who live in older rented sections of the city (and who are more mobile).

Even though quite simple measures of government intervention are used, their additional explanation of the variation in mobility rates after controlling for demographic and housing variation is 13 per cent. This result is powerful evidence of the important influence of government in the housing market. Despite considerable discussion of institutional impacts in urban areas, this is some of the first evidence in a comparative (across cities) framework on the size of these impacts.

Indirect intervention—mobility and the provision of services

A very different and more micro-example of the relationship between intervention (policy) and mobility arises in the connection between desegregation policies and mobility. In the United States, beginning in 1971, mandatory bussing of school children has been used to establish integrated schools throughout urban school districts. Although evidence, at the micro-level, of mobility behaviour in response to these programs is still fragmentary, a study of school desegregation policy and intra-district migration showed that in addition to a general suburbanization trend, there were a significant number of relocation decisions by households in response to the desegregation program (Lord and Catau, 1976). Those areas within the school district which were subject to significantly larger amounts of bussing, or which were transition neighbourhoods, were likely to have higher out-migration rates. In some cases, the relocation behaviour may have been in response to the fear of bussing, in addition to the bussing program itself. It is clear that there are impacts of policy interventions, and these impacts in turn may not be those which will be most beneficial for the continuation of the policy. This specific instance is a very good reason for further analyses of the links between programs and residential mobility outcomes.

Geographic contributions to policy analysis

We are still some distance away from any clear relationships between analytic models and public programs and their outcomes. The general procedure has not been to focus on the spatial aspects of the outcomes, even though most of the analyses of residential mobility are specifically concerned with the interaction of origin and destination areas. For example, in the analysis of population relocation in studies of school desegregation, most of the analyses have been undertaken at the district level, and have been aggregate studies of white population loss from central cities of metropolitan areas. In fact, this effect may average out individual neighbourhoods and their schools which have little loss of population, and other neighbourhoods and schools which have significant and large losses of school children. The specific effects of these are important for the policy-maker, because it is the local contextual effects which are critical in policy decision making, with respect to the opening and closing of schools, rather than the overall level of change in the district as a whole.

The future

The increasing evidence of links between mobility and policy have established that it is insufficient to study mobility out of its wider social context. It does appear, however, that it is appropriate to continue research in residential mobility in two general streams. The analytic studies focused on the individual decision-making processes will continue to be important, and in the long run may provide the most important structures for further detailed research. A second stream will emphasize the social interface of residential mobility and quite properly will emphasize the outcomes of mobility and its relationship to public programs.

A second point to be made in evaluating research on the links between policy and mobility is to reiterate that policy must be seen within local contexts and in terms of the socio-demographic processes that affect mobility. Adjustments in local market contexts which affect the supply of housing are certainly important elements in understanding mobility processes. Even more important is to recognize that the policy contribution to explanations of mobility (as in the example from the Dutch housing market) will be small, additional explanations. Demographic events—births, deaths, ageing, household formation and dissolution—will remain the significant elements in mobility and the impact of public programs is likely to be in the nature of additional rather than primary explanations.

Residential mobility (demand for housing) clearly involves the interaction of the household with the housing market (the supply side), and therefore the supply side of the equation is equally important. Research by British geographers and sociologists has emphasized the impact of institutions (Boddy and Gray, 1979), but in general there are still few studies which analyze the role of housing supply and its allocation, and those impacts on mobility patterns. Other notable exceptions in the British context include Bassett and Short (1980) and Murie, Niner and Watson (1976). A limited study of the role of information has been carried out in the United States (Smith, Clark and Onaka, 1982). But as studies of policy develop, they are likely to be interwoven with analyses of the supply side of the residential mobility equation. Whether the emphasis on the supply side and the role of institutions requires a totally new research paradigm, as has been suggested by some researchers, will be a topic for debate in the coming decade (Maher, 1980).

References

Bassett, K. and Short, J. (1980) *Housing and Residential Structure*, Routledge and Kegan Paul, London.

Boddy, M. and Gray, F. (1979) Filtering theory, housing policy and the legitimation of inequality, *Policy and Politics*, **7**, 39–54.

Clark, W.A.V. (1980) Residential mobility and neighborhood change: some implications for racial residential segregation, *Urban Geography*, **1**, 95–117.

Clark, W.A.V. and Everaers, P. (1981) Public policy and residential mobility in Dutch cities, *Tijdschrift voor Economische en Sociale Geografie*, **72**, 322–33.

Clark, W.A.V. (1982) Recent research on migration and mobility: a review and interpretation, *Progress in Planning*, 18.

Clark, W.A.V. and Heskin, A. (1982) The impact of rent control on tenure discounts and residential mobility, *Land Economics*, **58**, 109–17.

Clark, W.A.V. and Moore, E.G. (1982) Residential mobility and public programs: current gaps between theory and practice, *Journal of Social Issues* (forthcoming).

Clarke, J.I. (1979) Population geography, *Progress in Human Geography*, **3**, 261–6.

Frey, W.H. (1979) Central city white flight: racial and nonracial causes, *American Sociological Review*, **44**, 425–48.

Frey, W.H. (1980) Black in-migration, white flight, and the changing economic base of the central city, *American Journal of Sociology*, **85**, 1396–417.

Golant, S. (1980) Future directions for elderly migration research, *Research on Aging*, **2**, 271–80.

Harris, R. and Moore, E.G. (1980) An historical approach to residential mobility, *Professional Geographer*, **32**, 22–9.

Kobrin, F.E. (1976) The fall in household size and the rise of the primary individual in the United States, *Demography*, **13**, 127–38.

Lake, R.W. (1981) *The New Suburbanites: Race and Housing in the Suburbs*, Centre for Urban Policy Research, Rutgers University, New Brunswick, New Jersey.

Lord, J. and Catau, J. (1976) School desegregation, bussing and suburban migration, *Urban Education*, **11**, 275–94.

Maher, C.A. (1980) Intraurban mobility and urban spatial structure: a review of current issues, Monash University, Department of Geography, Unpublished paper, Monash, Australia.

Moore, E.G. (1981) Inter-city contrasts in residential mobility: some implications for public policy, *Association American Geographers, Conference Paper*, Los Angeles, California.

Moore, E.G. and Harris, R. (1979) Residential mobility and public policy, *Geographical Analysis*, **11**, 175–83.

Moore, E.G. and Clark, W.A.V. (1980) The policy context for mobility research, in W.A.V. Clark and E.G. Moore (eds.), *Residential Mobility and Public Policy*, Sage Publications, Beverly Hills, California, 10–28.

Murie, A., Niner, P. and Watson, C. (1976) *Housing Policy and the Housing System*, Allen and Unwin, London.

Palm, R. (1976) *Urban Social Geography from the Perspective of the Real Estate Salesman*, Center for Real Estate and Urban Economics, Institute of Urban and Regional Development, University of California, Berkeley.

Quigley, J. and Weinberg, D. (1977) Intraurban residential mobility: a review and synthesis, *International Regional Science Review*, **2**, 41–66.

Rossi, P. (1979) Housing allowances and residential mobility, The Brookings Institution, Conference Paper.

Rossi, P. (1980) *Why Families Move*, Second Edition, Sage Publications, Beverly Hills, California.

Short, J.R. (1978) Residential mobility, *Progress in Human Geography*, **2**, 419–47.

Smith, T., Clark, W.A.V. and Onaka, J. (1982) Information provision: An analysis of newspaper real estate advertisements, in W.A.V. Clark (ed.) *Modelling Housing Market Search*, Croom Helm, London, 160–86.

Stapleton, C. (1980) Reformulation of the family life cycle concept, *Environment and Planning A*, **12**, 1103–18.

Wiseman, R. (1979) Regional patterns of elderly concentration and migration, in S. Golant (ed.) *Location and Environment of Elderly Population*, Wiley, New York, 21–36.

10

Population Geography and Ageing

D. T. ROWLAND
(Australian National University, Australia)

Social science research on ageing has been gaining much momentum since the 1970s, reflecting the rapid growth of the elderly population, a wider recognition of their needs, and an escalation in public expenditure upon them for income maintenance, health services, domiciliary support and accommodation. There are many geographical research frontiers in ageing including: inter-regional and inter-community comparisons of the requirements and resources of the elderly; analyses of the influence of the environment upon aged persons' quality of life; assessment of the spatial impact of public policies; accounting for spatial variations in the size and composition of the elderly population; and examining the determinants and consequences of the mobility and immobility of the aged. These and other research issues are elaborated in the ensuing discussion.

Two wide-ranging reviews of social gerontology have recently appeared in the geographical literature (Wiseman, 1978; Warnes, 1981), and the aim here is to complement them through an overview of themes of particular interest in population geography. Ageing is an eclectic field, and it is inevitable that the geographical study of the aged will draw upon the experience of many disciplines. Similarly, ageing is a subject relevant to several branches of geography. Although the themes discussed here are addressed widely in research on ageing, their investigation in relation to spatial analyses of the size, composition and dynamics of older populations is the particular focus of population geography.

Diversity

Since 65 years is commonly used to define the start of old age, the older population is necessarily diverse in age composition, as well as in other characteristics. Diversity negates stereotypes of older people, and makes the targeting of programs and policies for the aged very complex. Documenting diversity by identifying and explaining the distribution of the aged with particular characteristics is thus an essential prerequisite for effective planning as well as for the development of a realistic perspective on the older population. In recognition of diversity, the age range of the older population is frequently dichotomized into the 'young–old' (65–74 years) and the 'old–old' (75 years and over). Use of this dichotomy helps to draw attention to marked contrasts within the older population by providing a simple and manageable approach to cross-classifying age with other population characteristics. Chronological age, however, is an imperfect measure of capacity, and it is important to recognize variations within age groups as well as between them. Recognition of diversity can also assist in avoiding research which Warnes (1981:328) described as having a 'somewhat narrow technical character' and 'an impersonal concern with average behaviour'.

Social integration

Failure to recognize variations within the aged population can give rise to the view that the elderly are isolated from family life, reliant upon others for support and constitute a mounting burden upon the resources of society. On the contrary, the elderly have problems similar to those of younger generations as well as problems associated with ageing, and the majority of the elderly are healthy, self-reliant and active, making useful contributions to family and community life. Yet stereotyping influences attitudes and actions and has led to the expectation that governments must assume increasing responsibility for the care of the frail, and that advanced chronological age is necessarily associated with dependency. Such thinking can cause the diversion of resources from support to families, an over-emphasis on material needs, and premature institutionalization, thereby setting the elderly apart and diminishing their social integration.

Social integration is a major theme in research on ageing, because it is a useful criterion against which the position of the elderly may be assessed and the impact of policies evaluated. Rosow (1967) argued that individuals are integrated into society through their values, roles and membership of formal and informal groups. The more the elderly preserve the patterns of middle age on these three dimensions, the greater the likelihood of their integration. For example, Rosow noted that ageing is accompanied by major role losses brought about through changes in marital status, employment, income and health. Economic changes in the twentieth century have eroded work opportunities for older people, thereby making loss of employment a usual consequence of ageing, and retirement commonly entails a substantial reduction in income, which may necessitate sacrifices in terms of previous life styles. Similarly, chronic illnesses, which become more prevalent with age, can seriously impair the performance of social roles. Ageing also affects group membership since retirement, residential movement and mortality undermine contact with family and friends. Thus integration is affected by changes associated with individual ageing, and by societal changes in production and family roles, which make social integration a matter of policy—to ensure the elderly maximum opportunity to participate and contribute to society (United Nations, 1975:24 and 51).

Social integration is a predictor of quality of life (Maddox and Wiley, 1976:13), but a person is not necessarily isolated or alienated simply through a low level of participation in society, since preferences as well as opportunities determine levels of participation. It follows that the issue is not whether particular aged persons are active in society, but whether opportunities are open to the elderly to remain in their own homes and to participate in family and community life to the extent that they wish.

A geographical perspective is central to the study of the social integration of the aged through the insights it can provide into the extent of residential segregation and spatial isolation of the elderly, the accessibility of services to them and the availability of domiciliary care facilitating the preservation of local ties. Maintaining the frail elderly at home through domiciliary services and community care programs is widely viewed as a desirable goal, and the failure of the community to provide adequate services is cited as a major reason for elderly people having to leave the family residence (United Nations, 1975:28). The aged in rural areas are often at a particular disadvantage in access to support services, because of the high cost of meeting the needs of widely scattered populations. The scale and accessibility of services, as well as the diffusion of knowledge about their existence, are considerations in planning to which geographical research can make a key contribution.

Nevertheless, it should be emphasized that the majority of the frail elderly do not use domiciliary support services, not only because of an under-supply, but also because of the availability of assistance from relatives. Thus sometimes the main issue is not whether the elderly themselves are receiving adequate care, but whether supporting relatives are being over-burdened by family responsibilities which community services could alleviate.

Dependency

Closely related to the social integration theme is that of dependency, sometimes defined in demographic terms as the ratio of elderly persons to those of working age. Such a definition, however, is only a starting point in the analysis of dependency, since the concept is multi-dimensional—the more material aspects include economic dependence and reliance on others for needs of daily living. While these types of dependency can be studied through statistics on incomes and health, there remain unresolved difficulties in identifying the needs of people (Pinch, 1979:203). For example, many pensions and benefits are granted on the basis of eligibility, assessed from age and income rather than from more sophisticated measures of need. Furthermore, some old people equate dependence with reliance upon family members, others with the use of support services (Russell, 1981:157–64), and old people's self-evaluated health—as obtained in household surveys—need not correlate strongly with objective indices of health (Shanas, 1968:67).

Despite these difficulties, dependency is a major issue because policy-makers interpret some of the main consequences of demographic ageing at the societal scale in terms of the 'burden of dependency', and because dependency, through its ties with the notions of role loss and the need for public and private support, is necessarily linked with social integration. Geographical analyses of demographic dependency ratios can provide useful background to the nature of the spatial allocation of resources to different age groups, as well as to the identification of places where the processes of individual and population ageing are potentially imposing an economic burden upon communities. Moreover, investigation of the relationship between the distribution of the vulnerable aged—in poor health or on low incomes—and the distribution of services and programs for them, is a means of determining the match between potential need and public support, and the consequences for the aged of living in particular places.

A further dimension of this theme is the interdependence of generations for different forms of assistance, spatial proximity being a prerequisite for the successful functioning of many kinds of support. While residential shifts may weaken or strengthen such linkages, individual mobility limitations associated with ageing can reduce the exchange of help; this places many of the elderly in a situation of dependence on relatives for aid with gardening, shopping, housework, cooking and, ultimately, personal care.

Environment

Since health impairments and withdrawal from the labour force increase the amount of time the elderly spend in the home and neighbourhood, they are most susceptible to the environmental influences of the residential setting. Characteristics of the environment can constrain or encourage independent living as well as limit or enhance social integration. Research on the influence of the environment on the aged has been guided by a wide variety of hypotheses, such as: (i) 'the less competent the individual, the greater the impact of environmental factors on that individual' (Lawton, 1980:14); (ii) the over-protective environment creates undue levels of dependency (Crandall, 1980:281); (iii) the residential location of the aged is a function of the age of their neighbourhood (Golant, 1972:43); (iv) changes in the spatial structure of cities, requiring greater individual mobility to obtain access to shops and services, have been especially disadvantageous to those elderly who have difficulties in driving, walking or using public transport (Wiseman, 1978:1); (v) as the person grows older there is a change of emphasis within geographic experience involving a constriction in the realm of action which is accompanied by an expansion of the role of geographical fantasy; (vi) and as the change of emphasis between action and fantasy occurs, 'there are consistent accompanying changes in the older person's orientation within space and in feelings about the places of his life reflecting a selective intensification of involvement' (Rowles, 1978:202).

Research has encountered many difficulties in identifying major environmental influences on behaviour, suggesting that single-variable analyses need to be replaced by approaches which recognize the interactions between different aspects of the environment (Lawton, 1978:63), including past associations as well as contemporary ones. For example, Rowles (1978:208) has explained some inconclusive findings about the relationship between morale and environment in terms of a neglect of the nature of the environment in the past, from which derives its familiarity, and its importance in reminiscence. Also, the contemporary elderly have a pronounced tendency to express favourable views of their circumstances:

> 'The apparently universal propensity of the elderly towards higher levels of satisfaction . . . has been attributed to a number of reasons: that today's old people were socialized to be happy with their lot; that they compare themselves with other elderly people; that they are less ready to express "failure" when questioned by strangers; that they remember the severe and almost universal hardships of the inter-war depression; that older people will have had more time to filter away from unsatisfactory physical and social environments; and that older people will have learned the emotional advantages of "dissonance reduction"—liking what they have and not liking what they have not got' (Knox & MacLaren, 1978:238).

Moreover, because of the diversity of the aged, there are conflicting findings about the desirability of living among age peers or in less segregated environments (Lawton, 1978:56), which poses one of a number of dilemmas in the application of research to planning the provision of housing and services for older people. Other dilemmas arise from inadequate assessment of the needs and wants of the aged, which can lead both to hardship through inadequate assistance and to socially created dependency through excessive provision of support. Achievement of the happy medium of a matching of requirements with social support is further complicated by the changing spatial distribution and composition of the aged population, an area in which geographical contributions to planning are much needed.

Mobility

In planning for the aged, opportunities exist to project impending developments quite accurately, since much of the growth in their numbers in communities is due to flow-on effects among existing residents, rather than to the effects of the inward migration of the aged. Indeed, although retirement migration is conspicuous and attracts much attention in the literature, residential stability rather than mobility is the dominant theme in the location of the elderly. For example, Kendig (1976:149) observed that the elderly moved infrequently, despite unfavourable housing and neighbourhood conditions, because of low incomes, high home ownership rates, limited opportunities in the housing market and the adaptational costs of change. Golant (1972:187) has also noted that low mobility could be attributable to the failure of the housing market to provide accommodation for the elderly that is suitable in terms of cost, size or location. Immobility provides a significant lead-time in planning, which is unavailable for many age-specific services and facilities for younger population groups.

While changes in the distribution of the elderly result more from individual ageing than from spatial mobility, migration remains a major consideration in accounting for areal variations in the growth and composition of older populations. Literature on the migration of the elderly draws particular attention to life cycle stage, housing and environmental considerations as precipitating factors in movement (Murphy, 1979; Svart, 1976). However, more attention appears to have been given to the redistribution of the 'young–old', emphasizing retirement migration, than to the movement of the 'old–old', whose motives for moving are probably quite different. Kendig (1976:149) noted that unanticipated forced moves can predominate over voluntary moves by elderly less capable persons; and widows, the poor and the very old move most frequently. There is evidence of a strong preference among the elderly for the familiar neighbourhood, and attachment to the place of residence contributes to an acceptance of overly large and sometimes poor housing.

Residential mobility of the elderly is often seen as conducive to social isolation, except perhaps where the elderly are participating in a chain migration of relatives (Rosow 1967:22) or are returning to a previous place of residence. Rowles (1978:22) observed that 'many older people experience severe (on occasion fatal) traumas during relocation . . . to new housing and especially to institutional settings.' He suggested that the reason for this may be not so much problems of adjustment to the new environment as grieving over the loss of the old.

Territorial justice

While there are many other research themes, those of diversity, integration, dependency, environment and mobility encompass some of the leading issues in contemporary social gerontology, and are especially appropriate in geographical enquiry. Because of the focus of population geography upon the spatial ramifications of population processes and characteristics, ageing and the aged comprise well-defined subjects for study. The geographical study of the aged is a significant research frontier because of the current dearth of such enquiries, and because of continuing and impending changes in the size, distribution and composition of the aged population and its position in society. In developing countries, for instance, projections reveal that demographic ageing early in the next century will produce unprecedented demands upon national economies and social support systems (United Nations, 1982), and even in the remainder of the twentieth century the numbers of the elderly there are likely to triple (Hauser, 1976: 84). The time lapse before developing countries experience the full effects of changes in their age structures should be viewed as an opportunity to prepare for this eventuality, rather than a reason for postponing research.

Geographers studying aspects of individual and population ageing will need to be acquainted with the subject matter of social gerontology, but they are in a position to make distinctive contributions to this field of knowledge, notably through the exploration of territorial justice. This concept refers to a matching of resources with the needs of areas, and provides a basis for determining allocations between competing local authorities (Pinch, 1979: 202). Problems with the concept arise in that, within areas, the most disadvantaged persons may not receive the support intended for them, either because of resistance to accepting welfare or because of difficulties in identifying needs, especially when such efforts are based entirely on aggregate population characteristics (Pinch, 1979: 204 and 219). Resolution of such problems, however, can be approached through small-scale follow-up studies, which may be used to verify and elaborate analyses emphasizing comparisons between areas. Territorial justice remains a little explored but promising concept; it could give geographical research on the aged a firm sense of purpose by stimulating thinking about the uses of such work in the development of social policies.

References

Binstock, R.H. and Shanas, E. (eds.) (1976) *Handbook of Aging and the Social Sciences*, Van Nostrand Reinhold, New York.

Crandall, R.C. (1980) *Gerontology: A Behavioural Science Approach*, Addison-Wesley Publications, Reading M.A.

Golant, S.M. (1972) *The Residential Location and Spatial Behavior of the Elderly: A Canadian Example*, University of Chicago, Department of Geography, Research Paper No. 143.

Hauser, P.M. (1976) Ageing and world-wide population change, in R.H. Binstock and E. Shanas (eds.) *ibid.*, 58–86.

Herbert, D.T. and Johnston, R.J. (eds.) (1978) *Geography and the Urban Environment: Progress in Research and Applications*. vol. 1, John Wiley, Chichester.

Herbert, D.T. and Smith, D.M. (eds.) (1979) *Social Problems and the City: Geographical Perspectives*, Oxford University Press, Oxford.

Kendig, H. (1976) Neighbourhood conditions of the aged and local Government, *The Gerontologist*, **16**, 148–56.

Knox, P.L. and MacLaren, A. (1978) Values and perceptions in descriptive approaches to Urban Social Geography, in D.T. Herbert and R.J. Johnston (eds.) *ibid.*, 197–248.

Lawton, M.P. (1978) Ecology and aging, in L.A. Pastalan and D.H. Carson (eds.), *Spatial Behavior of Older People*, Michigan, 40–67.

Lawton, M.P. (1980) *Environment and Aging*, Brooks/Cole series in Social Gerontology, Brooks/Cole, Monterey, California.

Maddox, G.L. and Wiley, J. (1976) Scope, concepts and methods in the study of aging, in R.H. Binstock and E. Shanas (eds.) *ibid.*, 3–34.

Murphy, P. (1979) Migration of the elderly: A review, *Town Planning Review*, **50**, 84–93.

Pastalan, L.A. and Carson, D.H. (eds.) (1978) *Spatial Behavior of Older People*, University of Michigan—Wayne State University, Ann Arbor, Michigan.

Pinch, S. (1979) Territorial justice in the city: A case study of the social services for the elderly in Greater London, in D.T. Herbert and D.M. Smith (eds.), *ibid.*, 201–24.

Rosow, I. (1967) *Social Integration of the Aged*, Free Press, New York.

Rowles, G.D. (1978) *Prisoners of Space? Exploring the Geographical Experience of Older People*, Westview Press, Boulder, Colorado.

Russell, C. (1981) *The Ageing Experience*, Studies in Society: 10, George Allen and Unwin, Sydney.

Shanas, E. *et al.* (1968) *Old People in Three Industrial Societies*, Routledge and Kegan Paul, London.

Svart, L.M. (1976) Environmental preference migration: A review, *Geographical Review*, **66**, 314–30.

United Nations (1975) *The Aging: Trends and Policies*, Department of Economic and Social Affairs (ST/ESA/22), 3, New York.

United Nations (1982) *World Assembly on Aging, Introductory Document: Demographic Considerations*, Report of the Secretary General, United Nations, Vienna.

Warnes, A.M. (1981) Towards a geographical contribution to Gerontology, *Progress in Human Geography*, **5**, 317–41.

Warnes, A.M. (ed.) (1982) *Geographical Perspectives on the Elderly*, Wiley, New York.

Wiseman, R.F. (1978) *Spatial Aspects of Aging*, Association of American Geographers, Commission on College Geography, Resource Papers, No. 78–4, Washington.

11

Geography, Epidemiology and Human Health

PETER CURSON
(Macquarie University, Sydney, Australia)

Introduction

Medical geography and epidemiology share a common interest in the occurrence, distribution and determinants of states of health in human populations. Neither discipline is new; both share a claim to a long heritage extending from the Hippocratic writings which speculate on the relationship between the physical environment and disease through the nineteenth century studies of disease mortality to the ecological research of the 1950s. Both rely on similar data sources and survey methods. In each case the concern is with patterns of health, illness and medical care in populations and groups. This concern is based upon the belief that these phenomena exhibit particular characteristics which can only be expressed in population terms. From time to time medical geography and epidemiology have also been described as medical ecology, involving a system the basic components of which are physical, biologic, socio-economic and spatial. Both fields have also been defined in terms of their methods and conceptual approach, a particular method of reasoning about a subject, so that 'epidemiology is a method of reasoning about disease that deals with biological inferences derived from observations of disease phenomena in population groups' (Lilienfeld, D.E., 1978:89) and 'medical geography . . . is the application of geographical methods and skills to medical problems' (McGlashan, 1973:220). It would also seem that epidemiologists have engaged in much the same internal debate and suffer the same doubts as geographers as to the definition and nature of their discipline. In the final analysis, however, both subjects would appear to subscribe to Hirsch's (1883) definition of historical and geographical pathology as '. . . science(s) which . . . will give firstly, a picture of the occurrence, the distribution and the types of the diseases of mankind, in distinct epochs of time and at various points of the earth's surface; and secondly, will render an account of the relations of these diseases to the external conditions surrounding the individual and determining his manner of life'.

Epidemiology and medical geography would appear to accept as a general premise the assumption that patterns of mortality, health and health care do not occur randomly in human populations but in ordered patterns which reflect underlying causes. Both would agree that knowledge of these patterns provides a key to understanding causation and leads to methods of prevention and control. Medical geography has tended to concentrate on the spatial patterns and relationships of health and health care in the belief that spatial interrelatedness of health and other variables provides an entrée to the search for causality. Epidemiology, on the other hand, has been more single-minded in its pursuit of causal associations between states of health and environmental exposures.

Despite such a commonality of origins and concern, epidemiology and medical geography remain largely introspective and have never developed a close working relationship. In addition, whereas epidemiology occupies an important place within medicine and public health, medical geography continues to remain at the periphery of geographical and population studies. Medical geography would further seem not to have been afforded the recognition extended to medical anthropology and sociology in the general field of public health and community medicine. Such is perhaps surprising, as Hellen (1979) points out, given the widespread interest in health and health care, the importance of preventive health in Third World countries, the role of spatial epidemiology in the U.S.S.R. and the fact that medical schools are incorporating more and more material of a bio-social nature in their teaching programs. The lack of communication between epidemiology and medical geography is a matter of some concern for those interested in unravelling the complexities of health and health care. To a large extent such a lack stems from the conceptual roots of the two subjects—geography with the social sciences and epidemiology with medicine, but it also stems from the nature of professional training. Medical geography still occupies a minority position within geography teaching programs, and, in addition, very few geography students have the opportunity of including any formal epidemiology within their degree. In consequence, few medical geographers possess any formal training in epidemiology. Even fewer epidemiologists, however, possess an acquaintance with medical geography. Most epidemiologists have approached their field via the narrow corridors of clinical medicine or in some cases via psychology or social work.

Geographical perspectives on health patterns

Research in the geography of health and disease has largely concentrated on three broad interacting themes which demonstrate the geographer's overriding concern for 'spatial relationships, patterns, processes and movements . . . their causes . . . and what they . . . influence . . .' (Woods, 1982: xii). Briefly these three themes are—

1. The spatial patterning of mortality, health and disease
2. The diffusion of disease through time and space
3. The spatial analysis of health care, behaviour and planning.

The spatial patterning of mortality, health and disease

It has long been recognized that mortality and many aspects of human health display distinctive areal distribution patterns. The literature on the ecological approach to the spatial distribution of mortality and disease is substantial and represents a significant area of the subject's concern. Most of this work, whether it be cartographic analyses of disease mortality or investigations of the spatial incidence of particular diseases, seeks justification in the claim that 'spatial variations in state of health can be regarded as an important element in spatial variations in the human condition in general' (Smith, 1982: 5). It is also claimed that identification of the spatial contours of mortality and disease may generate hypotheses as to causal associations. Although many of these studies remain at the broadly visual and descriptive level and treat the identification of spatial patterns of health as an end in itself, some have gone on to identify the spatial correlates of disease. In this, the concern has been primarily to use geographical methods and models to pinpoint those components of the local environment which are hazardous to human health. To this end some studies have simply relied on visual comparison of two or more distributional patterns as indicating some sort of causal relationship. Others, however, have incorporated a much more rigorous statistical methodology into their work (e.g. Armstrong *et al*, 1978; Glick, 1980; Meade, 1980).

The geographical approach is not without its difficulties. King (1979) has highlighted some of the problems inherent in the analysis of spatial patterns of disease. Broadly, these fall into four major categories: (a) the choice and applicability of disease measures or rates; (b) the problems attendant upon the cartographic representation of mortality and disease rates; (c) the constraints associated with spatial analysis *per se*, such as the ecological fallacy of inferring individual behaviour from aggregative data and the problem of scale in so far as ecological correlation coefficients are influenced by the size of areal unit employed; and (d) what King calls the problem of 'latency and mobility', that is, the time lag between exposure and death or the manifestation of disease. The situation may be further complicated by the fact that the areal distribution of mortality and disease may simply be one spatial expression of social class and 'that the search for causes . . . via ecological association risks confusing an intervening variable for the ultimate origin of differential health experiences' (Smith, 1982:5). Faced with such problems we may, like Girt (1980), be forced to question the ultimate utility of the geographical method in that it may be productive of little more than low-level hypotheses as to cause.

Diffusion studies of disease

Much of the work in medical geography has been static and cross-sectional in approach seeking to provide a pen-picture at a single point of time. While truly dynamic studies of health are still rare in geography, an emerging area of considerable importance has been the application of formal geographical techniques and models to epidemiological problems such as the diffusion of epidemics through time and space. Work by Hunter and Young (1971), Haggett (1972) and particularly Cliff, Haggett, Ord and Versey (1981) on the diffusion of particular epidemics of infectious disease show just what can be achieved by a subtle blend of epidemiology, spatial diffusion theory, time series models and cartographic techniques in 'formulating and testing hypotheses, of contributing to model building . . . [and increasing] our understanding of the spread of a disease which poses a continuing threat to public health . . .' (Cliff *et al*, 1981:191).

The spatial analysis of health care, behaviour and planning

The final area of geographical research into human health concerns investigation into the spatial patterning of health care facilities, the behaviour of health clients and the optimal planning of health services (e.g. Shannon and Dever, 1974). Work in this area has tended to concentrate on three broad areas. The first comprises the structure and spatial pattern of medical services and includes consideration of the spatial hierarchy of health care facilities and the distribution of health resources (individual practitioners, clinics, hospitals, etc). The second concerns the study of spatial variations in patient access and utilization of health facilities, and the socio-spatial factors which influence patient behaviour. In the final area of research, work has been mainly directed towards the identification of spatial clusters of inequality and deprivation in the supply, use and comprehension of health facilities and the planning of optimal health care services in terms of human need.

Epidemiological perspectives on health and disease

Although epidemiology has been variously defined, most would probably agree that the field concerns 'the study of the distributions and determinants of states of health in human populations' (Susser, 1973:3).

The discipline long ago escaped from its original preoccupation with epidemics of infectious disease, and has successfully applied its methods and focus to the investigation of chronic diseases and problems of health care. Like geography, the majority of epidemiological research is observational and descriptive rather than experimental and by consequence its output often differs little from that of medical geography in that it consists of measures of disease frequencies, spatial and temporal distributions, measures of health care usage and demand, distance travelled to service, distributions of bed-occupancy rates, etc. Where it differs from medical geography, however, is that it tends to concern itself more specifically with problem solving and hypothesis testing in search of causal associations between states of exposure and disease outcomes. Like geography, the discipline is heavily dependent upon the survey method and utilizes observations and measurements derived from randomized samples. In epidemiology, the central concern is with the evaluation of 'exposure' and the measurement of 'risk' (e.g. Lilienfeld, A.M., 1976).

Substantive work in epidemiology has tended to concentrate on three broad areas:

1. Broad descriptive studies of mortality patterns.
2. Descriptive studies of disease distribution.
3. Causal studies investigating the relationship between a particular exposure or agent and an outcome, often with the aim of establishing measures of risk.

In describing patterns of mortality and disease in time and space and according to a variety of population characteristics such as age, sex, ethnicity and socio-economic status, the work of epidemiologists bears close resemblance to that of geographers. It is with respect to the investigation of causal relationships that epidemiology has made the greatest contribution.

Methods of investigating causal hypotheses

Undoubtedly the main strengths of epidemiology lie in its precision in measuring outcome and risk, and in its development of particular methodologies pertinent to the investigation of well-defined causal hypotheses. To this end epidemiologists make use of a four-fold table, the cells of which indicate the frequency in a population with which an effect (the dependent variable) and a cause (the independent variable) occur separately or together (Table 11.1).

A typical approach to investigating a causal hypothesis is to select a population of cases and controls for comparison. Basically there are two main approaches, usually described as *retrospective* and *prospective*. In a retrospective or *case-control study* a population of cases with a particular disease is selected. One (sometimes more) set of controls free of the disease is selected and matched as closely as possible to the case population with respect to a

TABLE 11.1. *The epidemiological framework*

Exposure Status (Independent Variable)	Disease Status (Dependent Variable) Disease	No Disease	Total
Exposed	a	b	a+b
Not Exposed	c	d	c+d
	a+c	b+d	a+b+c+d

range of bio-social variables. Enquiry is thereafter directed towards establishing the history of supposed causal exposures and experiences. In terms of Table 11.1, the following applies: a+c represents cases, b+d the controls and the end point sees a/a+c compared with b/b+d.

Even in the area of health care research case-control studies have been useful, usually taking as their starting point the delivery of an item of service and then seeking to discover not only why the disease occurred but also why the patient presented where he did, at a particular time and in a particular manner.

In a prospective or *cohort study* the researcher begins with a set of people who are exposed to a specific risk factor and with a matched set of controls who are not exposed. Both groups are then followed through time to see how many ultimately manifest the disease. In terms of Table 11.1 the relevant equation is: a/a+b compared with c/c+d.

Both retrospective and prospective studies have their advantages and disadvantages but generally they have proved a valuable tool in investigating cause and establishing risk.

Epidemiology also uses a variety of other strategies such as *case series* studies (a+c Table 11.1), *cross-sectional* approaches where the data are collected cross-sectionally at one point of time and then allocated to the particular cells of Table 11.1, and finally experimental studies. Of the last, the *randomized controlled trial* occupies a central place in epidemiological method. This method involves the researcher in active and planned intervention whereby a new element is introduced into an existing environment and its effect monitored. Similarity of cases and controls is achieved by a process of randomization, that is randomly allocating persons to a treated or untreated group. The actual nature of treatment is also hidden from the participants as well as where possible from the person assessing the outcome (a double-blind trial). The attraction of such an approach lies in the fact that where a difference appears between cases and controls it can be put down to one of two causes, either the effect of the introduced element or the inadequacies of the randomization process.

If there are weaknesses in the epidemiological method, then they stem from the subject's conceptualization and use of socio-economic and environmental variables and its failure to adopt more sophisticated quantitative methods. As McQueen and Siegrist (1982) point out, much epidemiological work exhibits a simplistic approach to the definition of such variables as social class and ethnicity and a preoccupation with correlation research in the form of bivariate analysis with one variable controlled. Rarely have epidemiologists considered the causal relationships among multiple variables, and only very occasionally have they employed some of the more sophisticated multivariate techniques available to social scientists.

The problem of causality

Clearly one of the basic problems confronting epidemiologists and medical geographers is to develop causal models that will foster a closer understanding of the relationships between health and environment. The problem of establishing causality, of determining what sort of evidence is required to conclude that X causes YZ is of central concern to both subjects. In epidemiology as in medical geography outside an experimental framework, scientific proof of a causal relationship is an illusory and virtually unattainable goal. Statistical correlations or associations can be suggestive but never ultimate proof of a causal relation. What this means in practice is that the matter of determining causality normally rests with the researcher's personal judgement based on statistical association. With this in mind, the claims of medical geography to make a significant contribution to identifying the causative mechanisms of health need close scrutiny. Implicit in medical geography research is the assumption that spatial variations in health and health care will illuminate the underlying causative determinants. The basic objective in such research, therefore, has been to identify the environmental correlates of health that covary across space. A large amount of work has been carried out along these lines in urban areas, where the coincidence of distinct spatial clusters of disease with a number of so-called measures of social defect or deprivation is often striking. Geographers have been quick to investigate the association of these patterns, particularly the relationship between the spatial distribution of ill-health and that of urban social problems (e.g. crime, delinquency, broken homes, unemployment). The end point has been to establish causality from what has been called *variable association* (Pyle, 1979) or *associative occurrence* (McGlashan, 1972: 11). Usually the method has been to loosely hypothesize possible risk factors for a particular disease, assemble an array of bio-social and environmental variables and take the resulting significant correlations as indicating causality. Epidemiology has also tended to follow this method and in many cases the resulting studies are devoid of bio-social plausibility and constitute mere 'statistical fishing trips' (Mayer,

1982:218). The problem for both fields remains that statistical methods cannot establish proof of a causal relationship. Significant association does not imply a socio-biological cause-and-effect relationship, as there may be additional or intervening factors which constitute a bridge between the conditions shown to be associated. While epidemiologists have shown some concern for such *confounding variables* (see Miettinen and Cook, 1981), geographers have been less interested. Much medical geography research concerned with the inner-city environment, for example, either insinuates that there is something inherent in the local environment which either produces or aggravates ill-health or suggests that susceptible individuals are attracted or drift into such areas. Rarely do geographers consider confounders such as length of residence, place of work, residential and work history, history of exposure to harmful agents, personal and family history, etc. Neither do they take into account the time lag between exposure and the emergence of disease. Such is largely due to the particular research strategy adopted by geographers and the data they utilize, which are often uneven in quality and in a highly aggregated form. Epidemiologists, more single-minded in their search for causal associations, apply a regular check-list of criteria in an effort to gauge causality from statistical associations. Briefly, the criteria most widely applied concern strength of association, consistency of several studies, temporal sequence (cause precedes effect), socio-spatial and biological coherence, specificity, gradient of relationship and logical alternatives (see MacMahon and Pugh, 1970; Friedman, 1974).

Conclusions

It is clear that neither medical geography nor epidemiology is the sole proprietor of a well-defined and homogeneous field of endeavour concerned with human health. Rather, both are disciplines which have evolved relatively specialized methods for investigating patterns of mortality, health and health care. Each depends very largely upon material and skills drawn as required from a large number of other disciplines such as clinical medicine, pathology, zoology, demography, anthropology, history and sociology. The links between epidemiology and medical geography are both obvious and subtle. They share a common basis of experience in the use of population data sources and survey methods, as well as a common interest in the socio-spatial and environmental determinants of behaviour and the causal factors of disease. In theory, therefore, there would seem considerable opportunity for fruitful collaboration. Regrettably, however, the links between the two have not flourished and each has tended to remain within its traditional boundaries. Many epidemiologists and medical geographers have seen their roles in fairly limited terms, yet despite this, it is evident that each has much to offer the other and together they provide a formidable arsenal of techniques and methods for the investigation of patterns of health.

References

Armstrong, R.W., Kutty, M.K. and Armstrong, M.J. (1978) Self-specific environments associated with nasopharyngeal carcinoma in Selangor, Malaysia, *Social Science and Medicine*, **12**D, 149–56.

Cliff, A.D., Haggett, P., Ord, J.K. and Versey, G.R. (1981) *Spatial Diffusion: An Historical Geography of Epidemics in an Island Community*, Cambridge University Press, Cambridge.

Friedman, G. (1974) *Primer of Epidemiology*, McGraw-Hill, New York.

Girt, J.L. (1980) The future of Medical Geography, in F.A. Barrett (ed.), *Canadian Studies in Medical Geography*, Geographical Monographs, York University No. 8, 258–63.

Glick, B.J. (1980) The geographic analysis of cancer occurrence: past progress and future directions, in M.S. Meade (ed.), *Conceptual and Methodological Issues in Medical Geography*, University of North Carolina, Dept. of Geography, Chapel Hill, 170–93.

Haggett, P. (1972) Contagious processes in a planar graph: an epidemiological application, in N.D. McGlashan (ed.), *Medical Geography: Techniques and Field Studies*, Methuen, London. 307–24.

Hellen, J.A. (1979) Medical Geography and its place in university teaching, *Geographische Zeitscrift, Geomedizin in Forschung und Lehre*, 96–104.

Hirsch, A. (1883) *Handbook of Geographical and Historical Pathology*, Vol. 1, New Sydenham Society, London.

Hunter, J.M. and Young, J. (1971) Diffusion of Influenza in England and Wales, *Annals Association of American Geographers*, **61,** 637–53.

King, P.E. (1979) Problems of spatial analysis in geographical epidemiology, *Social Science and Medicine*, **13**D, 249–52.

Lilienfeld, A.M. (1976) *Foundations of Epidemiology*, O.U.P., New York.

Lilienfeld, D.E. (1978) Definitions of Epidemiology, *American Journal of Epidemiology*, **107**, 87–90.

MacMahon, B. and Pugh, T.F. (1970) *Epidemiology: Principles and Methods*. Little, Brown and Co., Boston.

Mayer, J.D. (1982) Relations between two traditions of Medical Geography, *Progress in Human Geography*, **6**, 216–30.

McGlashan, N.D. (1972) Medical Geography an introduction, in N.D. McGlashan (ed.), *Medical Geography: Techniques and Field Studies*, Methuen, London, 3–15.

McGlashan, N.D. (1973) Health, in J.A. Dawson and J.C. Doornkamp (eds.), *Evaluating the Human Environment: Essays in Applied Geography*, Arnold, London, 205–23.

McQueen, D.V. and Siegrist, J. (1982) Social factors in the etiology of chronic disease: an overview, *Social Science and Medicine*, **16**, 353–67.

Meade, M.S. (1980) An interactive framework for geochemistry and cardiovascular disease, in M.S. Meade (ed.), *Conceptual and Methodological Issues in Medical Geography*, University of North Carolina, Dept. of Geography, Chapel Hill, 194–222.

Miettinen, O. and Cook, E.F. (1981) Confounding: essence and detection, *American Journal of Epidemiology*, **114**, 593–603.

Pyle, G.F. (1979) *Applied Medical Geography*, V.H. Winston, Washington D.C.

Shannon, G.W. and Dever, G.E.A. (1974) *Health Care Delivery: Spatial Perspectives*, McGraw-Hill, New York.

Smith, D.M. (1982) Geographical perspectives on health and health care, in J. Cornwell *et al*, *Contemporary Perspectives on Health and Health Care*, Occasional Paper No. 20, Dept. of Geography, Queen Mary College, London, 1–11.

Susser, M. (1973) *Causal Thinking in the Health Sciences*, O.U.P., London.

Woods, R. (1982) *Theoretical Population Geography*, Longman, London.

12

Population Geography and Family Planning

GARY A. FULLER
(University of Hawaii, U.S.A.)

International family planning may be viewed by future historians as one of the strangest of man's innovations. Here is an undertaking conceived in a context of panic, born in the midst of confusion and bureaucratic morass, and nurtured in the Third World by vast sums of foreign currency. The original idea of family planning was to provide medical assistance to enable women to plan the timing and number of births, whether this would result in more or fewer children. However, by 1952, in the case of India, and by the 1960s for the majority of the Third World, family planning meant only fertility reduction. Physicians continued to dominate in this greatly expanded family planning movement, even though the goal of reduced fertility was no longer primarily a medical objective, but a social end. Pregnancy became akin to a disease, and contraception was the prescription. Perhaps the strangest thing of all is the fact that, despite the expenditure of billions of dollars over two decades or more, and despite volumes of program evaluation reports, it is not possible to prove conclusively that any national program reduced fertility to a level that would not have been reached in the absence of family planning provision. In fact, Casetti and Li (1979) have shown that even a program viewed as successful may owe its success to coincidence; their study of the family planning program in the Taichung area of Taiwan concluded that the family planning program did not have any significant impact on fertility.

The peculiarities of the international family planning movement notwithstanding, fertility reduction remains an important object of social science research. The close relationship between fertility and economic development has led the Third World to consider fertility reduction as a real variable in development. Even those societies that have had pronatalist policies, or that have found birth control repugnant on cultural or religious grounds, have often had to face costs arising from sustained high fertility which have proved even more culturally or religiously objectionable. Birth control technology, moreover, as it is distributed through family planning programs, is almost exclusively a foreign technology; its interface with the value systems and the institutions of the Third World is proto-typical of the overall process of economic development. Family planning, then, tends to mirror the developmental process in what it aims to do, in how it does it, and in the difficulties it encounters. The key words used earlier to describe family planning peculiarities ('panic,' 'confusion,' 'bureaucratic morass' and 'foreign currency'), of course, can be applied often to economic development schemes in general.

Geography potentially has much to contribute both to an understanding of fertility control and to the implementation of family planning programs. In fact, there has been only a small number of studies by geographers in this general area. The inevitable result is that other social scientists involved in family planning research have 'invented' research principles and paradigms that have been long used in geography. Given this situation, it is useful to consider what geography has to offer, the contributions that have been made, and ways to bridge the gap between the potential and the actual.

Geography's role in family planning

Family planning programs are aimed at human fertility, and human fertility is an individual behavioural attribute. More precisely, it is the reproductive performance of women. It might be presumed, therefore, that appropriate studies of fertility or its control must point ultimately at individual-level decisions. There exist, however, certain attributes of groups of people in specific areas that bear directly on fertility which are not present in individuals. For example, an imbalance of the sexes will affect fertility by depriving females of mates; a sex ratio is an attribute of a group, not of an individual. The spatial distribution of sex imbalances can be related to their effect on fertility. For example, high sex ratios and low sex ratios which exist in closely juxtaposed, mutually accessible areas probably would not affect fertility significantly, since mate selection can occur easily between the two areas of imbalance. On the other hand, imbalances occurring in inaccessible areas, or in widely separated areas, could affect fertility significantly.

Although the example of sex ratios offers justification for a geographic interest in fertility, as Wilson (1978a) observed, population scholars are generally more interested in behavioural, rather than structural, influences on fertility. Behavioural change resulting in new fertility norms seems a particularly fruitful area for the application of spatial diffusion models. Carlsson (1966) argued that fertility change was not amenable to diffusion models, but instead was an 'adjustment' process. Perhaps the reprinting of

Carlsson's work in a population geography reader (Demko *et al.*, 1970) caused geographers to eschew their diffusion hardware. Carlsson, however, was not concerned with spatial diffusion, but with the spread of norms through social structure; he was concerned with the trickle-down effect of values from the elites to the masses. The economist Demeny (1972), on the other hand, is the great apologist for spatial diffusion, and employed the term 'geographic diffusion' to describe the spread of demographic transition across Austria-Hungary. Demeny's findings, based on extensive empirical evidence, helped to give population geography's interest in fertility and its control a *raison d'être* among population scholars.

A rationale establishing geography's role in the study of fertility does not necessarily justify a geography of family planning. Indeed, some of the best examples of geographic studies of fertility have dealt with areas such as Scotland (Jones, 1975; Wilson, 1978a), Ireland (Coward, 1978a) or Australia (Wilson, 1971, 1978b) where high fertility is not a crucial problem. Family planning is, however, among other things, a problem in spatial allocation. There exists a set of spatial patterns of demand for information and services, and to meet this demand a supply network must be constructed. It seems reasonable to assume, therefore, that the effectiveness of a family planning program is partially (if not mainly) dependent on the ability of decision-makers to allocate manpower and contraceptive supply so as to best satisfy demand. In turn, this implies that decision-makers need to be well informed about the spatial pattern of fertility, the areal variation of complex linkages between fertility levels and demand for family planning services, and the location and impact of nodes in the supply network. These basic operational features of family planning involving the elements of allocation and logistics, are a program's strategy, while coping with local idiosyncratic demand and resistance are properly labelled tactics. It is in the development of strategy that geography as a research discipline has the most to contribute to family planning operation.

Strategy viewed from the level of a Third World family planning clinic is elusive. Blaikie (1975) begins his account of family planning in India by describing how, while sitting at the entrance of a family planning clinic, he envisaged a physician travelling by jeep to provide contraceptive supply at the right time and place. While thus considering jeep transport algorithms, he observed the medical jeep, stored in a shed, serving as a chicken coop. It is likely that sophisticated models can eventually aid in the development of rational family planning strategy since geographic models aim ultimately at answering relevant 'where' questions. The relevant 'where' questions for most Third World family planning, however, are currently elementary, and these must be answered first. It is ironic that national programs frequently set 'fertility targets', yet the location of the target is not known. Such a situation expends a great deal of ammunition with few positive results.

Geographic contributions to family planning

Geographers were late-comers to family planning research. There are several reasons for this, but perhaps the most important is that USAID, Population Division, has been a leading and early underwriter of international fertility control efforts. In the United States, neither geography in general, nor population geography in particular, possesses a high profile in most government-funded programs; sociologists and formal demographers have dominated the research scene in family planning. Today, there are perhaps no more than two dozen geographers who have published research on family planning in the English language and the bulk of these are from the United Kingdom or from Commonwealth countries.

When geographers became interested in family planning they were confronted by a large volume of research produced by other disciplines. It is not surprising, therefore, that they have carved a niche for themselves in an area not central to other disciplines. In particular, geographers looked at the diffusion of acceptance with an eye to the Hagerstrand model. Spatial diffusion and distance decay ('neighbourhood effect') are explicit themes or strongly implicit considerations in virtually every geographic study of family planning.

The concern with Hagerstrandian diffusion has produced two interesting effects. First, the concentration of interest on a single model in an already narrow field has produced a 'building-block' approach to knowledge. That is, authors generally have built each succeeding study solidly on the findings of earlier work, and one can detect a vertical development of understanding in the field. This construct, of course, is common in science; it seems rare in geography, where knowledge too often accumulates laterally. Second, despite clear gains in the field, there have been so few studies that true theory remains a future goal, and contradictory findings are yet to be reconciled.

Consider, for example, the role of distance in impeding access to contraceptive supply. Blaikie (1975), who has produced the most definitive geographic study of family planning, rejected the Hagerstrand model and argued that the tangled cultural web of Indian culture precluded the use of Western spatial diffusion models. The findings of Fawcett *et al.* (1967) in Thailand would probably support Blaikie's conclusion. Meanwhile, Fuller (1974), considering the service area of a single clinic, found that travel distance between a woman's home and the clinic was more important than any socio-economic variable in discriminating between acceptors and non-acceptors. Jones (1977) in Barbados, and Coward (1978b) in Ireland also found some evidence of distance decay in family planning acceptance.

The contradictions in findings, real or apparent, are not surprising since in each study particular objectives and different methodologies were used. The differences can be reconciled by reference to the unique features of each study, but the crucial point is that we do not yet fully understand how distance decay operates in family planning, or whether it is or can be a significant influence on acceptance. From a policy standpoint, this is an important issue because on it hinges the direction of family planning strategy. If physical accessibility is a significant determinant of acceptance, then the density of the clinic network and the siting of individual clinics are major strategic tools. If physical accessibility is not a significant factor, then strategy aimed at motivation, or which assumes economic development leads to 'adjustment' to new fertility norms, must dominate. Most family planning programs have put their eggs in the motivational or adjustment baskets, and most have not achieved their proclaimed goals. The role of the 'neighbourhood effect' in family planning is important, if for no other reason, because it is much easier to make contraceptive supply available than it is to 'motivate' or bring about 'adjustment'.

There are two recent developments in geography which offer considerable promise for application to family planning research. Brown (1975) has forced geographers to consider that the classic (Hagerstrandian) view of diffusion is a demand-sided view. The other side, supply, is critical in most modern diffusion processes, and certainly in family planning. Ali (1980) and Roberto (1977) have applied Brown's ideas to family planning. Both by-passed the distance decay question by advocating a greater integration of family planning supply and demand, and by developing a social marketing strategy. Unlike Blaikie (1975), who focused on disadvantaged areas of North Bihar, Ali examined high acceptance and low acceptance areas in eight villages in four Community Blocks in different regions of India. The advantage of adding a supply-side view of diffusion is evident in comparing the conclusions of Blaikie and Ali; at a surficial level, they are similar, but Ali shows much greater sensitivity to flows and trade-offs in the supply network which can be utilized to improve operation. Roberto's (1977) study of condom distribution in the Philippines deals explicitly with diffusion within the supply network, an important consideration, but one that has escaped the attention of those concerned only with the diffusion of contraceptive acceptance from the demand side.

A second methodological advance with potential for geographic research in family planning is Q-analysis. Gaspar and Gould (1981) used this technique to examine the structure of agriculture of the Cova da Beira in Portugal as it related to the acceptance of irrigation. Although the Q-analysis approach exudes a level of mathematical elegance which overpowers the quality of data that a family planning researcher is likely to uncover, it does offer the distinct advantage of requiring firm specification (or at least consideration) of the socio-economic matrix in which acceptance takes place. In a sense, Q-analysis can be a highly sophisticated ethnographic approach to diffusion and, as such, offers advantages in cross-cultural applications.

Future directions

The areas of diffusion of contraceptive acceptance and policy implications at the strategic level are two areas already carved out by geographers, and they should remain the principal focus of geographic research in family planning. The direction of the field, and cited methodological advances in other areas of the discipline, are likely to result in three areas of future inquiry.

First, modification in the Hagerstrand model, or perhaps total abandonment, is not only apt to occur, but perhaps already has occurred. The mean information field, central to Hagerstrand's model, is based on the cultural matrix of Northern Europe. Family planning is critical to the non-western world, and there, generally, information is not transmitted in the same manner as in Sweden. In particular barriers to, and channels of, information are often quite different, as Fuller (1973) showed for abortion patients in Chile.

Second, a much greater concern with the social and cultural context of contraceptive acceptance is needed. It is not adequate to simply reject existing diffusion models as 'inapplicable' or 'inappropriate'. Existing geographic studies show directional (Fuller, 1973) and ethnic biases (Ali, 1980) in acceptance. The differential behaviour of groups of people in space is an important disciplinary theme, and it is critical for a family planning program concerned not only with the immediate problem of fertility, but with the broader concerns of equity and justice.

Third, geographers engaged in family planning research are few in number and widely scattered. At the same time, I know of no sub-field in geography where the quality of research has been so impressive. For this high quality to continue, and for the research to have a greater impact on the problem, we need to have greater recognition and support from umbrella organizations, such as the I.G.U. Commission on Population Geography.

References

Ali, M. (1980) *The Demand and Supply of Family Planning Services in India*, unpublished Ph.D. dissertation, Department of Geography, University of Hawaii.

Blaikie, P. (1975) *Family Planning in India: Diffusion and Policy*, Edward Arnold, London.

Brown, L. (1975) The market and infrastructure context of adoption: a spatial perspective on the diffusion of innovation, *Economic Geography*, **51**, 185–216.

Carlsson, G. (1966) The decline of fertility: innovation or adjustment process, *Population Studies*, **20**, 149–74.

Casetti, E. and Li, W.L. (1979) The family planning program in Taiwan: did it make any difference?, *Geographical Analysis*, **11**, 395–403.

Coward, J. (1978a) Changes in the pattern of fertility in The Republic of Ireland, *Tijdschrift voor Economische en Sociale Geografie*, **69**, 353–61.

Coward, J. (1978b) Family planning clinics in The Republic of Ireland, *Irish Geography*, **11**, 189–92.

Demko, G., Rose, H. and Schnell, G. (eds.) (1970) *Population Geography: A Reader*, McGraw-Hill, New York.

Demeny, P. (1972) Early fertility decline in Austria-Hungary: a lesson in demographic transition, in D.V. Glass and R. Revelle (eds.), *Population and Social Change*, Edward Arnold, London, 153–72.

Fawcett, J., Soomboonsuk, A. and Khaisang, S. (1967) Thailand: an analysis of time and distance factors at an IUD clinic in Bangkok, *Studies in Family Planning*, **19,** 8–12.

Fuller, G.A. (1973) The diffusion of illegal abortion in Santiago de Chile: the use of a direction-bias model, *Proceedings of The Association of American Geographers*, **5**, 71–74.

Fuller, G.A. (1974) On the spatial diffusion of fertility decline: the distance-to-clinic variable in a Chilean community, *Economic Geography*, **50**, 324–32.

Gaspar, J. and Gould, P. (1981) The Cova da Beira: an applied structural analysis of agricultural and communication, *Space and Time in Geography, Lund Studies in Geography*, Ser. B, **48**, 183–214.

Jones, H. (1975) A spatial analysis of human fertility in Scotland, *Scottish Geographical Magazine*, **91**, 102–13.

Jones, H. (1977) Metropolitan dominance and family planning in Barbados, *Social and Economic Studies*, **26,** 327–38.

Roberto, E. (1977) The application of diffusion models to population programs: the Philippine case of the commercial contraceptive marketing program, *Studies in the Diffusion of Innovation*, Department of Geography, The Ohio State University, 46.

Wilson, M.G.A. (1971) The spatial dimension of human reproduction in Victoria, *Proceedings, Sixth New Zealand Geography Conference*, 258–64.

Wilson, M.G.A. (1978a) A spatial analysis of human fertility in Scotland: reappraisal and extension, *Scottish Geographical Magazine*, **94,** 130–43.

Wilson, M.G.A. (1978b) The pattern of fertility in a medium sized industrial city, *Tijdschrift voor Economische en Sociale Geografie*, **69**, 225–32.

13

Population Geography and Social Provision

R. M. PROTHERO and W. T. S. GOULD
(Liverpool University, U.K.)

Population geographers have always sought to make their work relevant to the needs of societies they have studied. They have focused on such vital issues as population/resources relationships, the population characteristics and patterns associated with cultural systems and economic and social change. Their analyses have often been applied directly in specific projects, but many studies have remained only of potential use and unused in any direct sense by governments or development agencies. However, in the Third World, where needs are greater and levels of social provision are less than in rich countries, the discrepancy between needs and provision is a matter of major planning importance. Not only are there too few facilities or service points, but these are more likely to be inappropriately distributed. Population geographers have much to offer in identifying the nature and structure of any deficiencies of basic needs and in the development of programs to alleviate them.

Our own work has contributed in these respects to the activities of individual governments and international agencies, particularly the World Health Organization (Prothero, 1961; 1963), the World Bank (Gould, 1978) and UNESCO (Gould, 1973), in their consideration of the problems of identifying needs at the most appropriate places and times and of providing appropriate medical and educational services to meet these needs. We have used our expertise in population geography to define and operationalize 'appropriate' as maximizing access by the users, to ensure an optimal match between the population and the facilities that are designed to serve their needs for improved health and education. In addition, we have used our knowledge of population patterns and processes to contribute to the understanding of some of the problems in the eradication or control of certain diseases and to examine the impacts of programs for health care and educational expansion. Our techniques of analyzing data of population distribution and of redistribution through movements of various kinds provide the starting point for our contribution to satisfying these basic human needs. This paper describes some of the general situations in which our work has been applied in the Third World, and is addressed to two main features that are of interest to population geographers: population distribution and population mobility.

Population distribution

The distribution of population is itself of direct relevance in service provision. Put at its simplest, concentrated populations are more easily served than dispersed populations. For example, programs for disease control and eradication, which may require the periodic application of insecticides to reduce insect vectors and/or drugs to be administered to people, are much more difficult to mount in areas with a dispersed population. People and their dwellings are more difficult to locate, so that total coverage, which may be essential for success, is significantly more difficult to achieve. Wear and tear on personnel and equipment, particularly vehicles, are much greater, and the costs of operations are therefore much higher. The majority of malaria eradication pilot programs undertaken in tropical Africa in the 1950s and early 1960s faced this range of problems and were seriously prejudiced by them. One of the most successful of these projects was in Kigezi District in south-west Uganda where planned resettlement of the population had taken place shortly before the project began. As a result the location of people was known, settlement dispersion limited, and the majority of the population accessible to eradication teams by motorable roads. However, the greater concentration of people in nucleated settlements and the resultant greater degree of physical contact between them provide more favourable conditions for the diffusion of certain contagious diseases.

Access to the service provided at a school or dispensary is severely constrained by distance. Children must walk to school; outpatients using a dispensary may be sick. Access is improved in nucleated settlements, and better access is regularly cited as one of the chief arguments in programs for population nucleation. Medical and educational practitioners prefer to provide fewer but larger health centres and schools respectively, with a better range of services and equipment in each and reaping *internal* economies of scale. A large school can have specialist teachers for particular subjects, and a full primary school with a separate class for each grade can have one teacher for each class. The 'threshold population' for any given facility, that population required to maintain a service at acceptable efficiency, is more likely to be reached where populations are living in nucleated settlements. But populations are not always in such settlements and the concern of population geographers for patterns of population distribution and density will identify the feasibility of different types of provision. In Botswana full primary schools with seven classes require a population threshold that is met only in the large agricultural villages that are the traditional settlement form of the area. However, since government is actively encouraging more people to live in smaller settlements away from these large villages it will need to provide, amongst other things, smaller schools with some grade amalgamations for the smaller numbers of children to be served in these settlements (Gould, 1982). Raw numbers might suggest one primary school per 1,500 people or one health centre per 10,000 people (Thomas, 1982), but how these people are distributed in space will affect the extent to which they can use the facility provided. Planners need to take local patterns of population distribution into account, and if providing better access is a major objective, the *external* economies of provision become much more important. Geographers can contribute by ensuring that census authorities provide tabulations of small area population data, and by using these data in cartographic and settlement analyses.

Population mobility

Studies of population movement are also constrained by the limitations of data. The constraints are greater for mobility analysis since the usual data collected in censuses provide essentially static snapshots of phenomena which are highly dynamic in character. Further problems arise from the failure to recognize the complex nature of mobility and the range of its forms. The relationships between mobility and disease and health are not as widely appreciated as they should be (Meade, 1977; Prothero, 1977). For example, the transmission of malaria is often associated with mobile groups within a population and in some instances with the mobility characteristics of the whole population. Problems associated with mobility are also to be faced in devising control and eradication programmes. Understanding the epidemiology of malaria in tropical Africa requires detailed knowledge of 'how many', 'where', and 'when' people move, and a range of other human factors (Prothero, 1965).

Mobility factors may be illustrated with reference to north-eastern Africa (the Republic of Somalia and adjacent parts of Ethiopia), occupied by ethnically homogeneous Somali-speaking people. Here in the 1960s traditional pastoralism and contemporary politics combined to prejudice progress for the improvement of public health in general and malaria in particular (Prothero, 1967; 1972). More than 75 per cent of the population were involved in nomadic pastoralism in a harsh semi-arid environment with limited water and pasture at all times and great scarcity for much of the year. In these conditions population movements and stock movements are essential to sustain life. These included major seasonal north/south movements across the international frontier from the sources of permanent water (though with limited grazing) to sources of pasture and water only available in the wet season. People were thus brought into contact with malaria vectors breeding in the water sources, affecting both stock and themselves. This north/south inter-country movement makes it difficult to maintain contact with people in order to spray dwellings (which were also mobile) with residual insecticide and to distribute anti-malaria drugs.

There were further complications from mobility. Frequent short-term, but fairly distant (e.g. 150–200 km) movements occurred in the wet season in response to the immediate availability of water and pasture depending on rain falling sporadically in time and space. Traditionally the composition of groups changed with continual fission and fusion—three or four families, coming together for several weeks and then breaking up to form new groups with other families. There were in addition changes in the composition of families—the young men with camels going long distances in search of pasture, the younger and older members of the family remaining with smaller stock but also moving over shorter distances. Such complex movement, while logical in relation to environmental constraints and traditional social organization, is seemingly chaotic for the design and function of anti-malaria measures, unless the need to monitor and understand changing dynamic circumstances is recognized. In the anti-malaria activities that were being undertaken this understanding did not exist.

Such complexity is at odds with the common assumption of many health officials that migration involves only a change of residence that is intended to be at least of substantial duration if not permanent. It is this kind of population movement which is most commonly considered in many epidemiological studies (Wessen, 1974). However, we have elsewhere argued for the need to distinguish between migration (involving a permanent change in place of residence) and circulation (mobility away from place of residence but with eventual return to it) (Gould and Prothero, 1975). Space and time dimensions may be combined to provide a typology in which 24 different categories of migration are identified. Considered in this variety, mobility as an epidemiological factor may be clarified (Prothero, 1977). Different types of mobility will have different factors in the exposure of population to disease, in the transmission of disease and in the development of programs for the improvement of public health. Various activities of people may be associated with the different categories of circulation and migration in the typology and in turn can be associated with several categories of health hazards to which people may be exposed (Table 13.1). Movement from one area to another with a different set of ecological conditions may mean exposure to disease, particularly disease which is vector-borne. Daily circulation to obtain water may result in contact with the fly vectors which transmit onchocerciasis (river blindness) and trypanosomiasis (sleeping sickness): seasonal circulation takes people from permanent dwellings which have been sprayed with residual

TABLE 13.1
Typology of mobility in tropical Africa, with examples of associated activities and health hazards

	Time					
	Circulation				Migration	
	Daily	Periodic	Seasonal	Long-term	Irregular	Regular
Rural-Rural	Cultivating Collecting (firewood, water) (1)	Hunting (1)	Pastoralism (1) (3)	Labouring (1) (3)	Gathering (1) (3)	Planned Settlement (1) (4)
Rural-Urban	Commuting (1)	Pilgrimage (1) (2) (3) (4)	Labouring (1)	Labouring (1) (2) (3) (4)	Drought Victims (1) (3) (4)	Labouring (2) (3)
Urban-Rural	Cultivating (1)	Trading (2)	Labouring (1)	Trading (2) (3)	Refugees (1) (4)	Retirement (1)
Urban-Urban	Intra-urban commuting (3)	Pilgrimage (2) (4)	Trading (2)	Official/ Commercial transfer (4)	Refugees (4)	Change of residence (4)

Health Hazards

(1) Exposure to diseases from movements through different ecological zones (e.g. malaria, trypanosomiasis, schistosomiasis, onchocerciasis)
(2) Exposure to diseases from movements involving contacts between different groups of people (e.g. smallpox, poliomyelitis)
(3) Physical stress (e.g. fatigue, undernutrition/malnutrition)
(4) Psychological stress-problems of adjustment.

insecticide to temporary dwellings which are unsprayed and therefore harbour malaria vectors. Movements bring different groups of people into contact with the increased possibility of the transmission of disease. Examples include the spread of smallpox in the past by the movement of refugees and the high risks of typhoid in crowded insanitary refugee camps. Movement may cause physical stress and thus lower resistance and raise susceptibility to infection. Enforced movements caused by natural hazard or political disruption bring both undernutrition, due to difficulties in making economic adjustments with periods of unemployment and limited means of acquiring food, and also malnutrition, due to the difficulty of adjusting to new kinds of food (for example through movement from cereal staple to root staple areas). There may also be nutritional difficulties associated with the preparation of foods when movements are sex-selective so that men move without their wives to support them. Psychological stress may result from movement because of socio-cultural-economic pressures in adjusting to new environments, and particularly in rural/urban movements where there are marked contrasts between the personal contacts in small cohesive rural communities and the impersonal nature of large heterogeneous urban communities. However, adjustment mechanisms which are socially and economically stabilizing may operate in urban communities to assist newcomers, and rural/urban/rural circulation allows the maintenance of contacts with places of origin.

Similar relationships between mobility and education may be identified both through going to school and after leaving school. The most common form of mobility in this respect is the daily journey-to-school within rural areas, within urban areas and between rural and urban areas. It may be of longer duration, where, for example, a student's home is far away from a secondary school in the nearest town, and he lives in that town during the school week, perhaps with friends or relatives, but returns home at weekends. In other circumstances, as in many parts of tropical Africa, many secondary schools are boarding schools, and admissions procedures mean that catchment areas of each school may be nationwide (Gould, 1975). In such situations most students are involved in periodic circulation of a termly duration at the beginning and the end of each term.

The daily journey-to-school is a mobility phenomenon where a geographical perspective has been effective in planning programs of enrolment expansion, particularly at the primary school level. Empirical research in several countries has shown how small is the distance that children walk to school each day, even in areas of low population density where there are few schools (Hallak, 1977). Most children come from within 2 km of the school, and usually over 90 per cent come from within 4 km, such that the range of a primary school, the maximum distance a child should be expected to walk, can usually be set at 4 km for practical planning purposes.

The planning implications of this fairly small range are considerable. In Area A (Fig. 13.1a) and Area B (Fig. 13.1b) there are 10,000 people, but in Area A they all live in three villages, and in Area B they are well distributed throughout the area. In the former there is a highly peaked demand surface, and if there is a school in each of the three villages, then all the potential students live within the range. There are some unserved areas beyond the range of any school, but these areas are uninhabited. If in Area B there are also three schools, located as in A, some students are now being denied access because these areas remain unserved. If in both cases only half the school children attend school, then the low enrolment rates in Area A may not be attributed to excessive journeys to school but to a combination of social and economic circumstances. In the case of Area B, the social and economic factors will remain important but are complicated by the spatial factor of access. Actual patterns of mobility in any given situation will differ from these theoretical distance minimizing assumptions, and will be affected not only by roads, but also by taking a longer route than necessary to avoid entering an

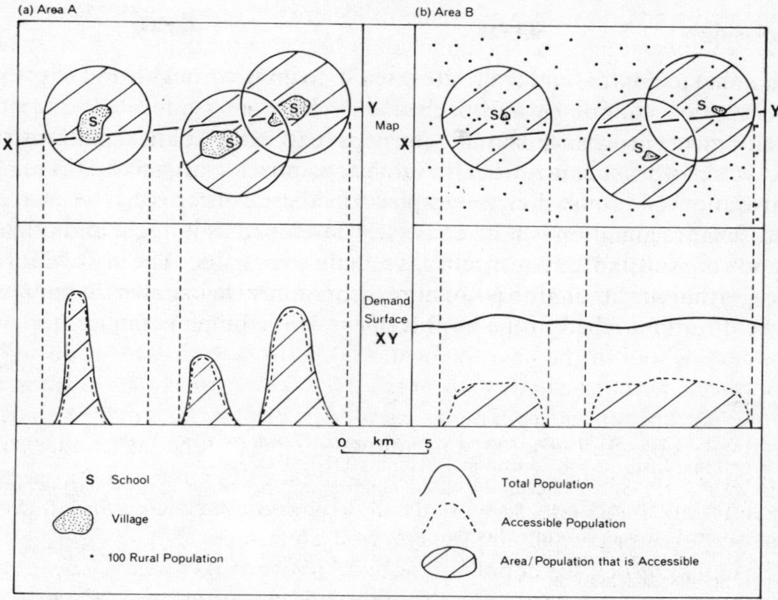

FIGURE 13.1 *Accessibility and spatial demand surface*

area (e.g. a swamp) perceived to be a health hazard or land of a hostile group, and by other attractions to children (e.g. a market). These can only be ascertained by detailed local study. In Ankole, Uganda, the observed overlap of primary school catchments in an area of dispersed rural settlement was due principally to denominational rivalry between Church of Uganda (Protestant) schools and Roman Catholic schools attracting their own adherents (Gould, 1973).

Educational status of an individual will also affect his or her mobility. Throughout the Third World the educated are attracted to towns in search of job opportunities for which they feel their education has equipped them, and which are available disproportionately in urban areas. Rural-urban movements of the educated may involve both circulation and permanent migration, but it is likely that the educated will remain for longer periods in urban areas and have greater commitment to them than will non-educated migrants. Programs for expansion of education at various levels in rural areas can be usefully examined to ascertain the extent to which they may lead to accelerated urban growth. In this respect the geographer's approach of examining conditions at both source and destination provides an essential corrective to the view, implicit in many econometric models, that migration of the educated is principally or even solely a response to urban wage rates (Gould, 1981).

Conclusion

Planning to control and eradicate disease, to improve health and to provide for education cannot be approached only from an aggregate perspective. Development programs should consider explicitly spatial patterns and processes of disease control, health provision and educational expansion. The contribution of population geographers in these concerns has been recognized. That recognition is not yet as fully developed as it might and ought to be, and very substantial contributions remain to be made. The use of data and concepts that are familiar to population geographers has shown that our work can be directly applied to the improvement of the human condition.

References

Gould, W.T.S. (1973) *Ankole, Uganda: Planning the Location of Schools*, Case Study, 3, International Institute for Educational Planning/UNESCO, Paris.

Gould, W.T.S. (1975) Movements of school-children and provision of secondary schools in Uganda, in D. Parkin (ed.) *Town and Country in Central and Eastern Africa*, O.U.P. for International African Institute, London, 250–61.

Gould, W.T.S. (1978) *Guidelines for School Location Planning*. The World Bank, Staff Working Paper, no 308, Washington, D.C.

Gould, W.T.S. (1981) Education and internal migration, *International Journal of Educational Development*, **1** (3), 103–10.

Gould, W.T.S. (1982) Provision of primary schools and population redistribution, in J.I. Clarke and L.A. Kosiński (eds.) *Redistribution of Population in Africa*, Heinemann, London, 44–9.

Gould, W.T.S. and Prothero, R.M. (1975) Space and time in African population mobility, in L.A. Kosiński and R.M. Prothero (eds.) *People on the Move*, Methuen, London, 35–49.

Hallak, J. (1977) *Planning the Location of Schools: an Instrument of Educational Policy*, International Institute for Educational Planning/UNESCO, Paris.

Meade, M.S. (1977) Medical geography as human ecology: the dimension of population movements, *Geographical Review*, **67**, 379–93.

Prothero, R.M. (1961) Population movements and problems of malaria eradication in Africa, *Bulletin of the World Health Organization*, **24**, 405–25.

Prothero, R.M. (1963) Population mobility and trypanosomiasis in Africa, *Bulletin of the World Health Organization*, **28**, 615–26.

Prothero, R.M. (1965) *Migrants and Malaria*, Longman, London.

Prothero, R.M. (1967) *Public Health, Pastoralism and Politics in the Horn of Africa*, Sixth Melville J. Herskovits Memorial Lecture, Northwestern University, Evanston.

Prothero, R.M. (1972) Problems of public health among pastoralists in Africa, in N.D. McGlashan (ed.) *Medical Geography: Techniques and Field Studies*, Methuen, London, 105–18.

Prothero, R.M. (1977) Disease and mobility: a neglected aspect of epidemiology, *International Journal of Epidemiology*, **6**, 259–67.

Thomas, I. (1982) Villagization in Tanzania: planning potential and political problems, in J.I. Clarke and L.A. Kosiński (eds.) *Redistribution of Population in Africa*, Heinemann, London, 182–91.

Wessen, A.F. (1974) The role of migrant studies in epidemiological research, *Israel Journal of Medical Science*, **1**, 584.

14

The Contribution of Population Geography to Development Planning, Especially in Africa

SIMEON H. OMINDE
(University of Nairobi, Kenya)

Introduction

The most challenging approach to the theme of this chapter may be summed up in the following quotation:

> 'Geography within the context of African development must contribute to the solution of the basic problem of poverty arising from under-development of resources in relation to population needs and from continuing imbalance between the high rate of population growth and the much slower rate of economic growth' (Ominde, 1972).

This general definition of the task of geography is the core of the challenge which scholars have translated into a sub-discipline of population geography, drawing on the methodological contributions of the study of demography. The population geographer is thus involved in the macro- and micro-studies of the dynamic relationships between population characteristics and the environmental and resource matrix which sustains the population base.

In a time dimension, the African region is experiencing a unique demographic change whose development impact has yet to be illuminated with improved data base and model building and testing. It has been summed up in terms of accelerating rate of population growth ranking Africa as the region of the fastest population change, indeed unprecedented in the demographic history of mankind. It is a result of combined effects of the impact of modernization on demographic processes strengthened by a basically pronatalist attitude towards fertility and survival in the region.

At the same time, the impact of development in the African scene is generating uncontrolled spatial population transfers on a scale that threatens to outstrip the capacity of planners to provide appropriate solutions. Implied in these spatial population changes are important changes in the characteristics of population and human settlements and related socio-economic needs arising from migration as a demographic process.

In the early stages of the development of the geographical discipline, the concern was with the static and macro-aspects of population in relation to environment and resources. Now we are seeing the emergence of population geographers once more to the forefront of the development challenge.

Major themes in population geography and development

Development theorists and policy-makers concern themselves with seven broad themes that are of fundamental importance to the study of population geography:

(i) population growth in relation to development at the national, regional and global levels;
(ii) components of population growth: fertility, mortality and migration;
(iii) population composition: age-sex differentials, marital status, households and family structure, ethnicity, race, religion and education;
(iv) population distribution: regional, rural and urban;
(v) labour force: agricultural and non-agricultural, employment status, occupational and industrial structure and age-specific activity rates;
(vi) projections at macro- and micro-levels; and
(vii) the economic and social implications of growth and spatial population change. This area of interaction with other social scientists has generated a vast and complex area of policy concern. The economic and social implications of growth to productivity, savings, agricultural land and what is produced from it, housing, education, medical facilities and transportation are of vital concern to development planning.

But the effective study of these major themes in population geography in relation to development planning is hampered by inadequacy of data or major data gaps that have so far not been satisfactorily closed. In comparison with similar data bases in the more developed parts of the world, the African population data base is still unreliable.

Population and development interactions

In order to appreciate the contribution of population geography to development planning in general, it is important to underline the essential dynamism implied in both concepts. The underlying concept is the dynamism of population changes and their impact on development planning. However, development planning is also by necessity a dynamic concept. The population geographer approaches development planning in a spatial and temporal context.

The purpose of development planning is to improve the standard of living of the people on the basis of available resources. Changes in the characteristics of the population or variables in turn affect the rate of achieving the social and economic objectives of the plan. The population/resource relationship is a changing one, both in time and in space. However, in a more specific way the interrelationship is very much affected by the population profile (Kazeze, 1980).

But there is an important distinction in the range of demographic data used by planners and the treatment of a much wider range of demographic indices by population geographers. Basically the planner is concerned with the following range of demographic indices which are given varying emphases by different censuses and in different sub-regions of Africa, the data coverage and quality varying greatly and thus limiting the population geographer searching for spatial and comparative data (Stamper, 1977):

(i) rate of population growth;
(ii) estimates of fertility;
(iii) estimates of mortality;
(iv) projection of future population size;
(v) estimates of current school-age population;
(vi) projection of future school-age population; and
(vii) estimates of current working-age population.

Rate of population growth

The rate of population growth is clearly one of the most critical measures used in defining the problems facing development planning. Although most African countries include such a rate in their censuses, not many of them actually use it in their development plans. This hesitation to use an important demographic measure at the national, sub-national or micro-level is due to the nature of disaggregation of growth data. The population growth data are in most cases limited to national level and to urban centres, but the frequent adjustment of boundaries makes the use of growth data below the national level unreliable.

Estimates of fertility

Estimates of fertility are not directly important to planners, but they are a major component of any good population projection. Information on the number of current and possible future births are of great importance to health planning. The basic problem is that fertility information usually comes in the form of crude birth rates which are difficult to use for spatial comparisons.

However, age-specific fertility rates, a more refined measure, have been used most successfully in depicting spatial patterns of fertility by Page and Coale (1972), Ominde (1975) and others. With more reliable data, population geographers can throw light on important aspects of spatial variation in fertility as a guide to planning population policy. The major problem facing planners is the difficulty of estimating indices of fertility in Africa. A concerted attack on this area will yield valuable data on the patterns, trends and determinants of fertility.

Estimates of mortality

Mortality data are vital in establishing health conditions and in the planning of needs and priorities for health programmes. They are also essential indices for monitoring the progress and effectiveness of health development plans. Of greater importance to the population geographer than the level of mortality are the causes, environmental and otherwise. We need information on age-specific rates, infant measures that can be analyzed geographically and environmental causes examined. The geographic distribution of mortality and morbidity are of crucial importance to population geographers interested in elucidating the environmental dimensions of health.

For example, Figure 14.1 showing child mortality in Kenya (Kibet, 1981) based on the number of children dying in the first two years of life per 1000 live births by district for mothers with no education, reflects the significance of altitude and level of education. The highland areas of Kenya show relatively low levels of infant mortality as compared to the Lake Victoria Basin and the Coast Region where malaria is endemic. On the basis of such data, health and educational planners can see more clearly the impact of development processes.

Mortality data are notoriously unreliable in Africa, but a number of techniques have been developed to improve their quality. The population geographer therefore has a largely unexplored field here in his effort to contribute to information on development planning.

Projection of future population size

The future is the essence of planning (Ominde, 1981). However, few countries have used population projections in their development planning documents. About 50 per cent of African countries studied in the mid-1970s did not give future population projections as a basic information, the major constraint being the absence of reliable information and models on which to base projection data.

Among the most crucial data gaps is the lack of information on projected resource availability, making it difficult to show the changing relationship

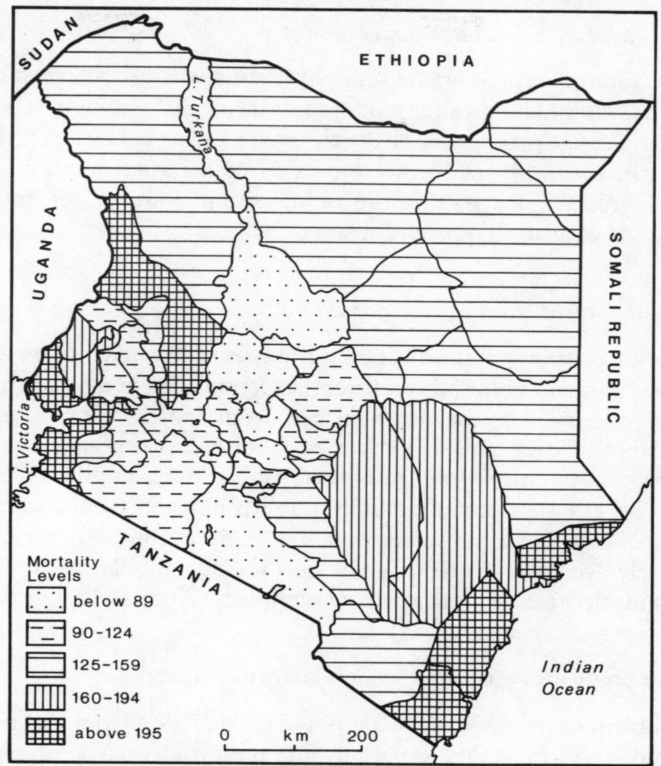

FIGURE 14.1. *Child mortality in Kenya, showing number of children dying in the first two years of life per 1000 mothers with no education (after Kibet 1981)*

between the population and resources, a relationship impeded also by the inherent practice of boundary changes which has thwarted the efforts of urban geographers concerned with the study of urbanization in Africa south of the Sahara. The contribution of the population geographer is thus limited to rather large and stable administrative units.

Estimates of current school-age population

By the mid-1970s approximately 55 per cent of African countries had data on current school-age population; the lack of such data in the development plans of other countries is attributed to lack of emphasis on educational planning as part of the overall development planning. Such data provide the population geographer with an interesting tool in analyzing the spatial impact of development policies.

Projection of future school-age population

In a situation of rapidly increasing population, the growth of school-age population is vital to long-range planning. Educational planning is by its very nature a long-range planning for a development strategy. However, the use of these data in the study of future impact of educational needs has lagged behind, a regrettable fact as they are an important source of information on inequalities of educational provisions and facilities.

Estimates of current working-age population

The working-age population between the ages of 15 and 65 years forms the principal component of the labour force projections. Broken down by age and sex, the figures need to be distinguished from indices such as economic activity, labour force and employment. However, although the current working-age populations are published by a large number of African countries, very few countries actually publish data on future working-age population, and in those countries the picture that emerges is of a progressively decreasing percentage of working-age population that can find employment, because of continuing acceleration of population growth.

Population problems recognized by development planners

The problem of a rapidly growing population arising from sustained high fertility and falling mortality, especially infant mortality, has been recognized as the main demographic issue in the African region for the remainder of the twentieth century and probably the greater part of the twenty-first century. It underlies the specific population problems faced by development planners.

The growth of working-age population is one such specific planning problem facing Africa, and the associated problem of unemployment. Many development plans for African countries cite this as a problem. Unfortunately, its spatial pattern has not been studied by population geographers and other scientists, largely owing to the poor data base.

The changing age distribution affects the demand for education and the capacity of society to supply the demand. The most striking example in educational planning in Africa is the effect of the demographic explosion of secondary school population on provision of tertiary education. African countries are acutely short of products of tertiary institutions, and the pressure of numbers on their limited facilities constitutes one of the most critical planning problems.

The problem of growing school-age population is related to the problem of a declining proportion of the population in the working-age cohorts that must continue to support ever-expanding numbers of youthful and aged dependants, a problem which needs to be studied in its rural and urban context and in the different regions of the national territory.

The reduction of economic growth by population growth is widely recognized as a critical population problem, but there are few studies that show how economic growth is influenced by population growth. There is need for studies that show not merely the national aggregate nature of the problem but the regional and sub-regional dimensions. This is an essential aspect of the national study of the geography of poverty.

Population geographers have carried out numerous studies on migration and urbanization, especially migration to urban areas, making a major contribution to our understanding of the causes, origins, destinations and consequences of such migrations in all the regions of Africa. Such studies have led to the emphasis currently being placed on rural development as a means to counteract excessive rural-urban population influx. They have also opened avenues for population geographers to make valuable contributions in United Nations plans of action on the Human Environment, Human Settlement and Population.

To development planners, however, migration continues to be a much more sensitive issue at the national population policy level. This is underlined by governmental policies regarding aliens, for example in Ghana, Nigeria and Sierra Leone, as well as the growing problem of refugees, seriously affecting Somalia, Sudan and a number of other countries. With inequalities in resource endowment and development, international migration will continue to be a thorny policy issue. Planners frequently cite high dependency ratios as a population problem of countries or regions with high fertility, and an increasing number of population geographers have carried out regional studies on dependency ratios and their implications.

The population factors that put pressure on education also affect health services. Population growth results in increased demand for all medical services. The current crisis being experienced in both rural and urban health services in Africa is due to the acceleration of population growth and inability of countries to provide the material and human resources needed. The geography of health care is as yet an unexplored field by population geographers and development planners. In particular, the imbalance between the rural and urban health services is a critical area of development planning to which population geographers can contribute.

Although an acute housing shortage has been recognized as a widespread problem, it has not been adequately documented except in a general way for urban centres. Very few African countries have prepared the data needed to assess the magnitude of the problem in both its rural and urban contexts.

With acute food shortages facing many African countries, and with the mounting foreign exchange implications of rising food imports, the problem of population pressure on food or agricultural systems has become an important area for development planners. The problem is made more acute by the fact that most people in Africa live in rural areas. Not much has been done in explaining the complex relationship between agriculture and population. African countries are just beginning to view food scarcity as a problem that may increase in intensity, but most are content merely to note or mention the problem. Basal studies on the relationship between population and food supplies in the context of nutritional needs are required.

The last area of concern is high population density. There is a wealth of literature by geographers on high population density as a development problem, but there are fewer studies on projected population densities. Despite the influx of population into urban areas the majority of African population will remain rural well into the next century. Rural population concentration will thus continue to present development planners with critical areas of concern, necessitating studies that relate the population to the limited land space.

Conclusion

Population geography is a relatively new sub-discipline in geography. Its emergence as a major area of concern to both geographers and planners is intimately linked to the development of demography and its contribution to informed planning. The main bottleneck limiting the contribution of population geographers is the inadequacy of data derived from censuses. The approach of population geographers has been selective in tapping those sources that explain more clearly significant spatial patterns in population characteristics.

Censuses, by virtue of their prohibitive costs, have provided a restricted range of data and levels of disaggregation. In this respect advances in the contribution of population geography to planning will depend on success in obtaining key demographic information of interest to planners and policy-makers concerned with population problems.

References

Kazeze, Z.W. (1980) Population and development in Africa, in Proceedings of FAO/UNFPA/PSRI Workshop on Population and Agricultural Planning, University of Nairobi, 26–49.

Kibet, M. (1981) Differential mortality in Kenya. Unpublished M.A. thesis, Population Studies and Research Institute, University of Nairobi.

Ominde, S.H. (1975) Regional patterns of fertility in Kenya, *Kenyan Geographer*, **1**, 13–29.

Ominde, S.H. (1981) Population and resource crisis: a Kenyan case study, *Geojournal*, **5**, 539–56.

Page, H.J. and Coale, A.J. (1972) Fertility and child mortality south of the Sahara, in S.H. Ominde and C.N. Ejiogu (eds.) *Population Growth and Socio-Economic Development in Africa*, Heinemann, London, 51–66.

Stamper, B.M. (1977) *Population and Planning in Developing Nations*, The Population Council, New Nork.

15

Government Policy and Population Distribution

ROLAND J. FUCHS
(University of Hawaii, U.S.A.)

The efforts of nations, particularly the developing nations, to regulate their natural increase through family planning programs have received wide publicity. Government programs intended to affect spatial distribution of population on the other hand are less well known, even though more governments are dissatisfied with population distribution than with fertility or growth. This chapter reviews the degree and nature of concern with population distribution, the objectives and types of policies and programs that have been adopted by governments, the general results of such policies, and possible future developments.

Governmental concern with population distribution

Most governments consider their nation as suffering from a maldistribution of population. In a recent U.N. survey, only 19 of 158 nations were satisfied with their spatial population distribution; 73 perceived their distribution as 'largely unacceptable' and requiring radical intervention while 66 found it 'unacceptable to some degree' and in need of more limited intervention [Table 15.1]. Although nations of both the more developed and less developed regions share a dissatisfaction with population distribution, this is obviously a matter of greater concern to governments of less developed nations, the great majority of which perceive their distribution as 'largely unacceptable' while among more developed nations the predominant perception is that of 'unacceptable to some degree.'

Why are so many governments dissatisfied with their current population distributions? There is no single explanation that holds for all nations. It is more appropriate to identify a variety of factors that may lead to dissatisfactions depending on national circumstances. In many developing nations, for

TABLE 15.1. *Perception of population distribution problems by governments and policies*

Adopted by World Regions—1978

Region	Perception of Overall Spatial Distribution						Policies Regarding Internal Migration								Policies to Modify					
	Largely Unacceptable		Unacceptable to some degree		Acceptable		Decelerate		Reverse		Accelerate		Maintain		Both Rural and Urban		The Rural Configuration Only		The Urban Configuration Only	
	no.	%	no.	%	no.	%	no.	%	no.	%	no.	%	no.	%	no.	%	no.	%	no.	%
Africa	35	70	15	30	0	0	33	66	6	12	0	0	11	22	19	38	18	36	1	2
Latin America	21	78	5	19	1	4	23	85	0	0	1	4	3	11	13	48	5	19	3	11
Asia and the Pacific	15	50	13	43	2	7	15	50	8	27	1	3	6	20	12	40	8	27	2	7
Western Asia	1	8	8	67	3	25	6	50	1	8	1	8	4	33	6	50	1	0	0	0
Europe and North America	1	3	25	64	13	33	24	62	5	13	0	0	10	26	7	18	4	10	15	38
More Developed Regions	5	12	24	57	13	31	25	60	6	14	0	0	11	26	6	14	4	10	18	43
Less Developed Regions	68	59	42	36	6	5	76	66	14	12	3	3	23	20	51	44	32	28	3	3
TOTAL	73	46	66	42	19	12	101	64	20	13	3	2	34	22	57	36	36	23	21	13

Compiled and modified from *World-Population Trends and Policies: 1979 Monitoring Report, Vol. II, Population Policies*, United Nations, New York, 1980, pp. 49, 116–20.

example, the rates of rural-urban migration are considered excessive in that they may be leading to population concentration in a limited number of urban centres which cannot adequately provide urban jobs and service; in the process rural areas may lose the most educated youth who might otherwise have been the most productive and innovative of the rural labour force. More generally, problems may develop of spatial disparities in labour availability and employment opportunities, with a relative excess of labour available in old settled agricultural regions as compared to newer frontier regions, or in the primate metropolitan areas as opposed to other urban centres. Population redistribution programs may be seen as necessary to reduce population pressure on fragile environments and agro-ecosystems (e.g. those in hill and mountain areas); to resettle nomads or consolidate rural villages in order to provide adequate health, educational or other services; to settle border areas for purposes of national security; or to increase national integration through redistribution of ethnic groups. Very commonly population redistribution programs have an equity objective: to reduce disparities in rates of growth among regions and the accessibility of jobs and services among individuals. A powerful but unvoiced concern underlying programs in many nations is the fear of political, social, or ethnic instability that may result from major shifts in population and rapid growth of large cities.

Policy objectives

The relative significance of major policy objectives may be assessed from U.N. surveys which categorize policies on the basis of their intended impacts on (1) the rates of migration from rural areas and small towns to major urban centres, (2) on patterns of rural population distribution, and (3) on urban configurations. Based on the results of a 1978 U.N. survey [Table 15.1]:

1. Policies that have as their objective modification of trends in rural-to-urban migration are the most common. Globally 124 of 158 nations responding to the U.N. survey had adopted policies to alter migration rates. The majority of both developing and developed nations, 101, were concerned with decreasing the rates of rural-to-urban migration; a significant number, 21, were intent upon reversing the trend of rural-urban migration. Only three nations, all in less developed regions, had as policy objectives the acceleration of migration to major urban cities.
2. Policies to alter rural and regional population distribution, either independently or in conjunction with urban settlement policies, were the next most common with 93 nations having such policies; they are particularly common in the less developed regions.
3. Alteration of urban configuration, often involving controls on primate city growth, and promotion of growth in small and intermediate-sized

TABLE 15.2. *Population redistribution programs, objectives, and instruments*

Type of Program	Migration/Mobility Objectives	Instruments Commonly Employed
I. *Urban Constraint*		
a. 'Closed City'	Reduce or slow in-migration to designated cities, including the metropolitan centre	— tax disincentives — identity cards or internal passports, residence permits; registration of address — limitations on investment in industry or housing — discriminatory treatment in access to services by non-legal residents — eviction of illegal residents, destruction of squatter housing
b. 'Rustication' Programs	Resettlement of urban residents in rural areas	— as above plus the following: assignment of rural residence and workplace — rationing coupons valid only in authorized place of residence
II. *Accommodationist Programs*		
a. Slum and Squatter Settlement Improvement	To accommodate to existing patterns of urban immigration and growth by improvements of urban habitat, especially housing and related services	— legitimization of tenure in squatter settlement — upgrading of services and utilities — provision of prepared sites and basic services prior to occupance
b. Dormitory Towns and Satellite City Programs	Deconcentration of growth within metropolitan area by development of settlements in periphery	— infrastructure investment in metropolitan periphery — development of public transport and commuting facilities — housing projects development in peripheral settlements — industrial relocation grants and subsidies

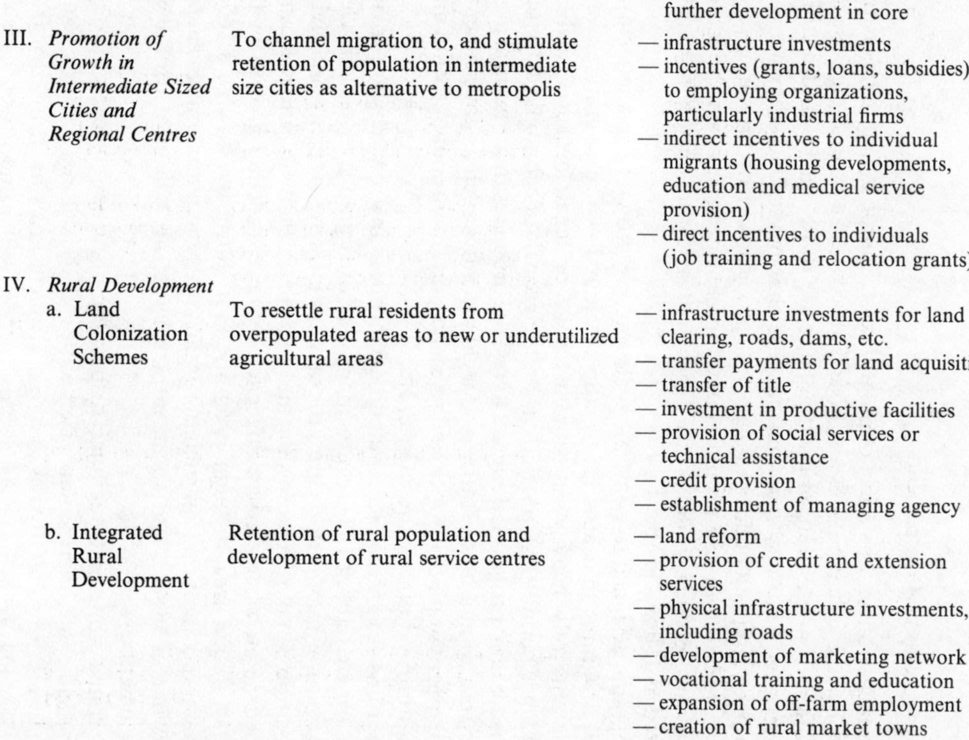

		— zoning and other controls on further development in core
III. *Promotion of Growth in Intermediate Sized Cities and Regional Centres*	To channel migration to, and stimulate retention of population in intermediate size cities as alternative to metropolis	— infrastructure investments — incentives (grants, loans, subsidies) to employing organizations, particularly industrial firms — indirect incentives to individual migrants (housing developments, education and medical service provision) — direct incentives to individuals (job training and relocation grants)
IV. *Rural Development*		
a. Land Colonization Schemes	To resettle rural residents from overpopulated areas to new or underutilized agricultural areas	— infrastructure investments for land clearing, roads, dams, etc. — transfer payments for land acquisition — transfer of title — investment in productive facilities — provision of social services or technical assistance — credit provision — establishment of managing agency
b. Integrated Rural Development	Retention of rural population and development of rural service centres	— land reform — provision of credit and extension services — physical infrastructure investments, including roads — development of marketing network — vocational training and education — expansion of off-farm employment — creation of rural market towns

Compiled from: Findley, 1977 and Demko and Fuchs, 1981.

cities, are policy objectives in 78 nations. Urban policies are relatively more common in developed regions which often adopt such policies even in the absence of rural settlement policies; this occurs only rarely in the less developed regions where urban settlement policies are generally implemented only in conjunction with rural settlement policies.

Policies, programs and instruments

Government policies that affect population distribution include *explicit* and *implicit* policies. Explicit policies are those that have as an express purpose the redistribution of population; implicit policies are those macro- and sectoral policies designed with a non-spatial purpose that nevertheless have strong spatial impacts. Explicit policies include both programs with a primary goal of affecting population distribution and development programs which include this as at least a secondary goal. These explicit redistribution programs may be categorized as follows [Table 15.2]:

1. Programs designed to constrain metropolitan growth: so-called 'closed city' programs that attempt to stop or slow down in-migration. Such programs rely heavily on administrative or legal measures such as residence permits and restrictions on the growth of economic activities.
2. 'Rustication' programs designed to resettle urban residents in rural areas also rest upon administrative and legal measures such as governmental assignment of place of work and residence, rationing coupons valid only in authorized place of residence, etc.
3. Programs designed to accommodate metropolitan growth by improving the urban habitat. There are many such programs; two with clear distribution implications are programs to improve housing and living conditions, in particular in slum and squatter settlements, and programs aimed at increasing urban efficiency by decentralizing growth in the metropolitan area through promotion of dormitory towns, satellite cities and commuting. In such programs investment and improvements in urban economic and social infrastructure are the most prominent instruments.
4. Programs aimed at regional dispersion of urban growth through expansion of intermediate-sized cities and regional centres. Such programs are generally based on government investment in infrastructure, such as transportation and utilities, as well as incentives—such as grants and subsidies—provided directly to employers.
5. Programs directed at retention of rural populations through rural development and the growth of rural service centres: so-called integrated rural development and 'agropolitan' programs. Such programs involve a variety of measures including land reform, physical infrastructure, extension programs, provision of credit and marketing facilities, etc.

6. Programs designed to shift rural population to frontier rural areas with underdeveloped land resources: land colonization schemes. Basic measures here include land acquisition and clearing, provision of transport and other infrastructure, as well as various services.

As is evident from the above classification, population redistribution programs are often subsidiary components of more general spatial modernization and economic development programs with the importance of the population redistribution component varying significantly from program to program.

Effectivess of policies

Some impression of the effectiveness of existing policies can be obtained from recent reviews of population distribution policies in developed countries (Sundquist, 1975; Fuchs and Demko, 1979), Asia (Oberai, 1981), and Africa (Abumere, 1981; Mabogunje, 1981) as well as from reviews of the various types of programs on a global basis (Findley, 1977; Gosling and Lim, 1979; Demko and Fuchs, 1981). A major conclusion of these reviews is that population distribution policies have had only limited effectiveness. However, the experience varies considerably depending on the type of program involved.

Closed city programs

The attempts by the U.S.S.R. to control the growth of Moscow and other large cities have been followed by similar programs in most Eastern European nations. Major examples in developing countries include the attempts to limit in-migration to Jakarta through registration, permits and controls on the informal sector, and to Seoul through taxes and land use planning (Simmons, 1979). Experience suggests that such programs may slow in-migration but risk creating undesirable side effects. Administrative measures are evaded, often through bribery; limitations on growth within the administratively defined 'closed city' are accompanied by increases in commuting and migration to adjoining areas of the metropolitan area that receive the displaced economic growth. If successful the program may result in undesirable demographic (e.g. ageing of the population) or economic consequences for the 'closed' city.

Rustication programs

Programs intended to transfer urban population to rural areas have been adopted by a number of the communist nations in Asia. Judged only demographically, they have been unsuccessful in accomplishing major population transfers in brief periods. In China it is estimated that between 10 and 15 million urban secondary school graduates were resettled in rural areas in the period 1969–73 alone (Chang, 1975).

While the demographic effects of these policies have been striking, the social and economic costs, including the impacts on the rural destinations, remain unknown. It is possible, if not probable, that urban problems of unemployment and underemployment were simply shifted to rural areas. Also, to be effective, such programs require stringent laws and administrative measures, massive propaganda and authoritarian political regimes (Simmons, 1979). Because of this, and their violation of widely accepted rights to movement and choice of residence and employment, rustication programs are unlikely to be adopted outside of the centrally-planned economies.

Urban accommodationist programs

In contrast to policies designed to reverse or constrain metropolitan growth, accommodationist policies attempt to adjust to in-migration and growth by improving the urban habitat (Laquian, 1981). Such programs, intended to promote urban efficiency, raise issues of equity: can the large investments involved, which generally reach only a small proportion of the national population, be justified in terms of overall welfare and development needs? Also the possible effect of such programs on encouraging further migration to the city, which would only aggravate the problems they were intended to relieve, requires further study.

Programs to promote growth in smaller and intermediate-sized cities

Such programs usually involve growth centre and related regional planning measures. The earlier optimism regarding such dispersal urbanization strategies has given way to widespread pessimism since the programs have generally failed to achieve expected growth in regional centres and the spread of development to surrounding regions (Hansen, 1981). However, it is possible that the shortcoming may have resulted from failures to implement promulgated policies or that inadequate time has been allowed for the expected results to be achieved. Since there are no clear alternatives to accommodating the enormous increases which will take place in urban populations of many developing countries, other than permitting growth of metropolitan populations to reach unmanageable proportions, what seems needed is a reassessment of these policies in order to frame more effective policies (Richardson, 1977).

Rural development programs

The disenchantment with the outcome of industrially based growth centre programs has led to an increased emphasis on rural development programs. The relative recency of many such projects has precluded definitive evaluation of the impacts upon migration, which appear to vary depending on the precise program components and the nature of the rural region and its population (Findley, 1981).

Land colonization programs

The record of sponsored colonization schemes is mixed, but failures outnumber successes (Bahrin, 1981). Even when successful, land colonization schemes have a high cost per settler. Also a serious drawback is the so-called 'second generation problem'; since land fragmentation is often prohibited most of the original settlers' children must eventually leave the project, which in effect then only serves to delay rural out-migration.

The future of population redistribution programs

The limited effectiveness of existing population redistribution programs in the light of the great concern of so many governments in achieving population redistribution raises the issue of how such programs may be improved. No single remedy will solve all the problems associated with the programs but at least the following steps would seem necessary (Fuchs and Demko, forthcoming).

1. A closer integration is required of spatial population planning and spatial and national economic planning. The complementary nature of these approaches must be recognized and expressed in appropriate institutional frameworks (Pryor, 1981).
2. The spatial impacts of macro- and sectoral economic (implicit) policies must be more carefully assessed. There is reason to believe that the unintended spatial impacts of these policies may outweigh the effects of explicit policies (Richardson, 1977). In many developing nations especially, modification of these policies is required in order to prevent the economic waste associated with the simultaneous implementation of policies with contradictory spatial impacts (Fuchs, 1981).
3. Governments should reassess the need for intervention and their policy goals. Nations may have assumed a need for intervention where none exists or adopted inappropriate goals (Richardson, 1981).
4. Programs can be improved by selecting instruments more closely matched to the determinants of migration behaviour (Fuchs and Demko, 1981). The effects of distance, migrant selectivity and information on migration behaviour are overlooked in most programs which rely largely on manipulating employment opportunities and social amenities.

Improvement of the effectiveness of population distribution policies is a major challenge for policy-makers, planners and scholars; whether it will occur is in large measure dependent on the degree to which the need for serious re-evaluation and modification of existing policies is recognized. Unless significant changes are forthcoming, further disappointment and a waste of scarce resources seem inevitable.

References

Abumere, S.I. (1981) Population distribution policies and measures in Africa South of the Sahara: a review, *Population and Development Review*, **7**, 421–33.

Bahrin, T.S. (1981) Review and evaluation of attempts to direct migrants to frontier areas through land colonization schemes, in G. Demko and R. Fuchs (eds.), *Population Distribution Policies in Development Planning*, UN, Department of International Economic and Social Affairs, New York, 131–43.

Chang, P.H. (1975) China's rustication movement, *Current History* **69**, 85–9.

Demko, G.J. and Fuchs, R.J. (eds.) (1981) *Population Distribution Policies in Development Planning*, U.N. Department of International Economic and Social Affairs, New York.

Findley, S. (1977) *Planning for Internal Migration: A Review of Issues and Policies in Developing Countries*, U.S. Bureau of the Census ISP-RD-4, Washington, D.C., U.S. Government Printing Office.

Findley, S. (1981) Rural development programmes: planned versus actual migration outcomes, in G. Demko and R. Fuchs (eds.), *Population Distribution Policies in Development Planning*, U.N., Department of International Economic and Social Affairs, 144–6.

Fuchs, R.J. (1981) Conflicts between explicit and implicit population distribution policies in Asian development plans, *Population Geography*, **3**, 41–56.

Fuchs, R.J. and Demko, G.J. (1979) Population distribution policies in developed Socialist and Western nations, *Population and Development Review*, **5**, 439–67.

Fuchs, R.J. and Demko, G.J. (1981) Population distribution measures and the redistribution mechanism, in G. Demko and R. Fuchs (eds.), *Population Distribution Policies in Development Planning*, U.N., Population Division, New York, 70–84.

Fuchs, R.J. and Demko, G.J. (1983, forthcoming). Rethinking population distribution policies, *Population Policy and Research Review*.

Gosling, L.A.P. and Lim, C.Y.C. (eds.) (1979) *Population Redistribution: Patterns, Policies and Prospects*, New York, U.N.F.P.A.

Hansen, N. (1981) Review and evaluation of attempts to direct migrants to smaller and intermediate-sized cities, in G. Demko and R. Fuchs (eds.), *Population Distribution Policies in Development Planning*, U.N., Population Division, New York, 113–30.

Laquian, A.A. (1981) Review and evaluation of urban accommodationist policies in population redistribution, in G. Demko and R. Fuchs (eds.), *Population Distribution Policies in Development Planning*, U.N., Department of International Economic and Social Affairs, 101–12.

Mabogunje, A.L. (1981) Effectiveness of population redistribution policies: the African experience, *Solicited Papers*, 1981 Manila International Population Conference, Liège, I.U.S.S.P., **2**, 527–42.

Oberai, A.S. (1981) State policies and internal migration in Asia, *International Labour Review* **120**, 231–44.

Pryor, R.J. (1981) Population redistribution: policy formulation and implementation, in G. Demko and R. Fuchs (eds.), *Population Distribution Policies in Development Planning*, U.N., Department of International Economic and Social Affairs, New York, 169–82.

Richardson, H.W. (1977) *City Size and National Spatial Strategies*, Staff Working Paper No. 252, Washington, D.C., World Bank.

Richardson, H.W. (1981) Defining urban population distribution goals in development planning, in G. Demko and R. Fuchs (eds.), *Population Distribution Policies in Development Planning*, U.N., Department of International Economic and Social Affairs, New York, 7–18.

Simmons, A.B. (1979) Slowing metropolitan city growth in Asia: policies, programs and results, *Population and Development Review*, **5**, 87–104.

Sundquist, J.L. (1975) *Dispersing Population: What Americans Can Learn from Europe*, Washington, D.C., The Brookings Institution.

United Nations (1980) *World Population Trends and Monitoring Report, Volume II, Population Policies*, U.N., Population Division, New York.

16

Population Geography and Population Education

K. E. VAIDYANATHAN
(UNESCO, Paris)*

Introduction

There are manifold interfaces between population geography and population education. Therefore it comes as no surprise that population geography as a discipline has contributed a great deal to population education, and population geographers are in the forefront of the world movement for population education. The interest of geographers in the study of population is as old as the science of geography itself, while other disciplines like sociology, economics and education have become interested in population questions only during the past two or three decades as a result of the crises facing mankind such as inadequate food supplies, poverty in Third World countries, energy resources and environmental problems in the developed countries.

Unlike other disciplines, geography has treated population as a endogenous variable and not as an exogenous variable. Population geography is the branch of geography concerned with the study of population and its interaction with the natural and man-made environment. There are variations in population characteristics and patterns of population distribution in the different parts of the world and at different points in time. Population geographers study these phenomena and their variations and have analyzed their relationships to natural factors like land, mineral and water resources, social and economic factors, and aspects of the man-made environment like roads, railways and ports. They have used tools like observations, interviews and mapping and analysis of secondary data from censuses, surveys and administrative records to draw their conclusions.

* The views expressed in the paper are those of the author alone and not of UNESCO.

Population education, on the other hand, is the educational process whereby the awareness and understanding of the causes, processes and consequences of population changes as they affect individuals, communities and countries is brought about (UNESCO, 1978). Population education is being introduced in many countries in formal education and in non-formal education. In formal education, the integration of population concepts is done through existing subjects like mathematics, science, social studies, civics, religious and moral studies at all levels of instruction—pre-primary, primary, secondary and post-secondary schools as well as teacher training courses. In some countries, population education occupies an important place in the formal training of health personnel, social workers and agricultural scientists. In non-formal education, population education is being attempted through rural extension programs, workers' education and women and youth programs. The concepts, objectives and modalities of population education are related to the needs and conditions in each country; they take into account the available personnel, facilities and equipment and the local beliefs, customs and superstitions, ethnic differences, religious taboos and family structure of the population as well as the physical, emotional and social needs of the target groups.

In this paper, an attempt is made to identify the contribution of population geography to the identification of population problems; defining the concepts and objectives of population education; developing the knowledge base, curricula and sourcebooks; developing the teaching methodologies; and providing the tools for research and evaluation. It must, however, be emphasized that population education is a multi-disciplinary educational process, for which several other disciplines like sociology, economics and demography have also made important contributions, and it is not the intention of this paper to belittle these contributions.

Identifying population problems

Before identifying the contribution of population geography to population education, a few characteristics of population geography need to be stressed: (i) it is a purposeful science, which has tried to identify problems and discover possible solutions; (ii) it is a dynamic science, which has not merely looked at the present or the past, but attempted to discover the successive links in the chain of causation which offer the key to the future; (iii) it has an international outlook which has viewed problems from a world perspective; and (iv) it is a science which has synthesized observations from other sciences like agronomy, geology and economics concerning the reciprocal interaction between man and his environment.

Because of these attributes, population geography has contributed to the process of problem identification and solution in the following sequence:

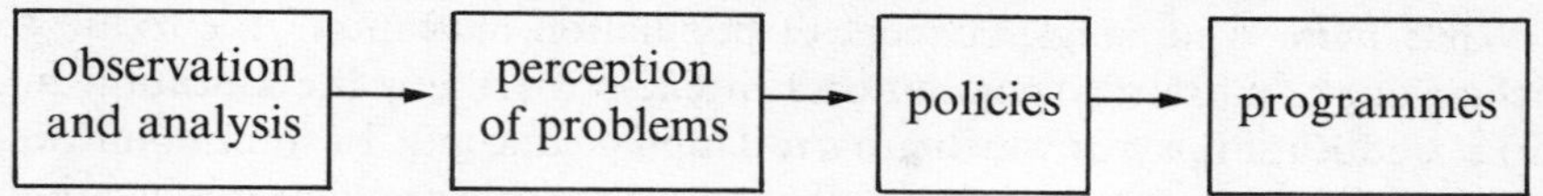

Population problems have been identified through a long continuous series of observations, field studies, interpretation of secondary data from censuses and surveys, mapping of resources and population, etc. By comparing the similarities and contrasts between areas having different population characteristics and variations in socio-economic variables, geographers have established the relationships between the two sets of variables and have sought to identify the lines of causation. Some relationships are easy to observe and explain, while others are highly complex and difficult to discover. Moreover the facts of population geography, in contrast to physical geography, change rapidly. People migrate, change the road system, grow new crops, set up new industries and so on. Such changes call for a constant review of the relationships observed.

The following are examples of the kind of problems identified by different countries:

(i) supplies of food, clothing and shelter are inadequate for the growing population;

(ii) the population growth rate is far too high in relation to the rate of economic growth;

(iii) high fertility has led to a high dependency burden, low savings and low productivity;

(iv) high infant and childhood mortality, poor nutrition and hygiene are detrimental to the welfare of the people;

(v) uneven distribution of population in relation to resources has led to excessive migration;

(vi) shortage of skilled manpower in some countries and surplus of skilled workers in others has led to excessive immigration and emigration respectively;

(vii) population pressure upon natural resources has led to deterioration of environment; and

(viii) population pressure upon social services has led to deterioration of standards of education, hygiene and housing.

This list illustrates the kinds of population problems for which solutions are sought through population education. Population geographers have helped to identify these problems, and have equally contributed to the methodologies of population education by emphasizing learning based on observation, ability to identify causal relationships and to 'discover' solutions.

Defining concepts and objectives of population education

While there is no single concept of population education, it is found to include one or more of (i) population awareness, (ii) family-life education and (iii) sex education, all of which are overlapping concepts. In some countries, health and nutrition education are also included within population education. There is a tendency to define population education in operational terms by identifying topics that population education should cover and the objectives that it should fulfil. The concepts and objectives adopted are influenced by the national perceptions of population problems. A comprehensive concept of population education would include knowledge about both quantitative and qualitative aspects of population and emphasize the cause and effect relationships and their multi-dimensionality.

In educational and behavioural terms, the objectives of population education are to help individuals and social groups to obtain:

(i) *awareness* of and sensitivity to population and related problems;
(ii) *knowledge* of the determinants and consequences of population size, composition, growth and distribution, and the associated factors;
(iii) *attitudes:* the social values and feelings of concern and the motivation for finding solutions to these problems;
(iv) *skills* for finding solutions to population problems;
(v) *evaluation ability:* an ability to evaluate population measures and development programmes in terms of demographic, social, economic, political, geographical and ecological considerations; and
(vi) *participation* in finding solutions to population problems and in actions that are appropriate to solve them.

Population education programs usually have a set of well-defined general objectives and operational objectives. Examples of *general objectives for formal education* are (NCERT, 1971: 9–10) to develop understanding of:

(i) demographic concepts and processes and the causes of rapid population growth in the present day;
(ii) the close interaction between population factors and the development process, and the influence of population trends on various aspects of human life;
(iii) the adverse effects of rapid population growth on the environment and the quality of life;
(iv) the fact that actions of each individual can affect others in the society and also have long-range consequences for the whole world;
(v) an attitude of responsibility in matters of personal and family living and problems of mankind; and
(vi) family size as a matter of deliberate choice and not an accident of forces beyond human control, and the desirability of a small family norm.

The *operational objectives of formal education* are defined on the following broad lines:

(i) to review the existing curricula and identify areas where population education themes can be integrated;
(ii) to revise the curricula and text books as appropriate;
(iii) to develop teaching materials, sourcebooks and audio-visual aids for use by teachers;
(iv) to carry out in-service and pre-service training programmes for teachers; and
(v) to carry out periodic evaluations and correct any deficiencies in the programme.

The *general objectives of non-formal education* may be defined as follows:

(i) to improve the quality of life of youth, women and other important groups by providing an understanding of the manner in which population factors affect their personal and social life; and
(ii) to encourage and assist youth and women's organizations to incorporate family-life themes in their education programs.

The specific *operational objectives of non-formal education* will usually include the following:

(i) to conduct orientation seminars for youth/women leaders on population and family-life themes; and
(ii) to prepare teaching-learning materials appropriate for each target group.

Population geographers have helped in identifying the general and specific objectives for different target groups and in delineating the themes that are appropriate for each target group. They have focused upon the impact of population growth upon human life and environment and how population factors affect food supply, living standards, natural resources, social and cultural conditions and even international relations.

Developing the curricula for population education

Population geography has contributed to the identification of areas of knowledge to be covered by population education and in defining them precisely in terms of factual information. The criteria for the selection of the information is determined by the general and specific objectives outlined for each target group. Some of the themes included are the following:

(i) effects of population growth on per capita income at the macro-level and living standards at the micro-level;
(ii) effects of population growth on food supplies, health, nutritional status and quality of life;
(iii) effects of population factors on labour supplies and productivity;

(iv) influence of natural resources on population patterns and vice versa; and

(v) effects of migration and urbanization on the human and physical environment.

These themes are neither mutually exclusive not exhaustive, and there is always a certain amount of overlapping of them in the different subject areas. In formal education, the 'infusion approach' is generally followed, whereby appropriate population concepts are integrated in the existing subjects rather than being handled as a separate subject. In non-formal education, population concepts are either integrated into the different subject areas or treated as a separate subject.

The syllabus can follow several possible patterns, but essentially it should be flexible to allow adaptation to the needs of the specific target groups and to the conditions of the community. The ultimate objectives and the expected outcomes should be kept in mind in developing the syllabus. The subject matter is organized in a systematic manner beginning with the immediate physical and social environment in classes I and II and then gradually widening the scope to the problems of the city, province, country and the world. At the elementary level, the essential aim is towards the acquisition of basic notions and facts about population and gradually leading the pupils to observe some associations and discover interactions. At the lower secondary level, the aim is to provide the knowledge and skills that are useful in life; while at the upper secondary level the students are encouraged to reason out and identify cause-effect relationships and to take part in group activities. While a presentation of the syllabus at different stages of instruction would be inappropriate, the following will illustrate the elements of population geography which are included (UNESCO, 1965: 190–200).

Elementary level:

(i) Basic geographical notions like direction, distance and area, and basic natural facts like heat and cold, weather, the water cycle, land utilization and natural landscapes.

(ii) Basic human facts like peopling of a locality, region or continent, population mobility and migration, number of inhabitants and their relationships to facts of nature, similarities and contrasts between populations.

(iii) Basic geographical facts which reveal intervention of man such as patterns of human settlements, types of dwellings and pattern of land use.

Lower secondary level:

(i) The local environment such as the school and its surroundings, village or locality, its location, population and activities, the natural environment, relief, climate, water supply, vegetation, etc.

(ii) Natural environments and landscapes in the region and country, to enable the student to correlate between the local environments and those beyond his immediate vicinity.

(iii) Peopling of the world and zones of civilization and the use and organization of space by man; for example, the availability of water, land and mineral resources and their utilization.

(iv) Settlement patterns and economic life in different parts of the world, development of towns, industrial centres, production and exports, means of transport and communications.

Upper secondary level:

(i) Geographic conditions of the world, including the natural environment, its components and dynamic conditions affecting the way it has been peopled and the conditions affecting different sectors of the economy.

(ii) Political and economic organization of the world, including demographic, social and economic conditions and problems of the world.

(iii) Impact of population growth on availability of food, shelter, clothing, employment, quality of life and economic development.

(iv) Measures taken internationally and nationally to alleviate poverty, maldistribution of wealth and other social problems.

Developing teaching methodologies

Population education has resulted in educational innovation in many countries, especially in the organization and methods of teaching (Vaidyanathan, 1982). Many countries have developed teaching modules for subjects indicating the contents of each lesson or unit, the class activities expected, source materials, teacher information and suggestions for evaluating the lesson or unit. Very great care has been taken in the preparation of these modules, taking into account the abilities, skills, knowledge and interests of the class, so as to contribute to the development of desirable attitudes and skills consistent with the objectives set forth. Selections of topics are based on educational and behavioural considerations and involve real-life situations, so as to interest and stimulate the curiosity of the pupils. Teacher activities and pupil activities outlined include topics for class discussion, terminologies to be learnt, questions to be answered, reading assignments, writing of reports, role playing, preparation or drawing of models, simple experiments, searching for illustrative materials and correlating topics with what is being learned in other subjects. Each unit is carefully evaluated taking into account the expected and actual outcomes in terms of knowledge, attitude, skills, pupil interests, difficulties, clarity and practicability.

The use of appropriate teaching methods is as important as the use of an appropriate curriculum or teaching plan. Population geography has contributed two kinds of 'participatory methods' to the teaching methodologies employed in population education: (i) methods which rely upon direct observation by the pupil (e.g. field visits, case studies and small sample observations); and (ii) methods based on indirect observations from second-hand materials (e.g. collection and interpretation of secondary data from censuses and surveys and use of visual resources like maps and models).

Field visits provide the learner with first-hand experience of the situations discussed in the classroom. Such visits can cover places like farms, urban centres, industrial establishments, hospitals and family planning clinics. Careful advance planning of such visits is needed in order to make it an effective learning experience. The visit should be related to classroom activities and the teacher should be familiar with the place of visit in order to be able to answer any questions that may be raised by the pupils.

Case studies and small sample observations help students to observe the facts studied in the class. For example, students may be asked to compare two families which are identical in many respects except the family size, and to discuss their differences in living conditions, attitudes and behaviour. Similar comparisons can be attempted between a typical migrant worker and a typical native worker and so on. Small sample surveys can be carried out in an agricultural community by the students who are asked to report on their observations. Some simple experimental studies can be built into these observations. For example an 'experimental village' exposed to an immunization programme may be compared with a 'control village' where no such programme was carried out. The possibilities for such case studies and small sample observations are so numerous that the teacher should make a judicious choice according to the level of the class and the subject matter dealt with.

Collection and interpretation of secondary data: students are encouraged to collect data from secondary sources like statistical yearbooks, census publications and survey reports and to draw conclusions from them. They are taught how to read tables and to develop simple indexes such as rates and ratios and to prepare charts and diagrams depicting the observed facts. The student is trained to analyze, compare and classify data, with a view to observing underlying relationships and connections and to formulating questions and seeking answers. The student is encouraged to identify and recognize intercorrelations between different variables and to find explanations of possible causes.

Exhibits and visual resources: There are four categories of visual resources: (i) charts, maps, graphs, written materials, exhibits, models and chalkboards, etc.; (ii) textbooks, workbooks, test sheets, etc.; (iii) photographs, slides, filmstrips, tapes, radio, television and video programs; and (iv) man-machine communication systems such as language laboratories, teaching machines, programmed self-instruction and teaching use of computers. From time immemorial geographers have encouraged pupils to develop their own exhibits like maps, diagrams and bar charts, and these methods have contributed to the development of visual memory and imaginative faculty of the students.

The aim of these methods is to involve the learners in the process of learning, to enable them to discover problems and find solutions, and to develop their faculties of observation, reasoning and judgement. It is obvious that the success of these methods would depend upon the capacity of the teacher himself, therefore there is need for adequate preparation of teachers in the application of these methods in the classroom situations they will be facing.

Research studies for program development

The tools of population geography such as collection of data through observations, sifting of information, analysis of cause-effect relationships and cartographic techniques are widely used in research devoted to program development. These studies could be broadly grouped into macro-studies and micro-studies. Macro-studies have helped to identify relationships at the macro-level of population factors to socio-economic development, quality of life and environmental conditions, and have helped to identify what constitute population problems and what are the educational themes appropriate for their solution.

Micro-studies have been focused upon finding the needs and characteristics of a specific target group or community or have addressed themselves to problems of curriculum design, teaching methods and developing tests. Micro-studies are in the nature of model or pilot projects, case studies, small sample observations or experiments, which try to obtain the following information on the target groups: geographic location, life-style, demographic characteristics (age, sex, marital status, etc.), socio-economic characteristics (education, occupation, etc,) and psycho-social characteristics (needs, interests, concerns, motivations, knowledge, attitudes, etc.). Such information enables the program planner to devise programs tailored to the requirements of the target group and to develop prototype curricula, teaching materials and training designs. The psycho-social information also serves as benchmark data for measuring changes in attitudes, motivations and commitment as a result of the educational project. The information may be obtained either through surveys of a small sample of the target group or through open-ended or unstructured interviews of a few representative persons of the target group.

Program evaluation

Evaluation of population education programs is another area where the methods of population geography are widely applied. The aim is to obtain a feedback on the strengths and weaknesses of the strategies and methods adopted and to assess the impact of the project in terms of the twin criteria of *effectiveness* (extent to which the objectives of the project are fulfilled) and *efficiency* (extent to which the results are commensurate with the resources used). There are two kinds of evaluations made: formative and summative evaluation (UNESCO, 1979).

Formative evaluation takes place during implementation of the project with a view to improving its effectiveness and efficiency. It addresses such questions as whether the appropriate target audience was selected, whether their needs are being met and whether their operational objectives are being fulfilled. An external evaluator may be asked to observe such aspects as lesson introduction, teacher-learner interaction, verbal presentation, use of visual aids and application of participatory methods. The participants themselves may be asked to give their reactions to specific elements of the training program, such as contents of the course, effectiveness of teaching, practical exercises, length of sessions, materials and equipment used and teacher-trainee relationships. Such analytical tools as unstructured interviews, questionnaires and score cards can be used in these evaluations.

Field trials of the program are among the activities included under formative evaluation. A field trial is an essential step in the curriculum-building process whereby the curriculum materials are tested for their suitability to a particular cultural milieu and whether they can fulfil the goals of the program. Field trials call for the application of survey and experimental design methodologies. For example, two homogeneous areas may be chosen, the 'treatment area' being exposed to the information campaign, while the 'control area' is not. The two areas may be compared before and after the experiment. A field trial can provide information on a wide range of parameters important in the design of curricula and teaching materials, such as the knowledge and attitude of the participants and the customs and taboos which can affect the program.

Summative or final evaluation is an attempt to discover to what extent the educational goals of the program have been fulfilled. Such an evaluation requires measurement of changes in knowledge, attitude and behaviour among the target groups. The usually adopted procedure is the Knowledge, Attitude and Practices (KAP) Survey before and after the implementation of the program. The 'before' situation should be established during the planning stage by obtaining the baseline data against which subsequent change may be measured. Similarly, the 'after' situation may be established by applying the same survey instruments at the end of the program. KAP Surveys before and after the project may be combined with an experimental design, whereby an experimental group and a control group may be compared before and after the program to test if the observed change in the experimental group is due to the program or some other factor. Population geographers have been involved in the preparation of the survey instruments in many countries.

Concluding remarks

This paper has shown the contribution of population geography and population geographers to the identification of population problems, the definition of the objectives of population education, selection of contents, preparation of exemplar materials, program development and its evaluation. By far the most important contribution is the mental attitude brought by geography, namely the powers of observation, reasoning and judgement and inculcation of the geographical outlook whereby the pupils see the individual phenomena as parts of the whole and vice versa. Moreover, the tools of population geography such as field observations, study of maps, models and diagrams and participatory methods have enabled students to identify problems and seek solutions themselves.

References

National Council for Educational Research and Training (NCERT) (1971) *Population Education: A Draft Syllabus*, New Delhi.

UNESCO (1965) *Sourcebook for Geography Teaching*, Longmans, London.

UNESCO (1978) *Population Education: A Contemporary Concern*, Paris.

UNESCO (1979) *A Manual on Evaluation in Population Education*, Bangkok.

Vaidyanathan, K.E. (1982) *Educators Training Programme for Out-of-School Population Education: A Methodological Guideline*, Paris.

17

Pre-Census Mapping

D. M. BOHRA
(University of Jodhpur, India)

Importance and need of maps in census operations

During recent decennial rounds of censuses there has been an increasing use of maps in the job of area control during the actual enumeration. In developing countries, often with poor areal coverage, the use of maps is now becoming a standard procedure in taking population and agricultural censuses. Current and precise maps provide an up-to-date spatial framework essential for population and housing censuses. Maps are required for a variety of pre-census operations: to establish the location of many types of boundaries, to canvass the enumerator-area, to avoid duplication or omission of census-count, to identify segments and sub-segments used in area sampling, to determine enumerator and supervisor workload and to foster comparability of data from census to census. An excellent discussion of geographical concepts, products and programmes and of the role of geography in taking censuses and in publishing the results may be found in *Census Geography* (United States Bureau of the Census, 1978a).

This chapter is not intended for use as a direct vehicle for the instruction of persons carrying out census mapping operations in a particular area. A comprehensive analysis and discussion of myriads of cartographic tasks which come before the enumeration is also beyond the scope of this chapter. It is intended more as a guide to persons responsible for initiating and maintaining an efficient and accurate system of mapping materials for different types of situations, for the development of control systems, and for adaptation of techniques.

Time required for mapping program

It is estimated that the geographic and cartographic work should extend over three-fifths (United Nations, 1954) or considerably more (Batschelet and

Archer, 1958) of the preparatory time for the enumeration of a population census. According to one estimate (United Nations, 1980), it is necessary to start cartographic work sufficiently early to ensure that an adequate supply of maps is available three to four months before the census is scheduled to begin. Mapping tasks undertaken too late or with insufficient planning almost surely will result in lack of maps or in maps that are inadequate for the enumeration of critical areas. On the average, even with an ongoing mapping program, lead time should be at least two or three years. Map inventory, in order to achieve sound area control, needs to be made three years in advance and map acquisition should start soon after. Base maps required for delineating enumeration areas (EAs) should be available one year in advance and the delineated EA maps should be ready for distribution at least three months in advance of the enumeration.

Functions and requirements of census organization

Among the variety of functions the census organization has to perform are: preparation of map inventory; acquisition of maps, necessary cartographic tools and equipment to make and reproduce maps; freezing of administrative area boundaries; training programs for census geographers and cartographers in the use of cartographic assessories; training of enumerators in field-work activities and careful handling of maps (United States Bureau of Census, 1976 chap. 3; Gordon, 1975). Among the requirements of census organization, the staff needs for census mapping operations include geographers, cartographers, draftsmen having a general training in geography, and clerks with some knowledge of mathematics required to train them in census mapping tasks. Census geographers and cartographers should be adequately trained in the task of map acquisition and aerial photography which are very important operations in census mapping programs in countries whose map coverage is poor.

The first operational step is to prepare, in a hierarchial order, a complete inventory of all the administrative and statistical areas and the maps available for these areas. Soon after starts the map acquisition work. The governmental census authorities should freeze the boundaries of various administrative units at last six months in advance of the census date so that no further jurisdictional changes are effected until the enumeration is over. This helps to minimize chances of omission or duplication (Economic and Social Commission for Asia and Pacific, 1978). The other major chores of the census organization include delimitation of administrative areas, delineation of statistical and enumeration areas and collection and revision of census maps. It is important that the national statistical offices should develop a continuing cartographic capability to serve their specialized cartographic needs. Such capability making available the appropriate, reliable and up-to-date cartographic materials can contribute to the population and housing census as well as to the analysis and presentation of census results.

Mapping and house-numbering

The mapping, house-listing and house-numbering of every dwelling structure preceding the population census, serve as the basis for estimates of population counts and as a reference frame for various types of survey. The house-listing and house-numbering maps divided sensibly into small land areas (called 'chunks') can well provide a frame to obtain multi-stage probability samples of the occupied dwelling units. The plan for listing and numbering dwelling units should be devised in such a way that new buildings can be added periodically as the need arises over a long period of time. The house-numbering system should be constant, reliable and expandable (Cooke, 1971). Different house-numbering systems, one of them being permanent (Office of the Registrar General, India, 1966), may be used in different places. In areas of poor mapping coverage for dwelling units, use of aerial photographs and timely maps prepared by the malaria eradication program (World Health Organization, 1978) can save a great deal of time and resources. Even when the aerial photography is quite old, it will give the structure and orientation of the dwelling pattern which can be updated by field check.

Pilot census

A pilot census (as well as pre-tests), also known as pilot study, pilot survey, trial census or rehearsal census, is almost a pre-requisite of an efficient enumeration. A pilot census helps to simulate actual conditions as closely as possible. The EA maps prepared during the pilot census provide (i) a base for assessing the quantum, quality and details of available base maps suitable for EA mapping, (ii) experience and a test for map reading and interpretation skills, (iii) suggestions for their improvements and (iv) a coverage check or housing unit (HU) estimates and average population per household.

Coding of areas

After compiling and verifying the list of areas, a unique location or identification (geographic) code should be assigned to each area down to the level of EA. Two coding systems available are: first, the traditional, hierarchical system, and second, the geocoding system having two approaches of segment allocation and area allocation to grid squares. The advantages of a geocoding system based on grid squares approach are its uniformity, clarity (finer geographic specificity) and permanence (Statistics Canada, 1971). A comprehensive literature devoted to national geocoding (Werner, 1974) and urban geocoding (Dueker, 1974) applications also exists. A geocoding system is more expensive than the traditional system and the technical pre-requisites for it may not be present in many countries.

A country should plan a code scheme that best suits its needs. *Mapping for Censuses and Surveys* (United States Bureau of the Census, 1978b) provides a methodology for coding the areas, based on the traditional, hierarchical systems. To make the coding scheme more scientific and standard, the census office should devise a scheme that requires minimum change from census to census, reserving gaps to allow for addition of places in alphabetical order.

Census map requirements and EA maps

All census maps (mainly EA maps) should contain some common features. Among these are: location of features in proper relationship to each other (direction should be correct but distance is slightly less significant); accurate and clear boundaries in appropriate relationship to other features; graphic scale to show distance; and correctly and commonly recognized and identified place-names obtained from survey maps, gazetteers and field sources.

An EA, also known as enumeration block (EB), collector's district (CD), enumeration district (ED) and census block (Cho, 1976), is a work assignment unit for an enumerator. EA maps form a major contingent of census maps. Maps should show those physical and cultural features identifying the location and boundaries of EAs: physical features like rivers, streams, water bodies, marshes and crest lines, and cultural features like railways, highways, roads, streets and trails with their available recognized names, transmission lines, telegraph and telephone lines, canals, drainage ditches and fence lines. The EA is the geographical base of the census and the design of this areal base is as important as the design of questions and tabulations for effective interpretation of census results (Denham, 1980). Better quality EA maps assure high order of accuracy and coverage in census counts. Accurate and updated EA maps showing each housing unit (HU) provide a good base for the design and implementation of post-censal multi-stage area sample surveys, including the selection of primary sampling units (PSUs) and their stratification (based on homogeneity principle), segmenting and sub-segmenting and exerting control on the sampling error of the results (United States Bureau of the Census, 1978c).

Use of aerial photographs for census work

Aerial photographs furnish information which can be used to produce, update, supplement and substitute maps for census taking. A vertical aerial photograph has advantages over an ordinary map in that it has more wealth of details, more reliability and quick production but requires special training in its use and interpretation. There are several sources which provide air photos usable for census work.

Recent air photos, accompanied at times by a certain amount of field work, are used for updating of the EA maps; in the preparation of base maps when there are no maps or the existing maps are unsatisfactory; in the preparation of uncontrolled photo mosaics for mapping of large areas and of controlled photo mosaics for precise mapping. Current air photos of proper scale with little foliage or ground cover can also be useful for approximating population (to delineate EAs) by counting the number of HUs. Boundaries of statistical areas can be identified and delimited on air photos.

Basic considerations in EA delineation

Delineation is the process of selecting and marking EA boundaries on the base map, on which crew leader (CL) areas or supervisory areas are also marked. There are certain basic considerations in delineating EAs:

(a) Size of an EA, especially the population size which can be enumerated by an enumerator during the scheduled period. The ideal size of an EA varies in different countries. On average, the ideal urban EA would contain 160 HUs or 800 persons and the rural EA 100 HUs or 500 persons. However, there are certain situations where EAs depart from the ideal size, such as where administrative areas have slightly more or less people than the ideal size, where visible feature boundaries are used, where there are areas of difficult terrain and scattered HUs, where the population is growing rapidly and where HU estimates are deficient.

(b) Special EAs: 'Large special dwelling places' designated as Special EAs should be assigned the prefix letter 'S' to distinguish them from other EAs. Special maps are not generally prepared; a circle is simply drawn around a special dwelling place.

(c) Comparability of EAs with last census: For reasons of changes in cultural features, administrative boundaries and population growth, it becomes practically difficult to use the same EAs from census to census.

(d) Obtaining population and HU estimates: Current estimates of HUs or population are needed to delineate EAs, and are generally obtained by way of a variety of procedures and sources: (i) knowledgeable local officials, (ii) field visits by the census officials, and (iii) recent air photos, maps and other sources. The HUs or population estimates with EA number should be entered on the EA delineation worksheet and shown on sub-areas (sectors) that appear on the EA maps. These estimates should be made with caution and for this some knowledge of current conditions in the areas concerned is essential.

Guidelines in EA delineation and numbering

EAs should be delineated in such a way that they prevent omission or duplication of land areas and overlapping of administrative area boundaries. There are certain guidelines which should be carefully observed in the efficient delineation of EAs (East-West Population Institute, 1978): (a) generally a wriggly line which does not obscure other features and administrative/statistical area boundaries should be used to delineate EA boundaries; (b) EA boundaries should not cross administrative and statistical area boundaries; (c) EA boundaries should observe easily visible and clearly identified physical and cultural features; and (d) if the use of imaginary or invisible lines like offset and extended lines is unavoidable for EA boundaries, they should be drawn with great care.

For EA numbering, one preferred systematic method is to begin at the north-east or north-west corner of an area and number in serpentine fashion. Generally 4 to 8 EAs, depending on enumeration workload, travel time and length of enumeration period, form one CL area. CL areas formed for control purposes observe the boundaries of district field offices.

After delineating and numbering of EAs, some important final tasks, like calculating the number of map copies required, cutting the EA maps from the base map copies, colouring the EA boundary lines and supplying the appropriate legend, should be accomplished.

Use of maps in enumeration

Three types of maps, namely EA, CL and field office maps, are used in enumeration and field operations. For effective use of EA maps in enumeration, the enumerators and crew leaders should possess certain basic skills like sense of direction, reading a map, comprehending written instructions and knowledge of simple calculations. They must be trained through classroom instruction and field exercises with the help of census cartographic manuals (United States Bureau of the Census, 1978d) in the whole process of efficient EA delineation and its proper canvass. There are certain important cartographic guidelines (Madigan, 1973) for preparing locality sketch maps, particularly in areas of deficient map coverage.

Special mapping problems

Mapping problem areas are not normally found in all countries, but include those with sparse population, difficulties of physical environment, pastoral nomadism, rapid population growth, population congestion, inadequate maps and undefined boundaries. Necessary changes in map specifications, modifications in EA maps specific to local conditions and use of recent air photos can serve as tools in dealing with mapping of such problem areas.

In some areas nomadic or semi-nomadic people cause specific problems during enumeration. Nomadic movements are not random; they tend to be systematic and often cyclical. Efforts must be made to prepare sector or zonal maps indicating nomadic movements, campsites, water points and springs as well as a special reporting form (World Health Organization, 1978). They should be completed for each individual group which moves about together, giving number of tents, population and information on movements (Economic Commission for Africa, 1977).

References

Batschelet, C.E. and Archer, A. (1958) Comments on geography and cartography for census purposes emphasizing map preparation for the 1960 Census of America, *Estadistica*, **16**, No. 58, 1.

Cho, L.J. (ed.) (1976) *Introduction to Censuses of Asia and the Pacific, 1970–74*, East-West Population Institute, East-West Centre, Honolulu, Hawaii.

Cooke, D.S. (1971) *Mapping and Housenumbering*, Manual Series No. 1, Laboratories for Population Statistics, The Carolina Population Centre.

Denham, C. (1980) The geography of the Census 1971 and 1981, *Population Trends*, **19**, 6–12.

Dueker, K.J. (1974) Urban geocoding, Review Article, *Annals of the Association of American Geographers*, **64**, 318–25.

East-West Population Institute (1978) *Unpublished papers presented at the Census Mapping Working Group*, October 4–November 17, 1978, East-West Center, Honolulu, Hawaii.

Economic and Social Commission for Asia and the Pacific (1978) *Asian and Pacific Recommendations for the 1980 Population and Housing Census*, Bangkok.

Economic Commission for Africa (1977) *Study on Special Techniques for Enumeration of Nomads in African Censuses and Surveys*, E/CN. 14/CAS, 10/16, Addis Ababa.

Gordon, M. (1975) Cartography for census purposes, *World Cartography*, United Nations, ST/ESA/SER.L/13, 3–18.

Madigan, F.C. (1973) *Mapping for Recurrent Research: A Philippine POPLAB Report*, Scientific Report Series No. 10, Laboratories for Population Statistics, The Carolina Population Centre.

Office of the Registrar General, India (1966) *Scheme on Permanent Housenumbering, Government of India*, New Delhi.

Statistics Canada (1971) *Population and Housing Research Memorandum*, PH-Geog-5, Ottawa.

United Nations (1954) Relative timing of various steps in a population census, in *Handbook of Population Census Methods: Studies in Methods*, Series F.No. 85, 14.

United Nations (1980) *Principles and Recommendations for Population and Housing Censuses*, Statistical Papers, Ser. M, No. 67.

U.S. Bureau of the Census (1976) *United States Census of Population and Housing: 1970, Procedural History*, PHC(R)-1.

U.S. Bureau of the Census (1978a) *Census Geography*, DAD No. 33, Revised October 1978.

U.S. Bureau of the Census (1978b) *Mapping of Censuses and Surveys*, Statistical Training Document, ISP-TR-3.

U.S. Bureau of the Census (1978c) *The Current Population Survey: Design and Methodology*, Technical Paper No. 40.

U.S. Bureau of the Census (1978d) *Mapping for Censuses and Surveys*, Statistical Training Document, ISP-TR-3W.

Werner, P.A. (1974) National geocoding, Review Article, *Annals of the Association of American Geographers*, **64**, 310–7.

World Health Organization (1978) *Geographical Reconnaissance for Malaria Eradication Programme*, PA/264.65.

18

Post-Census Mapping

PRITHVISH NAG
(National Atlas and Thematic Mapping Organisation, Calcutta, India)

Population censuses provide us basically with two types of information related to (a) the division of the country into census districts (CDs) or enumeration areas (EAs) and their hierarchical arrangement, and (b) population data for each of these units. Both these types of information are combined to produce census maps. There are several types of censuses, such as agricultural, industrial or livestock, but population censuses have been greatly used for mapping owing to the importance of population in development and planning. Therefore census maps are almost synonymous with population maps, although for population maps, information from extra-census sources can also be used, wholly or partly. For example, in preparing a map related to diseases, the census information is not sufficient; nor for making population maps when the theme is related to temporal phenomena, such as human movement during floods, earthquakes or wars. In such cases, the population map has to be based on sample surveys or official records. However, the census can also be considered as a record of several temporal phenomena effective on the day of operation. So a census cartographer has to be vigilant while using such data for population mapping.

Census districts and population grouping

At the national level, the census provides an aggregate picture of the composition of population. As we go through the hierarchical arrangement of data, we find deviations from this overall pattern. The spatial study of such deviations has been thought to be the focal theme of population geography. The mosaic of CDs provides the basis for the study of spatial patterns of population and its mapping. It has not been an easy task to prepare such a framework which links pre- and post-census mapping. The U.N. Population Division and Statistical Office, UNFPA, international organizations and national agencies have emphasized the colossal task of carving out CDs. For post-census mapping it is important to assess the intelligibility of such a framework while preparing population maps. How far does this framework resemble the physical, cultural, economic and urban structure of the country concerned, and how have these aspects been hierarchically organized in a system as a whole? In some countries, the tradition of taking a census has been established for over a century. Hence, such a framework is of historical importance as well. In countries like Zambia, the chiefs' territories have been accepted as the CDs, while in old-settled countries like India, Pakistan and Bangladesh, the revenue villages are recognized as the lowest order CD. In the case of British censuses, Local Authority Areas (along with their sub-divisions—wards in urban areas and civil parishes in rural areas) have been used as CDs (Dewdney, 1981). Other countries have evolved their own systems of forming CDs, which are probably best suited to their local conditions (U.N. Statistical Office, 1980b). Further, a viable framework also provides a basis for comparison of the data of successive censuses, and with the complementary information available from extra-census sources.

Census data and definitions

Apart from the framework of CDs being viable, the definitions of various terms occurring in censuses should be comparable. It has been felt that sometimes it becomes necessary to alter definitions owing to changing socio-economic conditions of the country. Such alterations should be kept to a minimum. Comparable definitions make it possible to use data of various censuses for mapping. Inconsistent definitions pose problems not only in the census mapping of a particular country, but also when certain aspects of population are to be mapped for a world region or whole of the globe. The U.N. Statistical Office and the I.L.O. provide globally applicable definitions for almost all population characteristics, such as occupational or industrial classification of workers, and these guidelines have been kept flexible in order to meet the requirements of each country. As a result, the vital data for developing countries on 'unemployment' cannot be used for mapping, if unemployment is explained variously as the number of persons seeking work, semi-employed or non-workers and the like. Obviously, it has always been less of a problem to prepare a map of a continent or a part of a globe depicting some basic features such as distribution or density of population. There is no problem of definition involved here.

Aspects of post-census operations

In all countries, the census operation is conducted by the government. The size of the country, its population, communications, and the number of census details determine the magnitude of the operation which includes data storage, retrieval and finally dissemination. There are several steps between enumeration and the transmission of census data to the potential users. Unfortunately, bureaucracy is involved at every step. 'The usefulness of a census will be affected adversely if census reports are not published on a timely basis' (U.N. Statistical Office, 1982).

National census operations in every country are facing these problems to varied extents. Some of the developing countries have very acute problems even after sincere efforts to produce the results on time. The U.N. has assisted about 100 countries, through various technical co-operation programs, in conducting national population and housing censuses during the 1980 census decade (1975–84). Census cartography is a part of the co-operation program and the scale of the assistance varies according to the needs of the country. At present, most countries have completed their 1980-round census enumeration, but there are still some 35 data-processing advisors including eight census cartographic advisors stationed in about 30 countries. International agencies and inter-governmental assistance are also helping developing countries in conducting their pre- and post-census operations. But, the least developed countries find themselves in difficulty. The foreign experts are trained in their own way and try to implement their methods. When they leave, the whole operation is left in a confused state. If there is more than one expert, conflicting opinions cause further delay, until a compromise is worked out. The level of technology to be applied as advocated by the experts and the aid from the funding agencies are often misfits. Use of computers in order to expedite the operation may instead jeopardize the process when program or repair experts are not available. For example, after the current census had taken place in Zimbabwe, the expected funds and equipment were not available, and reconsideration of the program has been necessitated. Other African countries are facing such problems.

There has always been a choice in the level of automation to be introduced in the whole operation, from data processing to printed census maps. In some countries this operation is done manually. India furnishes an example where an efficient system was used not only to conduct the census operation by enumerating 685 million persons in time, but also to produce the reports with several maps within a reasonable period. The example of India is not a prescription for all the developing countries. In some countries, there is an acute shortage of trained personnel. In contrast, the developed countries have been successful in producing census data and maps on time. The U.S.A., U.K. and Japan have not only produced their maps in time, but they are trying to find methods to accelerate their operations. The grid-method of census data collection has been experimented in some of the developed countries, and is expected to provide a better framework for data collection and post-census mapping. Computer print-outs, microfiche and magnetic tape files are already in use among the census users in developed countries, but the traditional publication of reports is still considered to be the most important form of data dissemination.

Delay in producing census results

One of the major problems which has been faced by census cartographers is the delay between taking the census and publishing the reports. Mapping can only be undertaken when census reports are available, and experiments with the techniques of mapping are largely based on the nature of data. The relationships between CDs and their population has to be worked out in order to prepare thematic census maps.

Recently, an attempt was made by the U.N. Statistical Office to find out the length of time taken to produce the reports on the censuses carried out in the periods 1955–64 and 1965–76. Almost all countries were able to publish a preliminary report during the year of the census enumeration, and about half produced the first report during the same year or the year after. Of the 137 countries, over half published their last report within 3 to 4 years after the 1965–76 enumeration, but half the countries in the 1960 census-round took 4 to 5 years to issue their last reports. A few countries have taken an exceptionally long time to publish their last report. These delays were due to unforeseen situations, such as political instability, wars, administrative changes, financial difficulties and the like (U.N. Statistical Office, 1982). On the other hand, there are about 18 out of 213 countries (or areas) where no census has been planned, including 4 European countries (U.N. Statistical Office, 1980a). Chad, Ethiopia, Guinea, Oman and Laos have never had a census of their population for similar reasons. In Djibouti, Equatorial Guinea, Jordan, Kampuchea, Lebanon and DPR Korea, the census was taken at least 20 years before 1980 (U.S. Bureau of Census, 1980).

If a map is to be published based on the census results, various printing options are available which may be time-consuming processes. The preparation of a census map is not merely a stage following the dissemination of data, but it is a cumulative process. There are several steps involved which need careful programming. Further, a printed map should indicate the year of census data used and the year of publication. The purpose of the census map is only partially served when the time gap is unduly long, as the map becomes obsolete or is only of academic interest.

Availability of census data and themes for post-census mapping

Not all the data collected for censuses are being used for post-census mapping. The following topics were given priority in the majority of the U.N. regional census recommendations:

1—Place of usual residence and/or place where present at the time of census (42); 2—Place of birth (57); 3—Duration of residence (16); 4—Place of residence at a past specific date (32);

5—Relationship to head or other reference member of household (64); 6—Sex (66); 7—Age (66); 8—Marital status (65); 9—Citizenship (14); 10—Children born alive (48); 11—Children living (34); 12—Educational attainment (60); 13—Literacy (30); 14—School attendance (54); 15—Activity status (62); 16—Occupation (65); 17—Industry (64); 18—Status in employment (58).

The figures in parentheses indicate the number of countries which have included these aspects in their programmes. These figures have been obtained from a survey of 66 countries which were involved in the 1980 census round (U.N. Statistical Office, 1982). Some of these themes have been popular for post-census mapping, such as sex, literacy, occupation and employment. There are themes for which data from successive censuses are required, for example mapping of growth or change in population. For some themes, additional information is required, not necessarily from censuses. Information about topography and settlement patterns is needed for population distribution maps, which have been considered the most significant census maps.

Another popular topic for mapping is the density of population, for which the geographical area of the CDs has to be known. The area of CDs is an aspect which is now finding place in some census programs. Further, researchers and planners are interested in making maps of agricultural or physiological densities of population. Data related to broad land use categories is available in some censuses, and hence the preparation of maps based on the census but not on the core population topics is becoming possible.

An additional set of information which is now being made available in almost all censuses is that related to housing. Housing conditions have been thought to be a most important socio-economic indicator of population composition. Data on related topics, such as crowding in houses, are also easily available in censuses.

Other common topics for post-census mapping are (i) occupational structure, (ii) age and sex ratio, and (iii) migration. Researchers on population-related issues have used census data for mapping. However, these maps are based on concepts, theories or hypotheses, such as internal density in urban areas.

Atlases are the most systematic users of census data. The topics of the atlas maps are directly related to the type of census data available. Some of the themes of the census maps are common to all atlases, while the themes of a few maps vary according to the scale of the map and population characteristics of the region (Thomas, 1972).

Post-census mapping techniques

There have been no radical recent changes in post-census mapping techniques. Dots, circles, squares and spheres for population distribution, and the choropleth technique for population density are widely used. Pyramids are still preferred for the mapping of age-sex patterns. Divided circles (pie-graphs) are found to be most convenient for the mapping of the occupational structure of urban centres. Again, there cannot be a better substitute for flow lines for the mapping of migration trends, while isopleths remain useful for developing statistical or trend surfaces.

There have been some attempts to use non-conventional techniques for census mapping. Model-maps are being developed in order to produce a better picture of the census data. Some of the models are known as three-dimensional maps or hardware models (Morgan, 1967), which enable an intangible distribution to be seen in a tangible or sensory format. They also provide an understanding of how choroplethic maps are created and of the form taken by the generalization (Jenks and Caspall, 1971). Smooth and stepped statistical surfaces and isometric block-diagrams are applied to show different population characteristics (Jenks, 1963; Coulson, 1968; Smith, 1975; Nag *et al.*, 1978). An attempt has been made to show 1970 population density in the U.S. by stepped statistical surfaces assuming that 'the geographical data are given by an at least piecewise continuous function Z(X,Y)'. Such notation is expandable as an infinite Fourier series in two dimensions (Tobler, 1975). Further, Tobler has stressed the use of geographical filters and their inverses in separating important from unimportant data. According to him, 'geographical versions of data filters occur frequently in cartography. Maps are generalized representations since it is clearly impossible to display the earth in all its complexity at a reduced scale'. Any operation which changes the values of the coefficients has been denoted here as a filter. If inversion of the transfer function is possible the effects of the weighted moving averages may be reversed. The effects of moving averages with weights declining from the central position have been variously called smoothing or blurring. Based on the above ideas, Tobler has shown the distribution of population in a portion of the Detroit region from 1930 to 1960 by trend surfaces using a non-linear vertical scale (Tobler, 1969).

The problem of class-intervals has increased with the size of the area being mapped and its scale. Population characteristics comprise many extreme figures, and it has been difficult to highlight such extremities along with the general pattern in the same map. We get more skewed distributions in population data with every new census and such a trend is likely to continue. Some attempts have been made to overcome this problem while preparing census maps. Tobler (1973) has suggested choropleth maps without class-intervals by appropriate spacing of orthogonal lines. Dasgupta (1965) has explained the density interval problem in population mapping by studying ten model cases. Density has often posed a problem for the grouping of data (Raychaudhuri, 1981). These problems have been faced while preparing maps of India, Nigeria and other countries (Chatterjee, 1962; Manshard, 1978). An attempt was also made to prepare a model-map of the density of houses in India (Fig. 18.1); since this density varied considerably, a vertical log scale was used in the model-map in order to produce a perspective view of the stepped statistical surfaces (Nag *et al.*, 1978). The mapping of such data by conventional techniques cannot explain the reality. New techniques are likely to emerge, though their acceptability in view of the conventional use of maps is debatable.

The third thrust area for the development of post-census mapping techniques is the multi-coloured map. It has been realized that multi-coloured

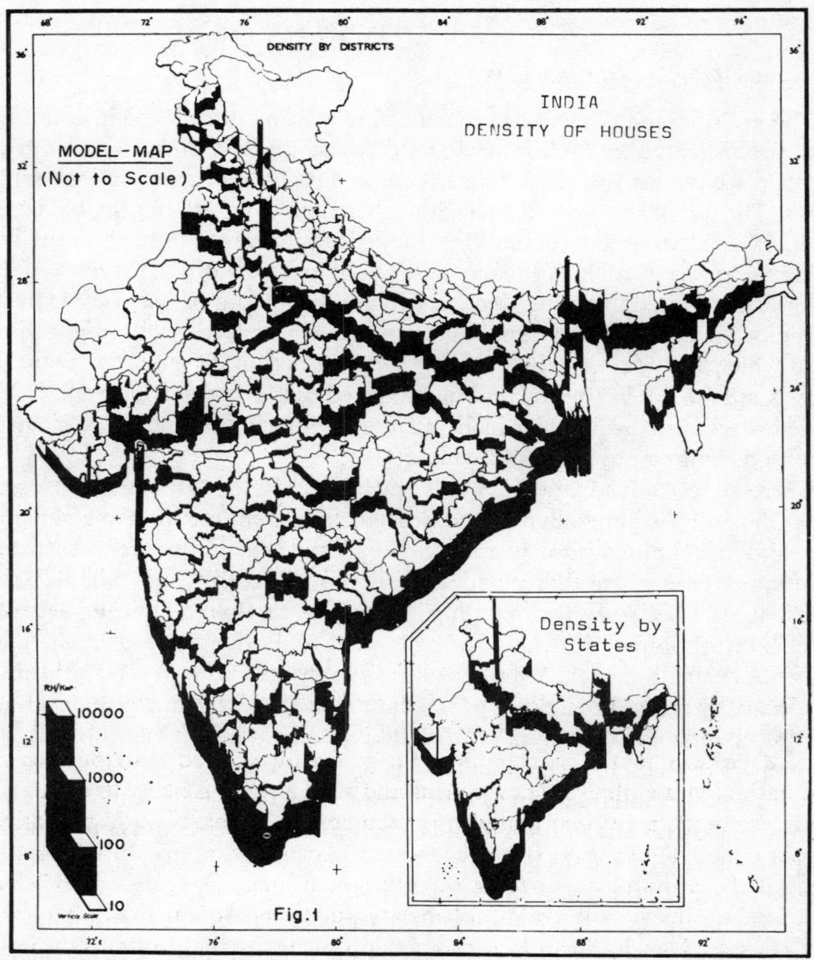

FIGURE 18.1. *A model-map of density of houses in India, using a vertical log scale to produce a perspective view*

census maps are not simply a step ahead of the monochrome maps including half-tone methods; additional information can be shown, and interrelated aspects can be highlighted in order of preference. Further, inset maps and diagrams have proved to be useful in explaining the secondary or related themes (Nag *et al.*, 1982). The development of printing and computer mapping technology have facilitated the preparation of coloured maps. With the help of modern printing technology, such as colour-troll, it has been possible to have a large number of class-intervals. Coloured maps are now being prepared keeping in mind their thematic significance and their potential users.

Computer-based census mapping

The grid-method of census data collection is being introduced in countries with sophisticated technology or no data-collection base. In both cases, grids provide a basis for the geocoding of census data and recording in computer tapes. The use of this system necessitates scrupulous programming of census data. Extra care has to be taken when the census data are to be rearranged into unit grid squares with locational codes. This is a pre-condition for most of the computer assisted mapping systems. Tomlinson and Boyle (1981) have developed a 'Basic System Capabilities' program after creating the digital data base which includes certain steps for mapping natural resources. Some of these steps are applicable in computer assisted census mapping as well. Other systems are also available which are useful for census mapping, such as Geomap, Linmap, Symap and Symvu (Hsu, 1973).

There are certain advantages and disadvantages with automated cartography. The following are the conveniences of having computer drafting of maps: (i) rapid calculations prior to mapping, e.g. construction of trend surfaces, running averages, residuals and land composites; (ii) fast and accurate interpolation decisions for mapping, e.g. where to align a contour between three control points; (iii) choice of scale, size, and orientation once the base map has been fitted to the template of the library programs; (iv) fast drafting, especially by the cathode ray tube (instantaneous) and the line printer (about 200,000 symbols per minute); (v) dramatic saving in effort, varying with the amount of the data to be handled; and (vi) greater accuracy with line printer, which can differentiate changes of direction down to 0.0125 mm. However, computer maps are not always found to be the best alternative to conventional maps owing to the considerations of (i) aesthetic quality, (ii) positional (planimetric) accuracy and (iii) readability (Fuller, 1978).

In view of the several advantages of automated cartography and scope for its improvement, some countries are introducing the grid-system of statistical mapping. In Japan, the maps based on the 1975 census depended on a high-technology computer for large storage of data and for computer mapping. This was possible because the data collected by CDs were later adjusted for a mesh of some 380,000 squares of one sq km each, based on longitude and latitude (Kosiński, 1980). Data from other sources (e.g. land use data and location of public facilities) are combined with census data to form the statistical maps. Similarly, the Geographic Information and Automated Mapping System (GIMMS) has been set up in the Republic of Korea in order to make possible more effective presentation of data. The purpose of the geographical system is to associate locational data (boundaries of administrative units etc.) with non-locational data (census variables). The data in this system can be reproduced on an inexpensive printer for low-resolution maps for rough analytic use or it can be used for high quality mapping that allows data manipulation (Asia & Pacific Census Forum, 1982). The U.S. Bureau of Census (1979) has developed its own system, Geographical Identification Code Scheme (G.I.C.S.), a set of tables which presents names, political and statistical subdivisions and their corresponding geographical codes for the 1970 census. In the U.K., population mapping of the 1971 census was carried out based on the one sq km national grid. The atlas *People in Britain* was prepared by the Census Research Unit of the University of Durham and the Office of Population Censuses and Surveys, using very sophisticated technology. Maps were made by computer firing of a laser beam on a sensitive film. Further, computer atlases and diagrams (graphics) are now available which have eliminated the time-consuming process involved in obtaining a spatial and synoptic view of the census data. However, owing to the cost involved, countries like U.K. and Japan have not continued with the grid-system of data collection after 1970-round censuses.

Conclusion

Post-census mapping is considered to be an emerging area for research and application. The spatial nature of census data is being studied in population geography, population cartography, statistics and demographic surveys. While population geographers are inclined to use maps as a tool for research on the spatial structure of population, cartographers have been involved in developing (i) techniques of production, and (ii) tools of communication. The combination of both the approaches with special reference to computer-assisted cartography in post-census mapping has been the focal theme of the International Cartographic Association (I.C.A.) Commission on Census Mapping (1980–84). Census cartography has been recognized as a specific area of specialization. National census organizations are trying to promote census cartography or geography, and some have published census atlases. The U.S. Bureau of Census (1979) has included aspects of pre- and post-census mapping in its volume *Census Geography*. Universities and institutions are not lagging behind. The Overseas Development Group of the

University of East Anglia has instituted a course on Population Census Geography for training of professionals from developing countries. The University of Durham has a Census Research Unit in the Department of Geography. Further, one of the workshops of the East-West Population Institute (1982) was on 'Computer Editing for Censuses and Surveys', using recently developed COBAL CONCOR computer package. The same institute publishes a newsletter called *Asia and Pacific Census Forum* regularly, which provides information on census related activities including census mapping.

The above activities indicate that there is an increasing awareness of the value of census data in teaching, research and planning. There is still scope for development in the approaches to census-based studies. Census mapping is certainly a good way of application of census data. How far can census maps contribute to the perception of reality or even to the interpretation of the concepts of population geography will depend on the efforts made in this field in future. How can mapping techniques be developed so as to increase the usefulness of census maps? Who are the potential users of post-census maps? How can such an expensive exercise be justified, especially in developing countries? These questions will remain with census cartographers (from the universities or national agencies or even from various U.N. organizations) in the years to come.

Acknowledgements

The author is grateful to Mr. William Seltzer of the U.N. Statistical Office, the U.S. Bureau of Census, the East-West Population Institute, the Department of Geography of the University of Durham, the National Atlas and Thematic Mapping Organisation (Calcutta), the School of Oriental and African Studies Library (London), and the Royal Geographical Society for assisting in the preparation of this chapter in various ways.

References

Asia & Pacific Census Forum (1982) Newsletter, East-West Population Institute, Hawaii, **8**, 18.

Chatterjee, S.P. (1962) Regional patterns of the density and distribution of population in India, *Geographical Review of India*, **24**, 1–28.

Coulson, M.R.C. (1968) The distribution of population age structure in Kansas City, *Annals, Association of American Geographers*, **58**, 155–76.

Dasgupta, S.P. (1965) A study of density interval problem in population mapping, in M. R. Choudhuri (ed.), *Essays in Geography*, Geographical Society of India, Calcutta, 99–108.

Dewdney, J.C. (1981) *The British Census*, Catmog 29, Institute of British Geographers, London and Geo Abstract, University of East Anglia, Norwich.

East-West Population Institute (1982) Thirteenth Summer Seminar in Population, Summary Report, East-West Center, Hawaii, 15–17.

Fuller, G. (ed.) (1978) *A Curriculum Guide for Population Geography*, East-West Population Institute, Hawaii, 120–2.

Hsu, Mei-Ling (1973) Cartographic application in population studies, in I. B. F. Kormoss and

L. A. Kosiński (eds.), *Population Mapping 1973*, I.G.U. Commission on Population Geography, Bruges, 8–12.

Jenks, G.F. (1963) Generalization in statistical mapping, *Annals, Association of American Geographers*, **53**, 15–26.

Jenks, G.F. and Caspall, F.C. (1971) Error on choropletic maps: definition, measurement, reduction, *Annals, Association of American Geographers*, **61**, 217–44.

Kosiński, L.A. (1979) *Population Maps*, Population Research Laboratory, Specialization Seminar Series (LA) No. 27, Dept. of Sociology, University of Alberta, Edmonton.

Kosiński, L.A. (ed.) (1980) I.G.U. Commission on Population Geography Newsletter No. 8.

Manshard, W. (1978) *Afrika-Kartenwerk* W8, Series W: West Africa, German Geographical Society, Berlin and Stuttgart (Map at 1:1 000 000).

Morgan, M.A. (1967) Hardware models in geography, in R. J. Chorley and P. Haggett (eds.), *Models in Geography*, Methuen, London, 727–76.

Nag, P. *et al.* (1978) Perspective mapping for a broad range of data: a case study of India, *Geographical Review of India*, **40**, 42–6.

Nag, P. *et al.* (1982) Importance of inset maps and diagrams in thematic mapping, in S. P. Dasgupta (ed.), *Essays in Thematic Cartography*, National Atlas and Thematic Mapping Organisation, Monograph Series 2, Calcutta, 20–3.

Raychaudhuri, R. (1981) Some problems of grouping data in mapping the density of population in Kerala, *Geographical Review of India*, **43**, 354–8.

Rhind, D. (1978) The reform of areal units, in J. Blunden *et al.* (eds.), *Fundamentals of Human Geography: A Reader*, Harper and Row, London, 124–5.

Smith, D.M. (1975) Mapping numerical information, Chap. 2 in *Patterns in Human Geography*, Penguin Books, 46–73.

Thomas, I.D. (1972) Census mapping in Tanzania 1967, in S. H. Ominde and C. N. Ejiogu (eds.), *Population Growth and Economic Development in Africa*, Heinemann, 3–9.

Tobler, W. (1969) Geographical filters and their inverses, *Geographical Analysis*, **1**, 234–53.

Tobler, W. (1973) Choropleth maps without class intervals, *Geographical Analysis*, **5**, 262–5.

Tobler, W. (1975) Linear operations applied to areal data, in J. Davis and M. McCullagh (eds.), *Display and Analysis of Spatial Data*, John Wiley & Sons, New York, 14–37.

Tomlinson, R.F. and Boyle, A.R. (1981) The state of development of systems for handling natural resources inventory data, *Cartographica*, **18**, 65–95.

U.N. Statistical Office (1980a) Social and Demographic Statistics: 1980 World Population and Housing Census Programme, Progress Report E/CN. 3/546.

U.N. Statistical Office (1980b) Principles and Recommendtions for Population and Housing Censuses, Series M, No. 67, New York; see Cartographic (mapping) Work, 18–20.

U.N. Statistical Office (1982) Demographic and Social Statistics: Population and Housing Census, Progress Report on National Experiences and Emerging Issues in Population and Housing Censuses, Report No. E/CN.3/1983/16.

U.S. Bureau of Census (1979) *Census Geography*, DAD No. 33, Washington, 12.

U.S. Bureau of Census (1980) *World Population Statistics in Brief: 1979*, Washington.

19

Population Geography in Britain

HUW R. JONES
(University of Dundee, U.K.)

In Britain, as elsewhere, population geography emerged in the 1950s as a systematic branch of geography in the sense that it dealt with a recognizably distinct group of phenomena and systematically related processes, the study of which involved a particular form of training. The roots of the subject in Britain were partly in traditional settlement geography of the Brunhes and Demangeon type, but more particularly in the mapping of census data. Indeed, the first five years (1963–68) of what has become the dominant forum and co-ordinating body of British population geography, the Population Geography Study Group of the Institute of British Geographers, were devoted entirely to the mapping of 1961 population census data (Hunt, 1968). The establishment, portrayal and inferential interpretation of population patterns thus formed the normative approach of British population geography in the 1960s, but the 1970s initiated more penetrative and intellectually satisfying analysis of the components and processes of population change, progressing most recently into assessments of, and tentative contributions to, population theory generally.

Teaching and training

Courses in population geography figure widely, but far from universally, in undergraduate syllabuses. The current Degree Course Guide of the Careers Research and Advisory Centre shows that courses in population geography are compulsory in 20 and optional in a further 22 of the 84 institutions offering degree courses in geography in British universities, polytechnics and colleges of higher education. A typical contemporary course is that offered to third-year students at the New University of Ulster:

Introduction

Scope and methodology of population geography; relations with other disciplines; importance of scale; data sources

Components of population dynamics

Fertility:	measurement; socio-economic and demographic variations; spatial variations
Mortality:	measurement; variations in time and space; medical geography
Migration:	measurement; socio-economic and demographic variations; spatial variations
Population change:	interaction of fertility, mortality and migration

Applications of population studies

Population projections and forecasting; the demographic transition model; relationships between population and resources; population policies; family planning programs

Regional studies of population growth

Ireland; England and Wales; Japan

Such emphasis on the nature and social relevance of population dynamics is paralleled in several 'Mark 2' undergraduate texts produced recently (Jones, 1981; Thomas, 1981; Woods, 1979, 1982).

Population specialists in geography, like their university counterparts in other social sciences, rarely exceed one per department, so that postgraduate training in population geography is acquired by supervised research rather than taught courses and is concentrated in those few departments where small groups of population geographers exist. Departments which have enjoyed such resources over several years are Durham (with a specialization in census mapping and Middle East populations), Liverpool (African and nineteenth-century urban populations) and Sheffield (census mapping and historical demography).

Research

A theoretical approach to the content of population geography would lead one to expect a research focus on understanding the changing size, distribution and composition of human population at various spatial scales, particularly through an appreciation of the spatio-temporal processes that fashion evolving patterns of mortality, fertility and migration. But British population geography research is characterized by specialization in parts of this field, notably migration, and serious neglect in others, notably mortality and fertility.

Currently the most exciting academic frontier in British population studies is in the construction and interpretation of pre-civil registration patterns of mortality and fertility under the leadership of the Cambridge Group for the History of Population and Social Structure, but the extent of geographical contributions (Smith, 1978) must as yet be regarded as modest. The spatial study of mortality is a central concern of medical geography, and while a strong theoretical case can be made out for regarding it as an integral part of population geography, the current status of medical geography is clearly that of an independent and active sub-discipline. Mortality or morbidity is mentioned in only five of 66 current research entries in a 1981 research register of the Population Geography Study Group, and only four persons have entries both in this register and the 1982 research register of the Medical Geography Study Group.

The neglect of fertility analysis by British population geographers is even more serious and indefensible since the field is not covered in any other branch of geography. Fertility is, of course, the core topic of demography, and demographers have increasingly been using territorially disaggregated data to throw light on the dynamic relations between fertility decline and socio-economic change, particularly when their preferred time-series data are lacking. There is no justification, therefore, for viewing spatial analysis of fertility as a distinctive preserve of population geography, but geographers have undoubtedly acquired valuable conceptual and technical skills in spatial analysis that other social scientists often lack. Such skills are exemplified in geographical studies of recent fertility patterns in Ireland and Scotland (Coward, 1978; Compton, 1978; Wilson, 1978) which demonstrate the persistence of inter-group and inter-area differentials, despite their long predicted demise as part of the process of demographic convergence in post-transition societies. That such differentials have important cause and effect relationships with spatial patterns of socio-economic malaise is shown in Compton's 'ecological' study (1981) of the unemployment differential between Protestants and Roman Catholics in Northern Ireland. This study is important in showing how population geographers can contribute powerfully to some of the most urgent socio-political debates of our time, although Compton's central argument that structural imbalances between the two denominational groups in population growth, fertility, class and location are the major cause of disparity in denominational unemployment rates needs to be examined critically.

Migration continues to be the dominant research topic in British population geography. Traditional approaches which establish intercensal net migration patterns and interpret them subjectively in relation to perceived socio-economic changes have been superceded by multiple correlation and regression techniques applied to spatial series of migration data and socio-economic indicators in attempts to identify and quantify relationships which are systematic and theoretically plausible. But as a reaction against what some geographers regard as the excesses of macroscopic analysis, of mechanistic quantification and of spatial fetishism, current migration work is focusing more on process rather than pattern by means of micro-level, behavioural and, occasionally, observer-participant studies. A growing appreciation that much complexity and variety is masked in aggregate migration studies is reflected in an increasing concentration of work on specific migrant groups or specific parts of the migration process: retirement migration (Law and Warnes, 1982), return migration (King, 1978); counter-urbanization (Fielding, 1982) and intra-organization migration (Johnson and Salt, 1980).

Elucidation of spatial variations in population composition no longer comprises a significant strand of British population geography. The one exception is ethnic composition, doubtless reflecting keen government and public interest as well as the formative role in such composition of international, regional and intra-urban migration. Much of the British work in this field, stemming from Peach (1981) and former colleagues at Oxford, falls as much into the field of social geography as population geography, particularly as it moves away from a narrow preoccupation with segregation indices towards a fuller integration with sociological theory.

So much for broad areas of specialization and neglect, of strength and weakness, in British population geography. Let us now consider several research developments found widely throughout British population geography which are enhancing the data base, methodology and conceptual context of the subject.

Information systems

In population geography as in all areas of demographic enquiry, the extent, quality and accessibility of data are of paramount importance. Study of the detailed spatial structure of population in contemporary Britain has been greatly enhanced by the availability of comprehensive standard sets of data from the 1961, 1966, 1971 and 1981 censuses for small areas (parishes, wards, enumeration districts, grid squares (1971) and postcodes (1981 Scotland)); the 1961 census also introduced the first question in British censuses on migration. But the most exciting development, long overdue and owing much to computerization, is surely in the creation of geographical information systems (Rhind, 1981) which, in theory, enable routine areal matching of census files with a host of other spatially referenced data files (housing, planning, electoral registration, social work, crime, vital registration, health, etc.). In Scotland, for example, postcodes (which at their highest resolution average about fifteen households) are being quickly developed as the basic building block in the incremental development of such information systems by central and local government (Hart, 1982).

On the other hand, pleas by researchers (Robertson, 1969) for more flexible access to census data tapes along the lines of the Public Use Sample in the United States have foundered against growing national concern for confidentiality of personal information. But freed of such constraints for earlier censuses, some population geographers have been providing valuable insights into nineteenth-century urbanization through their use of manuscript returns of census enumerators (Lawton, 1978; Pooley, 1979).

Population mapping

The traditional skills of population geographers in handling small area data have been put to good use in several innovative, computer-drawn, population census atlases for various regions of Britain, notably Durham, the West Midlands, Tyne and Wear, South Yorkshire and Northern Ireland. More ambitious has been a national atlas (Census Research Unit, 1980) of the 1971 census based on population data for about 60,000 one-kilometre squares. The technical achievements of this project are considerable: the initial translation and compaction of the massive data file supplied by the Office of Population Censuses and Surveys; the determination of class intervals by a chi-squared probability function which neatly takes into account both absolute and relative deviations from the national average value; and the achievement of remarkable clarity by high resolution laser plotting so that a kilometre square is represented by a coloured dot a quarter of a millimetre wide. Such atlases and their commentaries meet real educational needs in pattern presentation, but their analytical value must be regarded as limited.

Data analysis

For some time there has been nagging unease among British population geographers about what some regard as inadequate analytical rigour in much of their traditional work where quantification went little beyond the use of rates of incidence of population phenomena and only rarely considered how such rates could be explained quantitatively. Remedial action has taken two major forms. First, there have been explicit attempts (Woods, 1979) to incorporate in population geography a wide range of analytical methods from formal demography, introducing to population geography the 'search and plunder' approach to allied disciplines pursued somewhat earlier in other branches of human geography.

Second, expertise derived from the dominant paradigm of human geography as spatial science in the 1960s and early 1970s has been invaluable in the analysis of spatially arranged population data like the 1971 and 1981 census small area statistics which probably comprise the largest multivariate spatial series in human geography. There is growing appreciation that cross-sectional or 'ecological' studies by multivariate statistical methods comprise one field of population analysis for which modern geographical expertise is invaluable. This is especially because the pitfalls of multivariate analysis in spatial contexts are being increasingly appreciated, and often countered by: (a) the replacement of 'r^2'-enhancing statistical 'fishing trips' by the hypothesizing and testing of theoretically plausible relationships; (b) the realization of limitations in classical inferential procedures stemming from their assumption of independence of observations when, in fact, geographical data invariably exhibit systematic ordering in space (spatial autocorrelation); (c) the understanding that inferences about individual behaviour cannot readily be made from group or areal observation; and (d) the awareness of analytical problems posed by scale generally (Clarke, 1976) and, in particular, by the so-called modifiable areal unit problem (Openshaw and Taylor, 1981) in which different areal arrangements of the same data often produce different results. That analytical problems associated with multivariate work still remain, however, is illustrated by uncertainties on the weighting of units in correlation-regression analysis by population size.

The value of a technically sophisticated, yet distinctively geographical, approach to population analysis is also shown in the application of spatial diffusion theory. Blaikie (1975) considers the contribution such theory can make to understanding the spatial pattern of family planning acceptance in northern Bihar, but he finds that neighbourhood or contagious effects have little influence on female information networks compared with social factors like caste and literacy. On the other hand, Cliff *et al.* (1981) achieve promising results by using multiple-wave diffusion theory to identify and interpret spatial regularities in the recurrent epidemic waves of a specific infectious disease, measles, in twentieth-century Iceland. But perhaps the clearest exposition of population analysis successfully integrating advanced demographic techniques and modern spatial analysis is in the work of Rees and Wilson (1977) on the construction of spatially disaggregated, population-forecasting models.

Theory

Theoretical perspectives are being widened to embrace more fully than in the past the intricate relationship between demographic and socio-economic change. While Grigg's contribution (1980) to the long-standing controversy on relationships between agrarian change and population growth is representative of modest theoretical advance, Woods (1982) strongly advocates the need for much wider appreciation, and especially formulation, of population theory in geography. It is, however, important to realize that with the possible exception of diffusion theory there is no specifically spatial theory which is not part of more general theory, hence the profitable use by Woods of historic materialism to interpret the demographic transition as a transition between regimes associated with specific modes of production. The search for a comprehensive paradigm to provide a coherent theoretical frame to order information within the domain of population geography is surely a wild goose chase. Our effort can better be spent on refining spatial perspectives and modes of analysis in population study generally and then demonstrating their value to much wider academic and government audiences than we have reached in the past.

References

Blaikie, P. (1975) *Family Planning in India: Diffusion and Policy*, Arnold, London.

Census Research Unit, University of Durham (1980) *People in Britain: A Census Atlas*, HMSO, London.

Clarke, J.I. (1976) Population and scale: some general considerations, in L. A. Kosiński and J. Webb (eds.), *Population at Microscale*, IGU Commission on Population Geography, Christchurch, 21–9.

Cliff, A., Haggett, P., Ord, J. and Versey, G. (1981) *Spatial Diffusion: An Historical Geography of Epidemics in an Island Community*, Cambridge University Press, Cambridge.

Compton, P. (1978) Fertility differentials and their impact on population distribution and composition in Northern Ireland, *Environment and Planning*, **10**A, 1397–1411.

Compton, P. (1981) Demographic and geographic aspects of the unemployment differential between Protestants and Roman Catholics in Northern Ireland, in P. Compton (ed.), *The Contemporary Population of Northern Ireland and Population-Related Issues*, Queen's University of Belfast, 127–42.

Coward, J. (1978) Changes in the pattern of fertility in the Republic of Ireland, *Tijdschrift voor Economishe en Sociale Geografie*, **69**, 353–61.

Fielding, A.J. (1982) Counter-urbanisation in western Europe, *Progress in Planning*, **17,** No. 1.

Grigg, D.B. (1980) *Population Growth and Agrarian Change: An Historical Perspective*, Cambridge University Press, Cambridge.

Hart, S (1982) Year of the postcode, *The Planner*, **68**, 116–7.

Hunt, A.J. (ed.) (1968) Population maps of the British Isles, Special number of *Transactions, Institute of British Geographers*, 43.

Johnson, J.H. and Salt, J. (1980) Labour migration within organisations, *Tijdschrift voor Economische en Sociale Geografie*, **71**, 277–84.

Jones, H.R. (1981) *A Population Geography*, Harper and Row, London.

King, R. (1978) Return migration: a neglected aspect of population geography, *Area*, **10**, 175–82.

Law, C. and Warnes, A. (1982) The destination decision in retirement migration, in A. Warnes (ed.), *Geographical Perspectives on the Elderly*, Wiley, Chichester, 53–81.

Lawton, R. (ed.) (1978) *The Census and Social Structure: An Interpretative Guide to Nineteenth Century Censuses for England and Wales*, Cass, London.

Openshaw, S. and Taylor, P. (1981) The modifiable areal unit problem, in N. Wrigley and R. Bennett (eds.), *Quantitative Geography: A British View*, Routledge and Kegan Paul, London, 60–9.

Peach, C., Robinson, V. and Smith, S. (eds.) (1981) *Ethnic Segregation in Cities*, Croom Helm, London.

Pooley, C. (1979) Residential mobility in the Victorian City, *Transactions, Institute of British Geographers*, **4**, 258–77.

Rees, P. and Wilson, A. (1977) *Spatial Population Analysis*, Arnold, London.

Rhind, D. (1981) Geographical information systems in Britain, in N. Wrigley and R. Bennett (eds.), *Quantitative Geography: A British View*, Routledge and Kegan Paul, London, 17–35.

Robertson, I.M. (1969) The census and research: ideals and realities, *Transactions, Institute of British Geographers*, **48**, 173–87.

Smith, R.M. (1978) Population and its geography in England 1500–1730, in R. Dodgshon and R. Butlin (eds.), *An Historical Geography of England and Wales*, Academic Press, London, 199–237.
Thomas, I.D. (1981) *Population Growth*, Macmillan, London.
Wilson, M.G. (1978) A spatial analysis of human fertility in Scotland: reappraisal and extension, *Scottish Geographical Magazine*, **94**, 130–43.
Woods, R. (1979) *Population Analysis in Geography*, Longman, London.
Woods, R. (1982) *Theoretical Population Geography*, Longman, London.

20

Population Geography in France

DANIEL NOIN
(University of Paris I, France)

Geographical studies of population have known a remarkable development in France for a generation. Various reasons can be invoked to explain this expansion: the progress of demography with which geography maintains numerous links; the abundance of data provided by statisticians; the interest provoked by the fall in the birth rate in industrialized countries and by population growth in developing countries. These diverse factors have been able to operate simultaneously. Whatever the case, population geography is now the main subject of study for a group of French geographers, while many others are occasionally interested during research undertaken on other themes.

The growth of research since 1950

In France, the geographical study of population is relatively ancient. For three centuries at least, numerous observations have been made about populations. Some authors, of whom the most celebrated was the philosopher Montesquieu, have reflected upon the relationships between population and environment. However, it is only at the end of the nineteenth century that more profound studies appear about the spatial distribution of population in France or in the world, particularly by Levasseur. Soon after, during the 1910s, Vidal de la Blache devoted a part of his work to population; it occupied an important place in his publications. For him, the starting point of geographical analysis was the study of the distribution of mankind on the surface of the earth; man was considered as the central element of all geographical facts but, at the same time and to some extent in a contradictory way, he was seen as partially dependent upon the physical environment. Because of the influence exercised by Vidal upon the French school of geography, this last aspect, essentially ecological, has for long marked research during the inter-war years and even after the second world war.

An abrupt change occurred from 1950, basically under the influence of George, who published the first epistemological reflection on population geography (1950) and the first geographical text wholly devoted to population (1951). The approach was henceforth different; first because the action of man upon the environment is considered much more often than the action of the environment upon man, but also because of the field of investigation of geography moved in the direction of demography. The two disciplines, formerly separated, now have an overlapping domain; themes which seemed to be wholly within the competence of demographers, like age structure or fertility, are assimilated by geographers who devote part of their analyses to them. Population geography, sometimes called 'demographic geography', therefore appears as being at the intersection of the two disciplines.

This branch of geographical knowledge developed slowly a first, but then research works became more and more numerous during the 1960s and 1970s to the extent of representing at least one-tenth of the articles published in French geographical journals. Many doctoral theses have been undertaken on this theme over the last 15 years, and population geography constitutes a substantial part of the curriculum in university departments of geography. Scientific meetings concerned with population at the national level involve, depending on the selected topics, 50–100 geographers.

The multiplication of research themes

With the increase in the number of works, the research content has gradually evolved. The most remarkable fact from this point of view is undoubtedly the multiplication of the fields of inquiry.

During the 1950s the themes studied were still not very numerous. Spatial distribution of population, its explanatory factors and its diverse forms of settlement still constituted an important part of the research, but analyses concerning migration and, more gradually, demographic facts came to be added.

During the 1960s and more particularly the 1970s, the topics have become much more varied, precise and profound. The same basic themes still exist, of course, but their relative importance has changed and new fields of research have appeared. Only a glimpse will be given, simply to give an idea of the area covered by French geographers and to indicate some of the more outstanding works among the prolific output.

Studies concerning the geographical distribution of population, formerly so frequent, have become much more rare over the last 15 years. Those which have been done have focused on Third World countries, like Gabon, Congo, Mali, Morocco, Nepal and Indonesia (e.g. Sautter, 1966; Noin,

1970), or, at a pinch, on feebly developed countries like the Greek islands (Kolodny, 1974). The study of this theme is in fact logical in agricultural societies but of limited interest in industralized and urbanized societies. Anyway, in all cases there seems to be a preponderance of historical over physical factors. Several authors have considered the question of population pressure. In fact, what interests geographers, more than population distribution itself, is the way that it has evolved during recent years. A large number of analyses take this viewpoint, sometimes from a planning perspective or in response to a problem, as in Béteille's study (1981a) of the 'empty' areas of France.

Studies directed towards demographic characteristics, still rare during the 1960s, have since become more common. For a long time French geographers have hesitated to venture into this field, perhaps because of the dynamism shown by the French school of demography. It is no longer the case; geodemographic studies undertaken by specialists from both disciplines are now common, on several countries such as France (Noin, 1973), Greece (Kolodny, 1974), Ireland (Verrière, 1979) and Morocco (Escallier, 1981) or on French regions, including Limousin (Larivière, 1975), Nord (Thumerelle, 1979) and Savoie (David, 1980). Moreoever, several studies of medical geography have treated these aspects from the point of view of mortality or morbidity (Picheral, 1976). Certain texts cover the whole world for particular subjects like the diffusion of demographic transition (Noin, 1982) or the diversity of population policies (Verrière, 1978).

Studies of the active population, nearly non-existent during the 1950s and still rare during the 1960s, have increased during the 1970s. A general text has been recently published on this theme which has provoked discussion and will stimulate further research (George, 1978). Detailed studies have been impeded by the lack of statistical data and problems in their use. The French socio-professional classification has been frequently criticized by sociologists and geographers. Despite that, numerous studies have been published on questions as varied as the attitude of geographers faced with the study of employment (Pailhé, 1972b; Racine and Rouyre, 1982), socio-professional profiles of French towns (Pumain, 1976, 1982) or female employment in France (Sztokman, 1970). Many others are in progress. More recently, with the deepening of the economic crisis, unemployment has also become the subject of some research.

From the active population one slips easily to the study of society. Social geography now incites a very lively interest among French geographers and is in full flight; its limits with population geography are obviously fairly fluid and certain studies may be considered as of one or the other.

Studies of spatial mobility of population are by far the most frequent, and represent more than a third of all articles published in population geography during the last 15 years. They have constituted the theme of several symposia, as for example that in Lille in 1981 on internal and external migrations in Western Europe (Thumerelle, 1981).

Rural-urban migration has continued to attract the attention of some researchers, and diverse studies have been published of a general character (Pitié, 1979) or applied to a particular space (Merlin, 1971; Béteille, 1974).

Migration to retirement has been the subject of new and interesting studies in relation to France and other industrialized countries, especially by Cribier (1973–74).

International movements of workers have attracted much attention, not surprisingly when one considers the foreign presence in France. Almost all the migratory flows towards French territory have been investigated in detail; those concerning Italians, Spaniards, Portuguese, Algerians, Moroccans and Tunisians, as well as the more recent flows of West Africans, Turks, Yugoslavs, Vietnamese and Chinese. Among the most scholarly studies are those of Simon (1979) on the Tunisian migration to France. Seasonal and temporary movements of foreign workers have also been studied, particularly those of Spanish grape-pickers in the south of France. The research has not only been concerned with France; detailed investigations have also been undertaken elsewhere in the areas of departure and destination (Borris *et al.*, 1977). A general volume on the geographical aspects of international migrations has been written by George (1976).

Circulatory movements have equally been the subject of interesting analyses. Movements linked to work, previously well known, have been to some extent neglected whilst those linked to other activities, especially leisure, are more and more studied, despite difficulties posed by the lack of statistical data. Among the most original is Cribier's (1969) research on the summer migration of French citizens.

Cartographic works on population are numerous. Over the past 15 years a very large number of maps have been published on the demographic or social characteristics of populations, on migratory movements and, of course, on the geographical distribution itself. More recently, some high-quality documents concerning the French population in 1980 have been produced entirely by automated cartography.

Some books cover a large part, if not the whole, of the field of investigation of population geography as far as it can be defined precisely. They have been written in general for students, but can also, on certain problems, provide information and ideas to researchers (George, 1969; Noin, 1979).

In sum, there is a growing diversity of studies made in France in the domain of population. On the other hand, some aspects are rather neglected, as for example cultural geography, where there has been some interesting research on the geography of languages (Breton, 1976) but this is frankly exceptional. Moreover, the historical geography of population has been abandoned to the historians who have scarcely taken it up; yet it is an area where there is a lot to be done to understand the spatial patterns of today.

The diversity of areas studied should also be noted. Naturally, France continues to attract the most attention; it has been the focus of half of the studies about population by geographers over the last 15 years. Then come the francophone or partially francophone territories of Africa with about one-fifth of the studies. Thereafter, French geographers have worked in a wide variety of countries of Europe (above all those of Mediterranean Europe), the Near East, Central and South America and finally in South and South-East Asia. Nevertheless, it is regrettable that there are so few studies of Northern Europe and the anglophone countries.

The revival of approaches

The revival of population geography in France—and of French geography in general—would have undoubtedly been more striking if the contacts with the Anglo-American world had been closer and more frequent. During the 1960s and even at the beginning of the 1970s, when geography experienced a veritable scientific revolution in North America and in Britain, it continued on its own way in France. In the domain of population as in other fields, research had an essentially empirical character; it consisted mainly of monographs about a country, a region or a town; comparative studies were very rare; theories and models invoked mistrust. The existence of national competitive examinations and the preservation of the heavy state doctoral thesis for access to high levels of university research and teaching helped to impede or put a brake on change and to comfort tradition.

The 'new geography' therefore only arrived late in France, at the end of the 1960s and above all during the 1970s. It affected specialists of population at more or less the same time as other branches of the discipline. On the other hand, it has diffused more rapidly than in the countries which have been the first to be affected. In the space of barely a decade, the problems and methods have changed, not without giving rise to conflicts.

Interest in models and theories has evolved at the same time as a decline in the habit of producing monographs without a general perspective. A fair number of researchers make an effort to develop general concepts by varied processes. It is particularly clear in the case of migratory movements which, because of their regularities, lend themselves more readily to modelling (Courgeau, 1970; Béteille, 1981b), but it is also true for other themes. Models no longer provoke reticence. Borrowing of theories from other social sciences is no longer rare, as seen in Noin's (1982) utilization of demographic transition theory for a geographical study.

The treatment of statistical data has also spread during the 1970s, at first with fairly simple methods, then with more complicated ones. It is true that the analysis of data responds to a need in population geography where information is frequently presented in the form of statistical tables. Analytical processes of study therefore give way more and more to synthetic processes, which are much more satisfactory. However, researchers who have assimilated the most complex methods are still few in number (Courgeau, 1980; Pumain, 1976, 1982).

Behavioural and psychological studies have also been integrated, but more discretely, into the new research fields, notably those of migration (Cribier, 1973–74). The behavioural approach is little practised in France.

On the other hand, the radical or critical trend is fairly well represented. Among a number of French geographers, especially the younger ones, research has been reorientated towards population problems, whether these have a regional, national or international dimension, and the borrowings from Marxism are not rare when it comes to explaining observed phenomena. The increasing interest shown in the study of the structure, conflicts and dynamism of society lies within the same perspective.

In sum, the balance sheet is fairly favourable. Population geography constitutes a solid and well-developed branch of French geography. The diversity of research themes, the real sensitivity to problems, the acquisition of new and more rigorous methods and the interest shown in the development of theories comprise many comforting elements. The future therefore can be envisaged with some optimism even if, paradoxically, at the moment when there is a combination of favourable conditions, the eyes of French demo-geographers seem to be moving from population towards society and their attention from demography towards sociology.

Translated from French by John I. Clarke

References

Beaujeu-Garnier, J. (1976) *La population française après le recensement de 1975*, Colin, Paris.
Béteille, R. (1974) *Les Aveyronnais: essai géographique sur l'espace humain*, Poitiers.
Béteille, R. (1978) *Rouergue, terre d'exode*, Hachette, Paris.
Béteille, R. (1981a) *La France du vide*, Ed. Genin, Paris.
Béteille, R. (1981b) Une nouvelle approche des faits migratoires, *Espace Géographique*, **3**, 187–97.
Borris, M. *et al.* (1977) *Les étrangers à Stuttgart*, C.N.R.S., Paris.
Breton, R. (1976) *Géographie des langues*, P.U.F., Paris.
Courgeau, D. (1970) *Les champs migratoires en France*, P.U.F., Paris.
Courgeau, D. (1980) *Analyse quantitative des migrations humaines*, Masson, Paris.
Cribier, F. (1969) *La grande migration d'été des citadins en France*, C.R.N.S., Paris.
Cribier, F. (1973–74) *La migration de retraite*, C.N.RS., Paris, 3 vols.
David, J. (1980) *Du rural au rurbain: l'avant-pays savoyard. Analyse régionale et géodémographie*, Grenoble, Institut de Géographie Alpine.
Escallier, R. (1981) *Citadins et espace urbain au Maroc*, Tours, Poitiers, 2 vols.
George, P. (1950) Géographie de la population et démographie, *Population*, **2**, 291–300.
George, P. (1951) *Introduction à l'étude géographique de la population du monde*, P.U.F., Paris.
George, P. (1965) *Géographie de la population*, P.U.F., Paris.
George, P. (1969) *Population et peuplement*, P.U.F., Paris.

George, P. (1976) *Les migrations internationales*, P.U.F., Paris.
George, P. (1978) *Populations actives, introduction à une géographie du travail*, P.U.F., Paris.
Kolodny, E. (1974) *La population des îles de la Grèce*, Edisud, Aix-en-Provence, 3 vols.
I.G.N.-I.N.S.E.E. (1980, 1981) *La population française*, Paris, 2 vols.
Larivière, J.P. (1975) *La population du Limousin*, H. Champion, Paris, 2 vols.
Larivière, J.P. (1978) La fecondité en Bretagne, *Norois*, **100,** 495–510.
Lerat, S. (1978) *La population du monde*, Bréal, Paris.
Merlin, P. (1971) *L'exode rural en France* (Trav. & Doc. INED), P.U.F., Paris.
Noin, D. (1970) *La population rurale du Maroc*, P.U.F., Paris, 2 vols.
Noin, D. (1973) *Géographie démographique de la France*, P.U.F., Paris.
Noin, D. (1979) *Géographie de la population*, Masson, Paris.
Noin, D. (1982) *La transition démographique dans le monde*, P.U.F., Paris.
Pailhé, J. (1972a) Sur l'objet de la géographie de la population, *Espace Géographique*, **1**, 54–62.
Pailhé, J. (1972b) Population active et analyse géographique, *Trav. Inst. Géogr. Reims*, **12**, 3–14.
Picheral, H. (1976) *Espace et santé. Géographie médicale du midi de la France*, Montpellier.
Pitié, J. (1973) *Géographie de la population mondiale*, Sirey, Paris.
Pitié, J. (1979) *L'exode rural*, P.U.F., Paris.
Pumain, D. (1976) La composition socio-professionelle des villes françaises: essai de typologie, *Espace Géographique*, **5**, 227–38.
Pumain, D. (1982) *La dynamique des villes*, Economica, Paris.
Racine, J.B. and Rouyre, J. (1982) Perspectives critiques pour une géographie du travail . . . . , *Espace Géographique*, **11**, 56–66.
Revel-Mouroz, J. and Bataillon, D. (1977) Les migrations mexicaines vers les Etats-Unis et la frontière nord du Mexique, *Tiers Monde*, **18** (69), 55–76.
Sautter, G. (1966) *De l'Atlantique au fleuve Congo, une géographie du souspeuplement*, Mouton, Paris, 2 vols.
Simon, G. (1979) *L'espace des travailleurs tunisiens en France, structure et fonctionnement d'un champ migratoire international*, G. Simon, Poitiers.
Sztokman, N. (1970) Les Françaises et le travail, *Annales de Géographie*, **484**, 673–95.
Thumerelle, P.J. (1979) *La population de la region Nord-Pas de Calais* (thèse), 5 vols.
Thumerelle, P.J. (ed.) (1981) *Migrations internes et externes en Europe occidentale*, Hommes et Terres du Nord, no. spec., 2 vols.
Verrière, J. (1978) *Les politiques de population*, P.U.F., Paris.
Verrière, J. (1979) *La population de l'Irlande*, Mouton, Paris.

21

Population Geography in the German Democratic Republic

EGON WEBER
(Ernst Moritz Arndt University, Greifswald, G.D.R.)

The scientific results achieved in geography in the G.D.R. during the past three decades have increased the social significance of the subject. The goals set for research have been ever more consciously selected with a view to the requirements of society; at the same time international developments of the science have been taken into consideration; and findings have been made available for the benefit of the various spheres of social life (Lüdemann, 1980). This process has involved a deepening of the co-operation between geographers in the G.D.R. and also between geography and other sciences. Moreover, the activities of G.D.R. geographers on an international scale are very diverse, as for instance in the International Geographical Union.

The various sub-disciplines of geography have attained different levels of development in the G.D.R. Within the field of economic geography, settlement geography and population geography have come to the fore as objects of basic research (Jacob, 1981). The combination of these two sub-disciplines for research purposes is traditional in the G.D.R. (as in other socialist countries) so that the assignation of many publications (e.g. von Känel and Weber, 1976) either to settlement geography or to population geography is purely a matter of discretion. The significance of population geography derives from the central position accorded to the reproduction of the population, in particular of labour force, in socialist theory and development policy, including regional aspects (Schmidt-Renner, 1973b).

There is broad agreement within the numerically small group of population geographers in the G.D.R. on the object and aims of their science:

> 'Population geography is a discipline of economic geography which investigates the regularities of the distribution, development, structure and territorial organization of the population of economic and living regions in the process of the reproduction of society with an aim to creating certain conditions for the optimization of economic and living regions with regard to basic human needs (work, dwelling, recreation etc.)' (Weber and Benthien, 1980: 15, with detailed notes).

With this we have outlined the general scientific aims; the main objects of research are also determined by certain geodemographic and demographic developments and structural characteristics in the G.D.R. (Weber, 1976; Roubitschek and Weber, 1980), of which the following appear to be particularly important:

— uneven territorial distribution of population (north-south dichotomy) and high, still rising, degree of urbanization combined with a slightly decreasing population;
— great social, professional and spatial mobility (including very intense commuting) in the process of continuing urbanization;
— tendency to decline in fertility and an excess of deaths between 1969 and 1978, although a slight excess of births since then;
— unfavourable age structure, decreasing sizes of households and changes in the composition of households; and
— high levels of education and increasing professional qualification even in agrarian regions.

Such demographic processes and structures are of course characteristic of many highly developed industrial countries, but some of these features are particularly striking in the G.D.R., a prime example being the high ratio of old people to the total population as a result of the second world war and the great losses due to emigration in the 1950s (Lungwitz, 1974); the proportion of persons of pensionable age in the population of the G.D.R. is the highest in the world.

A number of studies on the above-mentioned points have been published (Weber, 1972, 1975; Lungwitz, 1979; Bose, 1980; Grünberg and Niemann, 1980; Mohs, 1980; Weber and Driebe, 1980; Neumann, 1981; Thürmer, 1981). In view of the continuing tendency towards concentration while the population level stagnates, research on migration is acquiring special significance. These and other studies have proved to stress two essential facts:
(a) owing to a long-term, directed policy of redistribution of population and intensification of communications (especially commuting), an ever-increasing part of the population of the G.D.R. can enjoy the benefits of an urban mode of settlement and life, but because of this concentration in larger towns the depopulation of certain agrarian regions has reached, and in places even exceeded, critical levels;
(b) the agglomerations of the G.D.R. (Halle—Leipzig, Karl-Marx-Stadt—Zwickau, etc.) are highly efficient economic regions, but reflect certain unfavourable proportions in the G.D.R. population particularly clearly in their own demographic structures.

Research on population geography in the G.D.R. was not consistently related to socially relevant topics until the 1970s, when research was more strictly organized under the guidance of the Institute for Geography and Geoecology of the Academy of Sciences in Leipzig and other central research institutions, with topics integrated into macro-research projects (e.g. studies of agglomerations: Scholz and Oelke, 1981; regions with agrarian structure: Weber, 1981). Since then, noteworthy results have been presented at all departments of geography of universities and colleges in the G.D.R. and at the Academy Institute in Leipzig; although so far not all have been published, these results have been made available for practical social use. In order to accomplish the more demanding tasks in which research on geographic processes and an integral approach to problems attain increasing importance, close inter-disciplinary co-operation with demographers, sociologists, labour economists, etc. has proved fruitful; the progress achieved in recent years by such co-operation is reflected in the activity of working groups involving more than one field and in publications (Lüdemann, Grimm, Krönert and Neumann, 1979; Khalatbari, 1980). The institutions for territorial planning, in which many geographers are active, have also carried out intensive geodemographic research of their own, which has, however, only in exceptional cases been published.

The increasing stress on practical use by no means implies that research on population geography merely performs preliminary work for planners engaged on short- or mid-term tasks. The increasing complexity of the territorial organization of social reproduction and the rapid advance of the sciences challenge us to form theories and apply new methods, so that the demands of the development of the science must equally be taken into account. Thus geodemographic considerations (development, structure, migration, communication, particularly commuting, etc.) play a special part in the theoretical explanation of settlement systems (Lüdemann, Grimm, Krönert and Neumann, 1979). A classification of communities based on the professional structure of the resident population and the structure of commuting was taken as the basis for economic regionalization (von Känel and Scholz, 1969). Scherf and Schilde (1974) undertook a regional classification of the G.D.R. according to functional district types with the help of population characteristics. Population development is increasingly being investigated in the context of dominant social processes, especially urbanization (von Känel and Weber, 1976; Margraf and Usbeck, 1981). Möbius (1982) supplied some elements of a general theory of population geography by deriving regularities of spatio-temporal variability of population development from the example of the G.D.R. Thus there have been many fruitful and promising beginnings, although the theoretical level attained cannot be judged satisfactory by international standards.

The same holds true for the range of methods used to date, in so far as analytico-descriptive techniques still predominate. Initial attempts to apply modern quantitative techniques (Kind and Steindorf, 1971) were for some time not followed up on a broad basis and a breakthrough has only recently been achieved (Mohs, 1980; Thürmer, 1981; Margraf and Usbeck, 1981) with factor, correlation and regression analyses and the like. The conscious inclusion in recent years of socio-geographic (and ecological) considerations both in theoretical works (Schmidt-Renner, 1973 a and b) and in a series of regional studies (Niemann and Grünberg, 1980; Hasenpflug, 1982), in which motives for migration and related problems are of central importance, has set the trend for research on population geography in the G.D.R. Schulze (1980) presents socio-spatial systems within the hierarchy of territorial structure and evaluates 'the social reproduction space of the population'. As a whole, however, research on the behaviour of people in space (locational preferences of the population, etc.) within the G.D.R. is still in its infancy.

Another important task of population geography is educational research to meet the information requirements of a broad circle of interested people and especially for the training and further training of students of geography. Topics of population geography are accorded due importance in the geography curriculum of universities and colleges in the G.D.R. (Lehrprogramme . . . . , 1982) and in the geography syllabus in schools. Studies in population geography occupy about 60–70 periods (including regional lectures) of a university or college geography course and there is a special textbook (Weber and Benthien, 1980). Geographic journals published in the G.D.R. strive in various ways (essays, reviews, congress reports, etc.) to promote the development of population geography and to propagate new findings of this sub-discipline. Let it be remembered that the very first volume (1855) of *Petermanns Geographische Mitteilungen*, one of the oldest geographic journals in the world, contained papers on population. After the second world war this tradition was successfully continued by K. Witthauer, whose monograph on world population was published initially in 1958 and later in 1969, and other authors. Papers in this field have also been published in the journal *Geographische Berichte* (Stams, Andreas and Reckziegel, 1980, 1981).

In conclusion, let us outline some development trends in research on population geography in the G.D.R. The level of theoretical and methodological demands and the topics to be concentrated on will be determined largely by co-operation in the 'General scheme for regional distribution of the productive forces in the G.D.R.', at present the main task of territorial planning in the G.D.R. The aim of this co-operation is to establish what parts of the national economy will need to be intensified in order to correspond to the territorial organization of the reproduction process. Population geographers, with a broad basis of current data at their disposal in the results of the census of population, professions, dwelling-space and buildings taken on 31 December 1981, have their part to play in making this prognosis. The general aim is to formulate the regularities of spatio-temporal variability of population in the context of the further development of economic regions which exhibit marked territorial differentiation within the G.D.R. (Kohl, Jacob,

Kramm, Roubitschek and Schmidt-Renner, 1976). Studies on the efficient use of labour power and all associated problems of the structural transformation of economic regions are accorded special importance, due in general to the growing significance of the population component in the question of social reproduction but also to the precarious manpower situation which is particularly pronounced in certain regions of the G.D.R. At the same time the manifold problems resulting from the consumptive functions of the population (provisioning, education, recreation etc.) are of great scientific importance. It is to be expected that these and other findings of research on population geography in the G.D.R. will also make a contribution to the further development of general population geography.

References

Bose, G. (1980) Ergebnisse und Tendenzen der Binnenwanderung in der DDR im Zeitraum 1953–1976, in P. Khalatbari (ed.), *Räumliche Bevölkerungsbewegung in sozialistischen Ländern*, Akademie-Verlag, Berlin, Beiträge zur Demographie, **4**, 121–80.

Grünberg, U. and Niemann, H. (1977) Die Analyse des Migrationsprozesses mit Hilfe der Bevölkerungsbefragung, *Geographische Berichte*, **83**, 109–16.

Hasenpflug, H. (1982) *Sozialräumliche Strukturen und Prozesse im Raum Radeburg—untersucht am Beispiel der territorialen Mobilität von Beschäftigten Radeburger Betriebe und Einrichtungen zur Befriedigung der Grundbedürfnisse nach Arbeiten und Versorgen*, Pädagogische Hochschule Dresden, Dissertation A.

Jacob, G. (1981) Entwicklung, gegenwärtiger Stand und Perspektive der Geographie in der DDR, *Geographische Berichte*, **101**, 197–208.

Känel, A.v. and Scholz, D. (1969) Wirtschaftsräumliche Struktureinheiten mittlerer Ordnung in der DDR, *Petermanns Geographische Mitteilungen*, **113**, 167–73.

Känel, A.v. and Weber, E. (1976) Aspekte der Entwicklung von Bevölkerung und Siedlungssystemen in den Nordbezirken der Deutschen Demokratischen Republik unter besonderer Berücksichtigung der Urbanisierung, *Petermanns Geographische Mitteilungen*, **120**, 120–4.

Khalatbari, P. (ed.) (1980) *Räumliche Bevölkerungsbewegung in sozialistischen Ländern*, Akademie-Verlag, Berlin, Beiträge zur Demographie; 4.

Kind, G. and Steindorf, H. (1971) Mathematisch-statistische Untersuchungen der Binnenwanderung, *Geographische Berichte*, **60**, 180–92.

Kohl, H., Jacob, G., Kramm, H.J., Roubitschek, W. and Schmidt-Renner, G. (eds.) (1976) *Ökonomische Geographie der Deutschen Demokratischen Republik*, 3rd ed., VEB Hermann Haack, Gotha, Leipzig.

Lehrprogramme (1982) Für die Ausbildung von Diplomlehrern der allgemeinbildenden polytechnischen Oberschulen im Fach Geographie an Universitäten und Hochschulen der DDR, Ministerium für Volksbildung, Ministerium für Hoch- und Fachschulwesen, Berlin.

Lüdemann, H., Grimm, F., Krönert, R. and Neumann, H. (eds.) (1979) *Stadt und Umland in der Deutschen Demokratischen Republik*, VEB Hermann Haack, Gotha, Leipzig.

Lüdemann, H. (1980) Geographische Forschung in der DDR—Entwicklung und Perspektiven, *Petermanns Geographische Mitteilungen*, **124**, 97–103.

Lungwitz, K. (1974) Die Bevölkerungsbewegung in der DDR und der BRD zwischen 1945 und 1970, eine komparative Untersuchung, *Jahrbuch für Wirtschaftsgeschichte*, 1974, **1**, 63–95.

Lungwitz, K. (1979) Zur Differenzierung der Geburten- und Fruchtbarkeitsentwicklung in den Bezirken und Kreisen der Deutschen Demokratischen Republik, *Petermanns Geographische Mitteilungen*, **123**, 251–5.

Margraf, O. and Usbeck, H. (1981) Bestimmung des Urbanisierungsgrades von Gemeinden mit Hilfe der Faktorenanalyse, dargestellt am Beispiel des Umlandes von Schwerin, *Petermanns Geographische Mitteilungen*, **125**, 245–52.

Möbius, D. (1982) *Zur Theorie und Praxis von Zeit-Raum-Feldern der Bevölkerungsentwicklung und ihrem Einfluß auf die Stadtentwicklung in der DDR*, Humboldt-Universität zu Berlin, Dissertation B.

Mohs, G. (1980) *Migration and Settlement: 4. German Democratic Republic*, International Institute for Applied Systems Analysis, Laxenburg, Research-Report 80–6.

Neumann, H. (1981) Tendenzen der stadtorientierten Migration in der DDR, *Geographische Berichte*, **98**, 49–56.

Niemann, H. and Grünberg, H. (1980) Die Migration der Bevölkerung als das Resultat des Wirkens objektiver und subjektiver Faktoren, in P. Khalatbari (ed.), *Räumliche Bevölkerungsbewegung in sozialistischen Ländern*, Akademie-Verlag, Berlin, Beiträge zur Demographie, **41**, 31–71.

Roubitschek, W. and Weber, E. (eds.) (1980) *Erläuterung der Karten zur Volks-, Berufs-, Wohnraum- und Gebäudezählung (VBWGZ) der DDR 1971*, Martin-Luther-Universität Halle-Wittenberg, Halle.

Scherf, K. and Schilde, L. (1974) Funktionale Kreistypen der DDR—eine Methode der statistisch-kartographischen Gebietstypisierung, *Petermanns Geographische Mitteilungen*, **118**, 19–24.

Schmidt-Renner, G. (1973a) Über territoriale Verhaltensweisen bei der Reproduktion von Arbeitskraft und Bevölkerung in der DDR, *Petermanns Geographische Mitteilungen*, **117**, 192–205.

Schmidt-Renner, G. (1973b) Zur territorialen Existenz- und Bewegungsform der sozialistischen gesellschaftlichen Reproduktion, *Petermanns Geographische Mitteilungen*, **117**, 259–67.

Scholz, D. and Oelke, E. (eds.) (1981) *Ballungsgebiete in der DDR*, Martin-Luther-Universität Halle-Wittenberg, Halle.

Schultze, E. (1980) Sozialräumliche Systeme in der Hierarchie der Territorialstruktur, dargestellt am Beispiel der DDR, in P. Khalatbari (ed.), *Räumliche Bevölkerungsbewegung in sozialistischen Ländern*, Akademie-Verlag, Berlin, Beiträge zur Demographie, **4**, 73–83.

Stams, W., Andreas, G. and Reckziegel, M. (1980, 1981) Kartenserie zur Bevölkerungsentwicklung der Erde von 1960 bis 1980, *Geographische Berichte*, **94**, 51–68; **96**, 205–20; **100**, 175–92.

Thürmer, R. (1981) Zur Planbarkeit und Steuerbarkeit von Bevölkerungsprozessen in Territorien niederer Ordnung, in P. Khalatbari (ed.), *Bevölkerungstheorie und Bevölkerungspolitik*, Akademie-Verlag, Berlin, Beiträge zur Demographie, **5**, 217–29.

Weber, E. (1972) Einige Aspekte der territorialen Struktur des Beschäftigtengrades in der DDR nach den Ergebnissen der Volks- und Berufszählung vom 31.12.1964, *Wissenschaftliche Abhandlungen der Geographischen Gesellschaft der DDR*, **9**, 135–52.

Weber, E. (1975) Die territoriale Differenzierung der Altersstruktur der Bevölkerung in der Deutschen Demokratischen Republik nach den Ergebnissen der Volks- und Berufszählung am 31.12.1964, *Wiss. Ztschr. d. Humboldt-Univ. Berlin, Math.-nat. Reihe*, **24**, 1, 17–31.

Weber, E. (1976) Bevölkerung, in H. Kohl, G. Jacob, H.J. Kramm, W. Roubitschek and G. Schmidt-Renner (eds.), *Ökonomische Geographie der Deutschen Demokratischen Republik*, 3rd ed., VEB Hermann Haack, Gotha, Leipzig, 55–101.

Weber, E. (1978) Gegenstand, Stellung und Aufgaben der Bevölkerungsgeographie, in W. Kuls (ed.), *Probleme der Bevölkerungsgeographie*, Wissenschaftliche Buchgesellschaft Darmstadt, Darmstadt, 59–80.

Weber, E. and Benthien, B. (1980) *Einführung in die Bevölkerungs- und Siedlungsgeographie*, 2nd ed., VEB Hermann Haack, Gotha, Leipzig.

Weber, E. and Driebe, B. (1980) Grundüge der Migration in den Nordbezirken der DDR, in P. Khalatbari (ed.), *Räumliche Bevölkerungsbewegung in sozialistischen Ländern*, Akademie-Verlag, Berlin, Beiträge zur Demographie, **4**, 305–38.

Weber, E. (1981) Greifswalder bevölkerungsgeographische Arbeiten-Ergebnisse, Probleme, Vorhaben, *Wiss. Ztschr. d. Ernst-Moritz-Arndt-Universität Greifswald, Math.-nat Reihe*, **30**, 25–31.

Witthauer, K. (1969) *Verteilung und Dynamik der Erdbevölkerung*, VEB Hermann Haack, Gotha, Leipzig.

22

Population Geography in Poland

ANDRZEJ JAGIELSKI
(University of Wrocław, Poland)

The geography of population is one of the youngest geographical sciences in Poland. In the 1960s, no longer a part of economic geography, it became a separate field of knowledge and a university subject. Its beginnings are also not ancient, because normal development of geography began with the independence of Poland in 1918. The development was again interrupted by the second world war, when all universities and scientific institutes were closed, and out of the small number of geographers many were either killed or remained abroad. Thus, historical events greatly affected the development of geography of population as well as the directions and subject of investigations of particular scientists.

Between 1916 and 1920 Polish geographers took greater interest in population; after 150 years of foreign occupation there was the problem of delimiting the boundaries of New Poland. This was not only the matter of armed fighting and theoretical discussions, but it concerned the geography of distribution of Polish population as the information according to official statistics of the invaders was unclear or false. Geographical and cartographical analyses of various sources allowed the reconstruction of the real state of affairs and to determine the territorial range of distribution of Polish population and its ethnic area (Romer, 1916). And so the beginnings of Polish geography of population are connected with political geography and cartographical analysis. On the other hand, they are also connected with practical demands of the people or the country for particular kinds of research.

This last factor has been of great significance in the historical development of geographical studies on population. In our case it has a distinctly pragmatic trend; for example, a quantitative prevalence of publications of an empirical character for practical application over theoretical publications or studies generalizing the results of various investigations.

Geographical studies of population were frequently carried out by non-geographers and non-geographic institutions or by official organs. After the second world war, due to social and economic development based on principles of centralistic state-controlled economy, the contribution of non-geographic institutions to studies on various spatial aspects of population growth and distribution increased considerably. Planners of territorial development and of cities utilize geographic methods, but are less interested in purely cognitive problems of population geography.

Thus the achievements and scientific range of population geography in Poland are not only the work of professional geographers in this field; its pragmatic character not only expresses a lack of deeper methodological reflection on the part of geographers, the anthropogeographic approach in the inter-war period did not favour research of a utilitarian character. But, for example, Marxist philosophical and methodological assumptions, adopted in the 1950s, distinctly stimulated investigations useful for planning the development of national economy. Therefore, empiricism and pragmatism, typical for studies on population in the last thirty years, were justified by obligatory methodological directives.

The development of geography of population in Poland

Scientific problems, investigation trends, methodological assumptions and the research of particular scientists in the course of the development of this discipline changed, but not independently. Thus, in the history of the development of population geography in Poland, three stages, unequal as regards time and significance, may be distinguished: pre-specialization, specialization within economic geography and the formation of a separate geographic science.

(1) ***Pre-specialization stage***

Between 1916 and 1948 population problems did not have a distinct scientific status in anthropogeography. These were secondary problems arising in various research fields, such as cartography and geomorphology (Romer, Pawłowski). At first, anthropogeographic problems and approaches dominated, the characteristics of population distribution in chosen historical and geographical regions being analysed from the point of environmental conditions (Mrazkówna, Niemcówna). Gradually, as more abundant statistical data became available, more frequent geographical and statistical analyses were made of various demographic phenomena (Wasowicz, Ormicki, Melezin). This orientation was called demogeography. It greatly developed after the second world war as a result of the ensuing serious changes in the distribution, demographic and socio-occupational make-up of the Polish population (Halicka, Leonhard, Migacz, Leszczycki, Uhorczak).

(2) *Specialization stage within economic geography*

After 1949 great changes took place as regards the basis for methodology and organization of geographic investigations, because '. . . . attempts were made to develop Marxist economic geography in Poland' (Leszczycki, 1975:112). This meant that the range of research problems for economic geography increased in closer cooperation with the requirements of the national economy. The Institute of Geography of the Polish Academy of Sciences was made responsible for the guidance and organization of this research. To this purpose a number of scientific departments and branches were used. Because of the significance of manpower spatial planning and planning requirements pertaining to population investigations, the position of geographical study of population became more important. Therefore, it was considered as a separate part of economic geography and a separate university subject. Simultaneously it was given a utilitarian orientation by linking it with the geography of settlement. This was justified by the fact that '. . . in principle, the population is distributed in settlements or groups of settlements (system: work place—place of residence). Thus the geographic population analysis should identify itself with the analysis of settlement network and the spatial structure of settlements' (Dziewoński, 1956).

This opinion had a great influence on the development of geographical studies on population in the following years as: (a) in centrally controlled and financed long-range programs the priority themes were subordinated to studies on the settlement system of the country; (b) preference was given to studies of practical significance for territorial development and urban planning; (c) a number of standard anthropogeographical subjects disappeared from the field of research; and (d) studies on various aspects of distribution, migration and make-up of population were of systematic and continuous character.

The resumption of publication of statistical data after 1955 resulted in numerous empirical investigations covering gradually a broader range of demographic phenomena and other aspects of population development (Litterer, Wełpa, Chramiec, Jelonek, Kosiński). Dziewoński and Kosiński have analysed the problem of population distribution on the present national territory in the twentieth century, where they have used statistical and cartographical methods to a greater extent than before. At present, this trend of investigations is the main one in the Institute of Geography and Spatial Organization, Polish Academy of Sciences, in Warsaw.

(3) *Stage of the formation of a separate geographic science*

The idea to subordinate the geographical studies on population for productive purposes or settlement investigations was criticized from both the theoretical and methodological points of view (Kiełczewska-Zaleska, 1958; Leonhard-Migaczowa, 1964), but ineffectively as regards the programs of scientific investigations. Nevertheless, the increasing interest in population problems and the influence of quantitative research techniques, inducing a more thorough methodological reflection, soon convinced many geographers that they were wrong in thinking that the geography of population should remain within economic geography. The recognition of the higher position of this scientific field was the publication, in a relatively short period of time, of two manuals for students of geography of population by Kosiński (1967) and Jagielski (1974). However, it has to be said, that even now, not all Polish geographers are quite convinced that geography of population is a science, and not just a field of research without its own methodological theories and basis (Chojnicki and Kozarski, 1980).

The use of quantitative methods and fast calculation techniques in recent years activated the development of geography of population and made it easier. This field of knowledge, as compared with other geographic ones, had at its disposal the statistics and mathematical research devices already used in demographic sciences, and a special modification was not necessary. Thus, the geography of population could use, in the first place, all available modern methods and research approaches (analyses of regression and correlation, taxonometric and modelling methods and simulation of processes etc.).

Apart from the demogeographical direction, there is also the recent development of socio-ecological studies (socio-spatial urban structures) and systems analysis, but above all the research centre of gravity has gradually moved from statistical problems of population distribution to problems of human behaviour in geographical space. For example, although in departments of the Polish Academy of Sciences population problems are still investigated from the point of the settlement system there is lately a tendency to develop the theory of spatial mobility including various migration forms and to study more thoroughly demographic problems, such as spatial analyses of components of natural movements (Dziewoński *et al.*, 1977a; Dziewoński and Korcelli, 1981a). In university centres, mainly in Wrocław and Kraków, studies are conducted on migrations, social ecology of towns, demogeographic regionalization, and various aspects of spatial systems of culture, standard of living and health characteristics of population. These studies are accompanied by discussions on methodological and epistemological problems. They have not been yet expressed to a sufficient extent in the literature, partly because they are new and partly because of new historical circumstances.

Subject-Matter and Approaches

The theoretical grounds of this field of knowledge have not been a subject of wide discussion; nevertheless some geographers pronounce their opinion on specific phenomena or processes, which they believe to be a part of studies on geography of population. These are mainly demographic problems. However, the authors of publications on this subject are rarely precise concerning the epistemological and methodological assumptions used when solving particular problems. It seems that the majority of them represent the chorological conception of geography and are of a similar opinion as Kosiński (1967) that the subject of population geography is the spatial differentiation of demographic phenomena and processes on the world surface. This conception is also convenient for many scientists as it justifies the pragmatic trend of investigations and the use of population data referring to territorial units that can be found in official statistical sources.

In these sources, the population is only a statistical aggregation of inhabitants in specific administrative territorial units. Thus it is a loose collection and not a substantial whole.

In the last ten years, the broader use of quantitative methods resulted in new methodological thought and approaches. According to Jagielski (1974), the statistical conception of population has a formal character and is not sufficient to study the reality. First of all, the significant attribute of the phenomenon 'population' is the duration, continuity in time. Thus, the population should be considered rather in categories of movement (flows) than in the sense of an aggregation of stable location of individuals or groups of people. Secondly, people do not occur singly in the geographical space, but as members of various kinds of entireties they are more or less internally integrated by special bonds (families, households, social groups, ethnic groups, societies, etc.). And so the conception of population as a geographical fact contains not only a formal content (numbers, structures and spatial relations), but also the substantial, qualitative content.

The substantial character of the phenomena is not the subject matter of geography, but the study of the relations between these phenomena and the world surface (geographical space), which are also expressed by determined relations and spatial patterns (distributions and flows). Therefore, the subject of geography of population is not the population 'in general', but population as a 'spatial phenomenon'. However, the 'spatiality' should not be understood in the formal meaning of the school of theoretical geography (e.g. Bunge *et al.*). Geography is not a variant of geometry. Its scientific purpose is to explain spatial relations of phenomena, i.e. treating these relations as the spatial form of the substantial content of the phenomenon. As regards the knowledge of the principles explaining the population facts observed in the geographical space, the geography of population is not limited to the recognition of geometric properties of structures and flows (networks) concerning population phenomena, but refers to the rules of systematic sciences, such as demography, biology of human populations, sociology and economics.

The methodological effects of such a conception of geography of population are considerable. First of all, it means a systematic approach to the objects of investigations instead of a chorological one, and furthermore the concentration of studies not on static problems (distributions) but on problems of movement and mobility. Methods of comparative statics should be replaced by methods adapted to studies of phenomena permanent in time and space. In reality, the geography of population is a geography of spatio-temporal processes, a geography of spatial behaviour of people living in specific social communities.

Research problems and application

The classic form of application of geographical knowledge, serving both cognitive and practical purposes, is the map. Thus, since the very beginnings of geographic studies on population, the mapping of population phenomena has been constantly in the mind of geographers. Several methodological approaches can be mentioned. For example, Romer (1916) has been first in the world literature to use the isorithmic method to show on a map the distribution of density of population, and later on he has differentiated the colours of the dots on the dot map showing the distribution of various nationalities, in order to illustrate the infiltration of cultural phenomena. In the 1960s and 1970s attempts have been made to present the distribution of population and other problems on maps with hexagonal or square grids with an equal surface area of cells (100 sq km) in order to eliminate the influence of uneven areas of administrative territorial units on population indices (Kosiński, 1967; Dziewoński, 1977a). Attempts to use this type of map in state institutions recording population data have been unsuccessful.

The studies and research within geography of population can be classified according to problems and their application:

(1) ***Research for a practical purpose***

This is mainly for recognition and diagnosis of various phenomena on a national, regional or local scale. The objects of investigations are mostly typical problems, such as distribution and concentration of population, spatial differentiation of growth and of demographic structure, migrations, urbanization, etc. In some periods there have been specific problems, to which more attention was paid: nationality problems after the first world war; mass migrations and settlement of the western and northern parts of the country after the second world war; country-to-town migrations and relative depopulation of some country areas over the last twenty years. This kind of investigation is frequently the result of studies conducted within government programmes and managed by various research institutes, not necessarily geographic ones.

(2) ***Research of a general cognitive and didactic significance***

One may mention here publications, also used as manuals, by Kosiński (1967) and Jagielski (1974, 1977), which apart from instruction contain a number of methodological postulates and substantial remarks. Maryański (1977) has published several books on the population characteristics of particular regions and states of the world, whereas Staszewski (1957, 1961) has analyzed the distribution of world population according to the distance from coasts and the height above sea-level, and also on the degree of density. Characteristics of the differentiation of population phenomena in Poland can be found in almost all studies of the economic geography in Poland (e.g. Srokowski, Loth and Petrazycki, Jagielski).

(3) ***Research of an analytical and scientific-cognitive character***

This is of basic significance for the development of geography of population as a science, and is also frequently a product of investigations for practical purposes, as for the requirements of spatial or urban planning. The authors expand not only the empirical knowledge by introducing new problems or more effective research methods, but also enrich the theoretical content in this field. For example, some research problems:
(a) *Population distribution.* Dziewoński and Kosiński (1967) have applied methods of population potential in order to illustrate in general the distribution of Polish population in several time profiles between 1910 and 1970. Jedut (1963) has studied the methods of analyses of population concentration, whereas Jerczynski and Kosiński (Dziewoński and Kosiński, 1967) have analyzed the changes in concentrations and their cartographical representation.
(b) *Internal migrations.* Migrations are an object of investigations in several fields of knowledge and the literature on the subject is vast. In the past, geographers were mainly concerned with these problems in order to determine areas with different rates of increase and decrease of population; at present, attention is paid to flows and migrational relations, and their role in urban development. Notions of spatial systems of migration flows and of the migrational region have been introduced (Zurek, Ksiezak, Rykiel, Jagielski), and studies on the properties of these constructs and their verification are being continued. These studies on migration have many aspects and cover some important forms of movement in space: migrations within the country

due to change of place of residence (intra-regional and inter-regional), mainly from the country to towns; commuting to work and to school; intra-urban movements of residential change, travel to work and shopping, etc. These studies provide great possibilities for using methods of statistical analysis and migrational models, e.g. gravitational models. The Rogers and Willekens method of inter-regional analysis has been applied by Dziewoński and Korcelli (1981a, 1981b) in the analysis of the settlement system. Gawryszewski (1974) has made an attempt to construct an index of spatial mobility, covering all forms of migration. In studies of the networks and systems of migrational flows, methods of spatial analysis have been also used, amongst others graphic and taxonometric methods.

(c) *Natural movement of populations.* A separate field, but a bit less interesting for geographers, are the problems of differentiated increase of population and natural movement of population. Iwanicka-Lyra (1980) has studied the effect of natural movement on migrations in Poland. Jagielski (1980) has investigated the relations between the fertility rate and the size of towns. He has used an iconographic model to represent the spatial process of demographic transition as a diffusion of a small urban family model from the centre of a town, previously inhabited by the social élite, towards suburbs and further along thoroughfares to rural areas. The impact of demographic transition on the spatial differentiation of population dynamics in various regions of the world has been also analyzed (Jakubowski, 1977). Demographic characteristics of territorial units have been especially frequently used in demographical typologies and regionalizations of Poland (e.g. Migaczowa, Czarkowska, Jelonek).

(d) *Generalization, classification and regionalization.* The chorological tradition and requirements of spatial planning demand geographers to give much attention to spatial grouping of territorial units, of similar population characters, or on the basis of special typologies, for example structures of population by age and sex in regions. Ormicki introduced in 1931 the concept of demogeographical region, and Kosiński (1967) the concept of Webb for the purpose of typological studies of demographic phenomena. Jelonek (1971, 1977) has worked out the demographic regionalization of Poland, a multivariate one using factorial analysis, and some other scientists, mainly demographers, have also applied various taxonometric methods. Problems of regionalization are broadly discussed and are of great significance for the administration and national economy.

(e) *Urban population.* At present, 59 per cent of Polish population live in towns. Population problems of urban agglomerations and large towns have become now a separate field of geographic studies on population. The main directions are: studies on spatial socio-ecological structures (Wecławowicz, Jagielski), distribution and population density profiles in towns (Bromek, Jagielski, Klimaszewska-Budzynowska, Mydel) and intra-urban migrations.

Studies of spatial social structures have been carried out on the basis of results of factorial analyses, and are significant for planning the development of towns.

Of course, these more important research fields, problems and applications, which have been mentioned, do not represent fully the interest of Polish geographers in population problems and in methods used for geographical research of aspects of these problems. Publications on the subject appear mainly in the quarterlies such as *Przeglad Geograficzny* (Polish Geographical Review), *Geographia Polonica*, *Czasopismo Geograficzne* (Geographical Journal) and in *Studia Demograficzne* (Population Studies), and also in special publications of the Institute of Geography and Spatial Organization, Polish Academy of Sciences, or particular universities.

References

Chojnicki, Z. and Kozarski, S. (1980) The development of the geographical sciences during 1973–1979 in the light of the decisions of the Second Congress of Polish Science, *Przeglad Geograficzny*, **52**, 251–70 (in Polish).

Dziewoński, K. (1956) Geography of population and settlement—achievements, theoretical bases and plan for research, *Przeglad Geograficzny*, **28**, 723–64 (in Polish).

Dziewoński, K. and Kosiński, L.A. (1967) *Growth and Distribution of Population in Poland during the XXth Century*, PWN, Warszawa (in Polish).

Dziewoński, K. *et al.* (1977a) *Distribution, Migrations of Population and Settlement System of Poland*, Prace Geograficzne 117, Ossolineum, Wrocław (in Polish).

Dziewoński, K. *et al.* (1977b) Population problems in geographical investigations in recent years, *Studia Demograficzne*, **50**, 71–86 (in Polish).

Dziewoński, K. and Korcelli, P. (eds.) (1981a) *Studies on Migration and Settlement System of Poland*, Prace Geograficzne 140, Ossolineum, Wrocław (in Polish).

Dziewoński, K. and Korcelli, P. (1981b) *Migration and Settlement: Poland*, I.I.A.S.A., Laxenburg.

Gawryszewski, A. (1974) *Spatial Relationships between Permanent Migrations and Commuting to Work. Factors Influencing Migratory Movements*, Prace Geograficzne 109, Ossolineum, Wrocław (in Polish).

Iwanicka-Lyra, E. (1980) An attempt at measuring the intensity of influence of demographic features on natural increase, *Przeglad Geograficzny*, **52**, 827–36 (in Polish).

Jagielski, A. (1974) *Population Geography*, PWN, Warszawa (in Polish).

Jagielski, A. (1978) Population and settlement, in St. Berezowski (ed.) *Geografia ekonomiczna Polski*, PWE, Warszawa, 137–212 (in Polish).

Jagielski, A. (1980) Urbanization and spatial aspects of "demographic transition", *Oeconomica Polona*, **1**, 84–104.

Jagielski, A. (1982) Problems and methods of research concerning migrations, *Studia Demograficzne*, **4**, 3–30 (in Polish).

Jakubowski, M. (1977) The theory of demographic transition and studies on the spatial differentiation of population dynamics, *Geographia Polonica*, **35**, 73–89.

Jedut, R. (1963) The application of the method of concentration analysis in the study of population distribution, the case of Poland, *Annales Universitatis Mariae Curie-Skłodowska*, **16**, Series B, 119–56 (in Polish).

Jelonek, A. (1971) *Demographic Regions of Poland*, Prace Geograficzne 30, Uniwersytet Jagiellonski, Kraków (in Polish).

Jelonek, A. (1977) Demographic regions and the regionalization of the population structures, in K. Dziewoński *et al. op. cit.* (1977a), 110–35 (in Polish).

Kiełczewska-Zaleska, M. (1958) Trends of development of human geography in Poland, *Przeglad Geograficzny*, **30**, 403–20 (in Polish).

Kosiński, L.A. (1967) *Population Geography*, PWN, Warszawa (in Polish).

Leszczycki, St. (1975) *Geography as a Science and Applied Knowledge*, PWN, Warszawa (in Polish).

Leonhard-Migaczowa, H. (1964) Population geography in Poland during the last twenty years, *Czasopismo Geograficzne*, **35**, 399–418 (in Polish).

Maryanski, A. (1977) *The Population of the World*, PWN, Warszawa (in Polish).

The Population of Poland (1975) CICRED Series, State Scientific Publishers, Warszawa.

Romer, E. (1916) *Geographical and Statistical Atlas of Poland*, Gebethner i Wolff, Warszawa-Krakow (in Polish).

Staszewski, J. (1957) *Vertical Distribution of World Population*, Prace Geograficzne 14, Ossolineum, Wrocław.

Staszewski, J. (1961) *Die Verbreitung der Erdbevölkerung nach dem Abstand von Meer, Eine Bevölkerungsgeographische Studie*, Prace Geograficzne 28, Ossolineum, Wrocław.

Zurek, A. (1975) *Spatial Structure of Urban Migrations in the Kielce voivodship*, Prace Geograficzne 113, Ossolineum, Wrocław (in Polish).

23

Population Geography in India

GURDEV SINGH GOSAL
(Panjab University, Chandigarh, India)

Among the various disciplines taught at the university level in India, geography is relatively young. In the early stages of development of this discipline the focus was on the study of regional geography and economic geography. During about the last thirty years, however, both in terms of teaching and research, the focus has shifted to the development of different areas of specialization within systematic geography. Urban geography and agricultural geography were the first favourites of most doctoral students in the beginning of the post-independence period. Subsequently in the late 1950s came population geography, and during a short span of about 25 years it has grown into a major area of research.

Consistent with the general philosophy of the subject, population geographers in India have been concentrating on studying population in the spatial perspective, dealing essentially with spatial distributions, spatial associations and spatial interrelations. The spatial approach has thus become the methodological basis of all geographic studies of population. However, the study of implications of population in its various aspects to the overall nature of places still remains neglected. A comprehensive development of population geography in India demands, therefore, greater adherence to conceptual as well as methodological norms.

In explaining the spatial patterns of population phenomena, there is a general tendency to confine consideration to elements of the physical environment. It is a legacy of the once dominant 'man-environment relationship' concept of the discipline. The social, economic, cultural and political correlates have received far less attention than they deserve. In fact, the whole universe needs to be searched to unravel the truth as far as cause-and-effect relationships are concerned.

Like studies in other branches of systematic geography, population geography is generally studied empirically in India. The 'from-facts-to-theory' approach is the chief guiding principle with most population geographers. Not that there is anything wrong with it, or that it is less scientific in any way, but there is an equal need to match this method with the theoretical approach—'from theory-to-facts'. There is no dualism between the two. The two are, in fact, interdependent and interrelated. The simultaneous use of the two approaches will serve better the cause of promoting not only population geography but geography as a whole.

To follow the theoretical approach in population geography would require comprehensive training in quantitative techniques, apart from reasonable exposure to psychology, sociology, economics and history. Model building must be studied in a major way. The hypotheses formulated and tested in most population studies by geographers, as evidenced in doctoral or M.Phil dissertations, leave much to be desired. Quantification should be used not only to bring in precision in description and explanation but also for developing theory.

The Census of India has been instrumental in the promotion of population geography in India. It is a rare treasure of population data available for the whole country covering a period of one hundred years. Among the countries of the developing world India is one of the most fortunate in having a well-developed census system for a long period, making it possible to examine its population in spatial-temporal dimensions. The data for most characteristics of population have been available by districts (equivalent to a county in the West) for almost the entire hundred-year period. During the post-independence period, however, additional comprehensiveness and depth have been added to the already efficient and well-established census. In 1951, the Census of India published for the first time what are called District Census Handbooks, containing population data of individual villages and towns. This is the ultimate in detail of data available in printed form anywhere in the world for a country of India's size. This has been a great incentive in developing research activities in population geography at the university level in India, more than what obtains in other sub-fields of geography. Accordingly, population studies have been carried out by geographers at different scales—national, regional and local—based on district, tahsil and village level data respectively. An indirect implication of the ready availability of so much and so detailed data from the census in printed, tabulated form, however, has been the neglect of fieldwork. Fieldwork is necessary not only for the collection of primary data but also for observing population in the total context of areas. What a perceptive mind can see in the field may not be obtainable even from the most sophisticated quantitative techniques and instruments of measurement. In view of the complex historical, cultural and political background of India, its population geographers must evolve their own methodology of fieldwork for collecting primary data on aspects which are not covered by the census and for observing the intricate reality of areas.

Another implication of the availability of such data from the Census of India is the overwhelming reliance on cartographic presentation as the basis of all analyses. In most population works the spatial patterns which emerge on the maps are the basis of description and explanation as a method of study. Such a technique does make the task simple and relatively easy, but a time has already come when cartography should be made to move along with quantification so that more complex and comprehensive targets in population geography can be achieved.

As far as contents of population geography in India go, they are predominantly confined to what is provided by the census. What are conspicuous by their practical absence are the data relating to vital rates. The registration of births and deaths is incomplete everywhere, although the degree of incompleteness varies widely from state to state. It leaves a significant gap in the available information required for studying the dynamics of population.

The actual accomplishments relating to India's population geography are incomplete both in terms of spatial coverage and contents. Many areas of the country and many aspects of the population still remain untouched by scholars in the subject. It is partly understandable in view of the short period of its growth, large size of the country and deficiencies and incompletenesses of the data referred to above.

Whatever studies have been carried out on the various regions of the country relating to different attributes of the population need to be subjected to a comparative analysis with a view to drawing generalizations of wider applicability.

India has a massive population which has been growing at an accelerated rate throughout the post-independence period, bringing its numbers to the staggering figure of 683 million by the 1981 census. It has had its paralysing effects on all attempts towards socio-economic development in the country. The socio-economic progress which has been registered under the various five-year plans has been remarkable in absolute terms, but it stands considerably neutralized in the face of spiralling population numbers. There is a need, therefore, to carry out population studies with reference to development in specific terms. Such studies have thus far been only a few. Improvement in the quality of population (in terms of health, education, income etc.) is not just a by-product of development. It is a primary lever for initiating the development process itself.

Lastly, it may be a measure of the growing importance of population geography in India that scholars interested in this area of specialization have formed an Association of Population Geographers of India as a registered body with the Department of Geography, Panjab University, Chandigarh as its headquarters. This association is regularly bringing out a journal entitled

Population Geography. The response and co-operation from colleagues in all parts of the world have been most encouraging in making this venture a success. It is hoped that, through this venture, India will be able to serve the cause of population geography in a positive and befitting manner, and bring about close collaboration among scholars of this sub-field working in different parts of the world.

Performance and prospects

It may be in order to make brief comments on the study of each aspect of the population as pursued by Indian scholars, suggesting future lines of action in each case. The references to different studies in the discussion are only illustrative of the trend and not exhaustive by any means.

Despite the availability of fairly detailed data for the whole country extending over the past about one hundred years, very few studies were carried out by Indian geographers on this vital subject up to the early 1950s. The ones which were done, were related to distribution and density of population only. Gosal's (1956) doctoral dissertation, supervised by Glenn Trewartha, was the first attempt to do a systematic analysis of India's population, using district data relating to 1951. It included chapters on such aspects of population as distribution and density, growth, internal migration, sex ratio, literacy, occupational structure and urbanization, followed by regionalization of the country on the basis of significant characteristics of population. Throughout this study the discussion was based on the spatial patterns that emerged on maps based on data by districts. In a sense, it provided an initial framework of India's population geography. Subsequently, particularly from the mid-1960s onwards, studies using similar methodology but on local areas, based on data by individual villages and towns, were carried out at the Panjab University (e.g. Krishan, 1968; Chandna, 1970; Mehta, 1971). These studies examined the realities relating to the spatial distributions and relationships of various population characteristics of smaller areas from much closer angles. When subjected to a comparative analysis, such studies are bound to be rewarding in producing a meaningful body of knowledge relating to the theoretical aspects of India's population.

Distribution and density

The most exhaustive account of distribution of population in India is available from the population sheets published by the National Atlas Organization under the direction of S.P. Chatterjee (1959). These sheets are on 1:1,000,000 scale and depict the (i) physical background and administrative boundaries in light shade, (ii) distribution of rural population by villages in terms of their size and dominance of agricultural/non-agricultural population and (iii) distribution of individual urban places by their size and functions. The back of these sheets provides useful description on the distribution of population in the area covered. There is hardly any area of comparable population and size in the world where population distribution has been mapped in such great detail as in these sheets. But the population distribution has rarely been analyzed in terms of size and spacing of settlements, and densities (other than arithmetic) have seldom been mentioned. There is a need to analyze in detail the distributional pattern of population in different regions of India in the context of not only the physical environment but also the history, economy and culture of each region.

Growth of population

This is a much discussed aspect of population at different scales, using data for the post-independence decades and based on well-drafted maps. But in all such studies, the analysis is handicapped by the paucity of data on birth and death rates, and direct information on migration—the three basic determinants of population change. Every scholar of studies on population change in the Indian context has therefore to face a challenging task of making precise and detailed statements on the role of each of the three determinants (Trewartha and Gosal, 1956; Gosal, 1962). While precise description and interpretation of the spatial patterns of population change are an integral part of the population geography of India, it is most desirable to highlight the socio-economic implications, particularly in the present context of the country. Gosal has briefly done this in his study of recent population change in India (1982), but such implications need to be examined at different spatial levels and in greater detail. The findings of such detailed studies would be useful for future socio-economic planning as well as for planning population control in specific terms.

Considerable development effort has been made in India with the aim of freeing hundreds of millions of people from the grip of poverty which is the country's most pressing human problem. Since poverty is a condition characterized by hunger and malnutrition, lack of education, unemployment, lack of health care, sub-standard housing and poor sanitation and general living conditions, one can see clearly that any of these problems is directly linked with the size and growth of the country's population. Thus the relationship between population and development is inseparable, and in a country like India with a massive base of population, the implications of demographic growth have to be deciphered in concrete terms. Conversely, every development effort should be planned in relation to the size and growth of the population. In other words, the interrelationships of the demographic factor with policies on education, health, housing, food and agriculture, industrialization, employment and improvement of the status of women, etc.

must be given a pivotal consideration. Likewise, in all such considerations of population and development, the environmental issues must receive simultaneous attention.

There is an absence of studies on the regional variations in birth and death rates in India due largely to lack of information on this subject by small areal units like districts. In recent years, however, based on sample studies, the Census of India have prepared estimates of birth and death rates and changes therein by states which may be subjected to close scrutiny.

Equally important are studies of internal migration in the country during the post-independence period. Geographers have done a few studies on internal migration covering the whole country (Gosal, 1961a; Gosal and Krishan, 1975; Roy, 1979) on the basis of 1951, 1961 and 1971 census data relating to place-of-birth. Migrational studies of regions and smaller areas need to be undertaken on the basis of census data supplemented with primary data collected in the field. Not only are the streams of internal migration a measure of the processes of redistribution of population in the country, but they also produce a mixing of people of diverse linguistic, religious and cultural affiliations. While such mixings may strengthen the forces of secularism, they are also, in many instances, sources of social tension. Apart from identifying the areas of in- and out-migration, assessing the magnitude of such mobility, and analyzing its correlates in each case, there is, therefore, a need to unravel the impact of migration (both in- and out-) on the social, economic and political aspects of areas—nay, on the total character of areas. However, the census data on place-of-birth on which most of the migrational studies in India are based have certain inherent shortcomings. It is only indirect information: (i) a person's place-of-birth does not necessarily coincide with his residence, as Indian wives generally return to their parents' home for their first confinement, and if this happens to be just across a state or a district boundary or in an adjoining village, the child becomes an in-migrant at the next census; (ii) the difference between the place-of-birth and the place-of-enumeration gives no indication of the number of moves the individual may have made during his lifetime; (iii) the place-of-enumeration may be entirely accidental and may have nothing to do with the individual's regular place of residence and work; and (iv) the place-of-birth data give no precise indication as to when the migration took place and for what motives. Till 1951, the entire population was classified into categories of those enumerated within the district/state/country of birth along with those born abroad but enumerated in India. It was only in the 1961 census that the number of persons enumerated at the place-of-birth was also given, making it possible to assess the intra-district migration. The 1961 census also provided for the first time rural/urban classification of both place-of-birth and enumeration of migrants. Such data facilitate an estimation of rural-rural, rural-urban, urban-urban and urban-rural patterns of migration. Also, the new data on duration of migrants' residence at the place-of-enumeration make it possible to discern the temporal-spatial patterns of mobility. In addition, in the case of cities (places with a population of 100,000 or more), data on age, literacy and occupation of migrants were published. Thus the 1961 census added several new facets to the study of migration. Notwithstanding recent improvements mentioned above, studies on internal migration in India remain only attempts towards what can be accomplished from meagre and indirect data. Direct and comprehensive information on migrants must be collected in the field to get a realistic picture of the various facets of human mobility in the Indian context. Such a pioneer study is being conducted by S. Mehta on the Bist Doab (Punjab).

Age and sex structure

Despite the great importance of age and sex structure to understanding any population, very few studies have been made by geographers in India on these aspects particularly on age structure. In view of prevailing illiteracy in the country, the available information on age is of low reliability. Even on sex composition, there are only a few geographic attempts (Gosal, 1961b; Sen, 1963), and Lall's (1962) is the only comprehensive study of age and sex structure of Indian cities. There is a need to make a detailed spatial analysis of changes in the sex composition of India's population, particularly during the past three decades.

Literacy

Some studies have been conducted by geographers on the spatial patterns and progress of literacy in India (Gosal, 1964; Schwartzberg, 1961; Tirtha, 1966). Likewise, rural literacy (Gosal, 1967) and literacy in cities (Krishan and Shyam, 1974) have been separately subjected to areal analysis using data for different census years. The rural-urban differential in literacy and the regional disparities therein, which assume so much importance in a country of India's background, have been studied by Krishan and Shyam (1978) on the basis of 1971 data. Of equal interest would be a spatial study of male/female differentials in literacy in the country. Throughout the post-independence period the national and state governments have provided special facilities for the extension of literacy and education among scheduled castes and scheduled tribes—the traditionally neglected sections of the Indian society. It would be of practical interest to carry out geographic investigations into the progress of literacy and education among these people, with special reference to their rural-urban and male/female differentials. Such a study would be of special utility in planning the future welfare of these sections of the population. Another dimension which needs to be added to future studies of literacy and education in India is the impact of the progress of literacy on the socio-economic life of the people.

Religious composition and languages

In a country like India where religion is directly or indirectly involved in practically every aspect of life, spatial studies of religious composition and changes therein from time to time assume a significance of their own. A few studies on the distribution and relative strength of major religious groups in India have been brought out by geographers (Brush, 1949; Gosal, 1965; Gosal and Mukerji, 1970). Studies on individual religious groups have also been accomplished by some scholars; Surinderjit Kaur (1979) has produced a doctoral dissertation on changes in the distributional pattern of Sikhs in India during 1881–1971, and Siddiqui (1976) a detailed study on the population geography of the Muslims of India. There is also a need to develop a geography of languages in India. Apart from Tirtha's (1966) work, very little has been done in this regard.

Caste

Caste is another aspect of India's population which deserves to be studied in all its dimensions for a fuller understanding of the society. The scheduled caste population first attracted the attention of Gosal and Mukerji (1972) who analyzed the distribution and relative concentration of persons belonging to these castes using district-level data pertaining to 1961. Similar studies have been conducted at regional levels ever since. Mukerji (1971) studied the patterns of distribution and density of scheduled caste population of Andhra Pradesh, while Chandna (1972) mapped and interpreted the patterns of all attributes of the scheduled caste population of rural Haryana. Chandna is working on a project dealing with a comprehensive study of the various characteristics of the scheduled caste population in India. A study of trends in the various characteristics of the scheduled caste population in the spatial perspective will provide a measure of the social change taking place in India.

Working force and occupational structure

Changes in the definition of worker and occupational categories from decade to decade have rendered vast amounts of census data non-comparable, making it difficult to carry out vital studies of working force and occupational structure.

The 1951 census data related to livelihood categories, not to workers. Allowing for a certain percentage of the population deriving livelihood from non-agricultural activities that must be needed for the local populace, Gosal's (1958) was the first geographic study of the economically active non-agricultural population of different parts of rural India. Implicit in this innovation was the basic and non-basic concept of economy operating in India's countryside. Following the same idea and using 1971 census data, Krishan (1979) did a study of non-agricultural workers in rural India. The definition of worker as adopted by the 1961 census was a little liberal in favour of the females but, when made rigorous in 1971, it showed up a general decline in the female working force. Similarly some changes in occupational categories cost the data its comparability during this period. Based on 1961 data on workers, Mehta (1967) and Chandna (1967) studied the female working force in rural India and rural Punjab respectively. Krishan is doing a study on the patterns of unemployment and under-employment in rural Punjab based on data collected from sampled villages, but, despite its great practical relevance, India's working force and its occupational structure continue to remain inadequately studied in their various dimensions. Intensive studies are, therefore, needed on: (i) changing pattern of the occupational structure of India's working force; (ii) extent of unemployment and under-employment among educated and uneducated persons in different parts of the country, both in urban and rural areas; and (iii) future supply of labour and availability of employment opportunities at national, regional and local levels. It goes without saying that such studies would require the census data to be supplemented with primary information collected in the field.

Urbanization

Urbanization as a characteristic of population, as distinct from geography, has received increasing attention in recent years. Raj Bala's doctoral dissertation (1978) dealt with the process of urbanization in India during the present century focusing interest on the discovery and understanding of the spatial patterns. Several studies in urbanization at regional levels have been done during the past two decades; remaining to be done is an analysis of urbanization in relation to socio-economic development. The development strategy may be reflected in the planning of new towns or the expansion of old ones. Of particular interest would be decentralization of industrial development and spatial dispersal of the process of urbanization. An initial but interesting work on this theme has been done by Raza and Kundu (1982). The authors have formulated an analytical frame within which this problem has been studied in the Indian context. Such studies can be, no doubt, of great value in developmental planning and, as such, should receive more attention at the hands of population geographers in India.

Conclusion

From the brief observations made above, it emerges that population geography in India is coming up very satisfactorily and is showing all potentialities of playing its full role in academic as well as practical terms in the years to come. The potential areas of future research in this sub-field in the Indian context are:

(i) distribution of population with special reference to size and spacing of settlements;
(ii) regional inequalities in birth and death rates and their impact on the patterns of population change;
(iii) internal migration and regional development;
(iv) study of age structure with reference to future growth of population and patterns of employment;
(v) growth of literacy and education in all its dimensions and its impact on socio-economic development;
(vi) spatial analysis of changes in occupational structure (rural and urban) during the post-independence period;
(vii) urbanization and regional development;
(viii) comprehensive study of the population geography of scheduled castes and scheduled tribes with reference to changes in their characteristics during the post-independence period;
(ix) exhaustive studies of the population geography of small areas in different parts of the country (using data by individual villages and towns) and comparative analysis thereof; and
(x) population-resource regionalization.

References

Bala, Raj (1978) *A Spatial Perspective on Urbanization in India*, Panjab University (Unpublished Ph.D. Thesis).

Brush, J.E. (1949) The distribution of religious communities in India, *Annals of the Association of American Geographers*, **39,** 81–98.

Chandna, R.C. (1967) Female working force of Rural Punjab, 1961, *Manpower Journal*, **2,** 47–62.

Chandna, R.C. (1970) *Changes in the Demographic Character of the Rohtak and Gurgaon Districts, 1951–61: A Geographical Analysis*, Panjab University (Unpublished Ph.D. Thesis).

Chandna, R.C. (1972) Scheduled caste population in Rural Haryana—a geographical analysis, *National Geographical Journal of India*, **18,** 177–86.

Chatterjee, S.P. (Director) (1959) *Population Plates*, National Atlas Organization of India.

Gosal, G.S. (1956) *A Geographical Analysis of India's Population*, University of Wisconsin (Unpublished Ph.D. Thesis).

Gosal, G.S. (1958) The occupational structure of India's rural population—a regional analysis, *National Geographical Journal of India*, **4,** 137–48.

Gosal, G.S. (1961a) Internal migration in India—a regional analysis, *Indian Geographical Journal*, **34,** 106–21.

Gosal, G.S. (1961b) The regionalism of sex composition of India's population, *Rural Sociology*, **26,** 122–37.

Gosal, G.S. (1962) Regional aspects of population growth in India: 1951–61, *Pacific Viewpoint*, **3,** 87–99.

Gosal, G.S. (1964) Literacy in India: an interpretative study, *Rural Sociology*, **29,** 261–77.

Gosal, G.S. (1965) Changes in the religious composition of Punjab's population during 1951–61, *Economic Weekly*, **23,** 119–24.

Gosal, G.S. (1967) Regional aspects of rural literacy in India, *Transactions of the Indian Council of Geographers*, **4,** 1–15.

Gosal, G.S. (1982) Recent population growth in India, *Population Geography*, **4,** 33–53.

Gosal, G.S. and Krishan, G. (1975) Patterns of internal migration in India, in L.A. Kosiński and R.M. Prothero (eds.) *People on the Move*, Methuen, London, 193–206.

Gosal, G.S. and Mukerji, A.B. (1970) The religious composition of India's population: a spatial analysis, *Tijdschrift voor Economische en Sociale Geografie*, **61,** 91–100.

Gosal, G.S. and Mukerji, A.B. (1972) Distribution and relative concentration of scheduled caste population in India, in *Economic and Socio-Cultural Dimensions of Regionalisation: An Indo-USSR Collaborative Study*, Census of India, Census Centenary Monograph No. 7, 473–83.

Kaur, Surinderjit (1979) *Changes in the Distributional Pattern of Sikhs in India, 1881–1971—A Geographical Appraisal.* Panjab University (Unpublished Ph.D. Thesis).

Krishan, G. (1968) *Changes in the Demographic Character of Punjab's Border Districts of Amritsar and Gurdaspur, 1951–61*, Panjab University (Unpublished Ph.D. Thesis).

Krishan, G. (1978) Impact of population growth on rural housing, *Geographical Review of India*, **40,** 138–43.

Krishan, G. (1979) Non-agricultural workers in India, *Population Geography*, **1,** 109–25.

Krishan, G. and Shyam, M. (1974) Literacy pattern of Indian cities, *Geoforum*, **19,** 77–80.

Krishan, G. and Shyam, M. (1978) Regional aspects of urban-rural differential in literacy in India: 1971, *Journal of Developing Areas*, **13,** 111–21.

Lall, A. (1962) Age and sex structure of cities of India, *Geographical Review of India*, **24,** 7–29.

Mehta, S. (1967) India's rural female working force and its occupational structure, 1961: a geographical analysis, *Indian Geographer*, **12,** 49–68.

Mehta, S. (1971) *Some Aspects of Change in the Demographic Characteristics of Bist Doab, 1951–61*, Panjab University (Unpublished Ph.D. Thesis).

Mukerji, A.B. (1971) Regional contrasts in distribution, density and relative strength of scheduled caste population in Andhra Pradesh, *Indian Geographical Journal*, **46,** 23–49.

Raza, M. and Kundu, A. (1982) Agglomerated and dispersed patterns of urbanization in India: a spatial analysis, *Regional Development Dialogue*, **3,** 117–44.

Roy, B.K. (1979) *Geographic Distribution of Internal Migration in India*, Census of India.

Schwartzberg, J.E. (1961) Observations on the progress of literacy in India, 1951–61, *Indian Population Bulletin*, No. 2, Census of India, 295–300.

Sen, J.C. (1963) The sex composition of the population of India, 1961, *Deccan Geographer*, **2,** 43–62.

Siddiqui, N.A. (1976) *Population Geography of Muslims of India*, S. Chand, Delhi.

Tirtha, R. (1966) Areal patterns of literacy in India, *Manpower Journal*, **1,** 88–118.

Trewartha, G.T. and Gosal, G.S. (1957) The regionalism of population change in India (1891–1951), *Proceedings of the Cold Spring Harbor Symposia on Quantitative Biology*, **22,** 71–81.

24

Population Geography in Mexico

MARÍA TERESA GUTIÉRREZ DE MACGREGOR
(Universidad Nacional Autónoma de México, Mexico)

The purpose of this brief paper is to provide available information on the characteristics and development of population geography in Mexico, mainly in research and teaching aspects.

Interest in population studies in our country may be traced back to prehispanic times and has continued through the colonial period until now. Currently in excess of 70 million, the population in Mexico is growing rapidly, as it registers one of the highest annual rates of increase in the world, averaging 3.0 per cent during the last three decades. It should also be noted that rapid urban growth is one of the most spectacular features of Mexico. In 1900 there were only 1.6 million inhabitants living in urban areas; in 1980 the figure estimated was 35.9 millions, representing a rise from 12.0 to 51.5 per cent of the total population. Moreover, the percentage of urban population living in cities with more than 100,000 inhabitants increased from 27 per cent in 1900 to 81 per cent in 1980. The population of the Metropolitan area of Mexico City which is now estimated in 15 millions, is also impressive, representing at present more than 20 per cent of the total population.

Population growth, together with uneven population distribution, are important problems of Mexico. A large part of the country is uninhabited or very lightly peopled. In the central temperate zone, at an altitude above 1000 m, live more than 50 per cent of the total population on 16 per cent of the area. For this reason some Mexican geographers have concentrated their studies upon distribution and evolution of population and processes of population change such as internal migration. In 1980, 14.5 per cent of the population have changed their place of residence. These studies have been conditioned by the quantity and quality of available statistics. Moreover, the introduction of population geography as a subject in the curriculum in the Colegio de

Geografía of the Universidad Nacional Autónoma de México (UNAM) has also played an important role as a stimulating agent on population studies.

Sources for population data in Mexican history

It is a fact that people of all times have been worried about population problems, which have been recorded according to their cultures and development, especially those relating to population migration. Mexico has not escaped this phenomenon, which is detected through its cultural development during the centuries before the Spanish conquest. Diverse facts in relation to population were registered in those times; for example we have knowledge of migration through the Indians codex (pictograph maps). Unfortunately very few of these have reached us. One of the most significant, 'La tira de la peregrinación', shows us the importance they gave to registering population movements through time. A band nearly 20 m long and 25.5 cm wide drawn at the beginning of the sixteenth century in 'amate' paper made of wild fig, it represents the mobility of the Aztecs from their place of origin, Aztlan, located on an island in the north-west of Mexico, to their place of destination, also an island located on a lake in the basin of Mexico, where they founded Tenochtitlan. All the places where they stayed for a period of time were indicated in the codex. The hieroglyphs represent the places and the number of years they stood in each place (Fig. 24.1 A and B). It is evidence of the existence of a stepwise movement of Aztec population in prehispanic times.

During the colonial period the Spaniards were very much interested in obtaining information about New Spain, especially demographic data. They wanted to know the number of Indians and Spaniards living in the provinces, and obtained that information through the bishops and Franciscan and Dominican monks.

The interest in population continued to increase, and Mexico was one of the first countries in Latin America where research on population was important. The development of population geography as a university discipline started in 1944 at the Colegio de Geografía of the UNAM, although the term demography was used. In 1963 a seminar entitled 'Demographic Geography of Mexico' was introduced at postgraduate level at the same university, but really population geography was established as a systematic branch in university syllabuses only from 1970, when the name demography was changed to population geography and the seminar on the demographic population of Mexico became the seminar on the population geography of Mexico. Today the institutions that offer courses on population geography are Colegio de Geografía of UNAM, Escuela de Geografía of the Universidad Autónoma del Estado de México and Facultad de Geografía of the Universidad de Guadalajara.

FIGURE 24.1A. *Pictograph showing the migration of the Aztecs from Aztlan in the north-west of Mexico*

FIGURE 24.1.B *The arrival in Atzcapotzalco (ant hill) and the village of Acalhuacan (place of canoes), places where the Aztecs stopped for 4 years on their journey to Tenochtitlan in central Mexico*

Statistical sources

The recording of data has represented an important problem for population geographers. It is known that enumeration of population in New Spain was carried out before 1528 by Hernan Cortés, who wanted to know the population of the conquered lands. From then until the end of the nineteenth century only estimates were available. In 1895, the first national census in Mexico was taken. Five years later in 1900 the second census was taken and subsequently censuses of population occurred almost every 10 years.

In Mexico the concept of censuses has varied. Those of 1895, 1900, 1910 and 1921 were taken with a *de facto* approach, each individual recorded at the place where he was found at the time of the census. In the last six censuses, from 1930 to 1980, the *de jure* approach was used, people being recorded according to their usual residence.

The demographic data covered by the national censuses vary over time, but the basic data that appear in all censuses are: name, sex, marital status, literacy, place of birth, economic characteristics such as active and inactive population, language and religion. Less common data such as physical and mental disabilities, race and change of nationality, have been eliminated. In Mexico vital registration started during colonial times in which the priests were in charge of recording births, deaths and marriages. The first government intervention in vital registration occurred in 1857, when a law for civil registration was promulgated, giving priests and civil servants charge of registration. In 1859 a new law was promulgated which removed the priests from this task. The registration of data was interrupted during the revolutionary period (1910–1921) and some archives were destroyed. The Dirección de Estadística started to work again in 1922. At present the data registered are births, adoptions, marriages, divorces and deaths, but in general their accuracy varies between regions, being least satisfactory in rural areas.

Population research studies published

Most of the studies on population published in Mexico are written by demographers, sociologists and economists. In order to know the present status of research on population geography in Mexico a bibliography was compiled in 1982 at the Instituto de Geografía, UNAM. According to the available information, the bibliographic references showed that 75 studies were published by geographers while 452 were published by professionals of other disciplines, although it must be accepted that a complete coverage of the studies on population might not have been recorded. In this paper we are going to mention only those studies published in Mexico written by Mexican geographers.

One of the first articles on population, written by Antonio García Cubas

(1870) a well-known geographer of the nineteenth century, was entitled *Apuntes relativos a la población de la República Mexicana*. Subsequently, no articles on population appeared until well into the twentieth century, when two periods may be identified. The first period was from 1940 to 1959, when papers written by geographers were scarce—only three papers in 20 years were devoted specifically to population, two by Vivó (1941, 1949) and one by Gutiérrez de MacGregor (1957). The second period, from 1960 to 1982, is much more important, because 72 studies were published and the number of authors increased to 26; 21 studies during the 1960s, 32 in 1970s, and 19 in only three years in the 1980s, almost as many as were published in the 1960s.

The growth of research in topics of population geography is closely linked with the establishment of population geography as a subject in higher education and also with the creation of a specialized section on population geography at the Instituto de Geografía at UNAM in 1970.

Mexican geographers concentrate their studies mainly at the regional and at the national levels; the number of articles at each level reached 39 and 36 per cent respectively, while only 16 per cent were at local level and 9 per cent on general population matters.

Although the research interests of Mexican geographers are very uneven, certain topics can be distinguished. The major research topics are: distribution, growth and development, and composition of population.

The studies on distribution of population represent 29 per cent of all those written. Most are descriptions and analyzes of maps of population distribution and density. More than half are studies at national level. The most important analysis on distribution of population was published by the Instituto de Geografía (1962), in which Lopez de Llergo made a very good description and analysis of population according to the 1960 census. In other papers the authors analyze distribution of population in relation to different factors: climate, latitude, hydrographic basins and geoeconomic zones. It is interesting to mention that more than half of the papers focus on the distribution of the Indian population, who numbered 3,412,000 in 1970, or 6.7 per cent of the total population.

The 21 per cent of the papers devoted to growth and development of population arise mainly from the rapid increase of population as a result of declining mortality and high fertility. During the period 1930–75 the death rate and infant mortality rate decreased from 25.6 to 7.5 and from 145 to 46.7 per thousand respectively, while the average expectation of life passed from 36.8 to 64 years of age and the birth rate remained superior to 40 per thousand. Mexican geographers interested in the composition of the population have treated only some aspects—age structure, sex composition, economic composition and education—but 24 per cent of the studies analyzed this theme.

The rest of the studies (26 per cent) focus on the following topics: migration, population in general, population and resources, patterns of mortality and population monographs. Most of the studies have been written by research workers of the Instituto de Geografía at UNAM. In addition, 20 per cent of the theses on human geography of the Colegio de Geografía of UNAM study problems related to population geography.

The main serial publications on geography in Mexico are the Anuario de Geografía and Boletín del Instituto de Geografía both published by UNAM; and the Boletín de la Sociedad Mexicana de Geografía y Estadística. Over 62 per cent of the studies of population geography have been published by UNAM: 38 per cent in its Anuario de Geografía and 24 per cent in the Boletín and books of the Instituto de Geografía. The Sociedad Mexicana de Geografía y Estadística has published 33 per cent of the papers in its Boletín and memoires of meetings. There are six books published on population geography: *Análisis de los mapas de distribución de la población del Estado de Tabasco* and *Chilpancingo ciudad en crecimiento* (Falcón, 1965, and 1969); *Desarrollo y distribución de la población urbana en México* and *Geodemografía del Estado de Jalisco* (Gutiérrez de MacGregor, 1965 and 1968); *Composición por edad y sexo e índices de dependencias de la población de la República Mexicana, 1930–1970* (Holt Buttner, 1973); *La población y las lenguas indígenas de México en 1970* (Oliveira, Ortíz and Valverde, 1982).

Population cartography

It is important to stress the development of population cartography in Mexico. Many valuable population maps are published in conjunction with various monographs, books and articles. Of special importance are the Atlas of Internal Migration in Mexico and the maps of the distribution of population speaking Indian languages, designed by research workers at the Instituto de Geografía, UNAM, that have not been published yet.

The interest of Mexican geographers in collaborating with the I.G.U. Commission of a World Population Map must be mentioned. A great effort was made by members of the staff of the Colegio de Geografía, UNAM to draw a map showing the distribution of population in Mexico in 1960 within the limits of the scheme proposed by the I.G.U. Commission, and Mexico was the only country in Latin America that published its map, in 1966.

Meetings

Several meetings partially concerned with population were organized in Mexico by geographers and other specialists, mostly in the 1970s. The meetings organized by geographers did not have population as a central theme, but there was a special section for papers focusing on population geography; five of them were National Congresses and one was the Latin American Regional Conference of the I.G.U. There were twelve meetings organized by other specialists mainly demographers, in which population was the central theme.

Government institutions and policies for population

Mention must be made of the increasing interest of the Mexican government in population problems, as shown in the creation of the following institutions dedicated to population studies:

1958 Centro Latino Americano de Demografía
1964 Centro de Estudios Económicos y Demográficos at the Colegio de México
1968 Comisión de Población y Desarrollo del Consejo Latinoamericano de Ciencias Sociales
1974 Consejo Nacional de Población.

There are also centres for demographic research in four states of the Mexican Republic: Veracruz, Jalisco, Chiapas and Nuevo León. Most of these institutions are managed by demographers, sociologists and economists; only one geographer is collaborating with them.

In 1974 the Consejo Nacional de Ciencia y Tecnología formulated the Programa Nacional Indicativo de Investigación Demográfica, in order to increase research on population in Mexico. This program supports studies on population realized in different government ministries.

The demographic policies have been established by the government through the Consejo Nacional de Población; in its publication *México Demográfico* (1982), the Consejo indicates that the objectives of these policies have been fixed at national and regional levels in two main aspects: natural growth policy and migration policy. The objective of the former is to try to reduce population growth through measures to decrease natality; and that of the latter is to obtain a geographic redistribution of the population, taking into account the considerable regional inequalities manifested particularly by the immense growth and urban primacy of Mexico City, predicted by the U.N. to be the world's largest city before the end of this century.

Conclusions

(a) The ancient Mexicans were the authors of the first pictograph maps in America showing demographic phenomena like mobility of population and stepwise movement using symbols (hieroglyphs) that indicate the places they passed through and the number of years they stood in each place.
(b) From the preceding review, it is apparent that studies on population geography have received very limited attention by geographers, in spite of increased interest shown over the last twenty years.

(c) Traditional descriptions and regional approaches are the most common among the papers of Mexican geographers.
(d) Theoretical aspects of population geography have not yet generated much interest among Mexican geographers.
(e) There is no participation of population geographers in the institutions created by the central government for population studies.

Acknowledgements

I want to express my sincere thanks to Lourdes Godínez, Ignacio Kunz and José Manuel Campos, for their collaboration, and to Silvana Leví de López for useful comments.

References

Consejo Nacional de Población (1982) *México Demográfico. Brevario 1980–81*, México.

Falcón de Gyves, Z. (1965) *Análisis de los mapas de distribución de la población del Estado de Tabasco*, Instituto de Geografía, UNAM. México

Falcón de Gyves, Z. (1969) *Chilpancingo, ciudad en crecimiento*, Instituto de Geografía, UNAM. México.

García Cubas, A. (1870) *Apuntes relativos a la población de la República Mexicana*, Imprenta del Gobierno de Palacio. México.

Gutiérrez de MacGregor, M.T. (1957) Importancia de las cartas demográficas en los trabajos de planeación y métodos para construirlas, *Revista de la Escuela Nacional de Ciencias Políticas y Sociales*, **9–10**, 425–31.

Gutiérrez de MacGregor, M.T. (1965) *Desarrollo y distribunción de la población urbana en México*, Instituto de Geografía, UNAM. México.

Gutiérrez de MacGregor, M.T. (1965) *Desarrollo y distribución de la población urbana en México*, Instituto de Geografía, UNAM. Mxico.

Holt Buttner, E. (173) *Composición por edad y sexo e índices de dependencias de la población de la República Mexicana 1930–1970*, Instituto de Geografía, UNAM. México.

Instituto de Geografía UNAM (1962) *Distribución Geográfica de la Población en la República Mexicana*.

Oliveira, M., Ortiz, M.I. and Valverde, C. (1982) *La población y las lenguas indígenas en México en 1970*, Institutos de Geografía e Antropología, UNAM. México.

Vivó Escoto, J.A. (1941) Razas y lenguas indígenas de México: su distribución geográfica, *Instituto Panamericano de Geografía e Historia*, Publicación Núm. 52.

Vivó Escoto, J.A. (1949) Los problemas demográficos. Los recursos naturales, *Boletín de la Sociedad Mexicana de Geografía y Estadística*, **68** (1–2) 227–67.

25

The Japanese Approach to Population Geography

ATSUSHI OTOMO
(Utsunomiya University, Japan)

A Japanese approach to population geography can be said to have started in the 1920s, when the returns of the first national population census conducted in 1920 became available. Since then, population data have been used prolifically, in various fields of human geography in Japan. Nevertheless, studies of population geography have not always been numerous. The comparatively small number of studies have focused mostly on contemporary population phenomena reflecting the social and economic situations which have changed with the passage of time. This paper is chronological in treatment, being divided into four sections corresponding to the four stages of demographic changes in Japan since 1920.

Population geography in the pre-war period

The first important paper on population geography in *Chirigaku Hyoron* (*Geographical Review of Japan*), the most influential academic journal of geography in Japan, is the one entitled 'On population geography' by Mugitani (1926). He pointed out that the previous researches on population had focused on practical aspects such as population problems and population policies, and he emphasized the necessity of studying population geography in its theoretical aspects rather than in practical ones. During the same period, using the first national population census data, researches on measurement of population distribution were performed. Above all, Ono (1925) prepared the map of population distribution of Japan by *shi* and *gun* (minor administrative divisions) for the first time, covering the whole territory of Japan and being based on reliable data. Compared with the studies on population distribution, those on migration of population at that time were few.

During the period 1930 to 1940, the Japanese population experienced steady growth, due to a slowly declining but still high fertility and a declining mortality, and heavy concentration of population to urban or industrial areas from rural areas resulting from industrialization since the last decade of the nineteenth century. Studies of population distribution got underway, mostly disclosing the patterns of changes in population distribution, in particular the pattern of population increase in urban areas against the decrease in rural areas and that of the declining trends in population growth rates in the western part of Japan against the increasing trends in the eastern part. Meanwhile, the researches on the internal migration of population pointed out a growing tendency of the movement of people from rural to urban or industrial areas during this period (Hama, 1976).

Thus, it can be said that Japanese population geography during the pre-war period had focused mainly on the study of population distribution.

Population geography during the second world war and immediate post-war period

From the 1930s the Japanese population had experienced resettlement in overseas regions, particularly in Manchuria as a result of governmental policy. During the second world war a considerable number of people transmigrated voluntarily or involuntarily to South-East Asian countries occupied by Japanese armies as well as to Manchuria. With the aggravation of the war fewer studies of population geography were performed.

Immediately after the war more than four million Japanese returned to the homeland from overseas areas and the Japanese population experienced extraordinarily high growth, also because of the increase in fertility. The population in rural areas showed an increase, while the people in urban areas indicated a decrease due to the evacuation from urban to rural areas and the loss of lives of urban people by air-raids during the war. As a consequence the density of population in rural areas, which had declined since 1930, tended to increase, and in 1947 it recorded its highest level since 1920. Rural areas experienced high pressure of population, and the main concern was how to solve the high population densities per land area and per economic capacity. Accordingly, population geography still focused on the study of geographical distribution of population.

Beside those studies, one by Kiuchi (1951) disclosed the changes in the geographical distribution of city population for 1888 to 1947, and the concentric structures of population increase rates and their changes for the intercensal periods of 1920 to 1946 in the metropolitan areas of Tokyo and elsewhere.

Population geography from the mid-1950s to 1970

From the mid-1950s the movement of population, which had been directed toward rural areas from urban areas during the latter part of the second world war and immediately after, tended to change direction. A great deal of people in rural areas under high population pressure began to move to urban areas, particularly to major cities. Thus, rural-to-urban migration prevailed again, and the geographical distribution of population experienced a drastic change. For instance, of the 47 prefectures in Japan, the number recording population increase during 1955–60 augmented remarkably to 26, against 3 or less for the periods of 1920 to 1935.

Under such situations the geographical approach to population focused on urbanization and metropolitanization. Among the related studies, the discussions on the formation of Japanese 'megalopolis' were of great concern to regional administrators and planners.

During this period unevenness in the spatial distribution of population between metropolitan and non-metropolitan areas augmented further, and how to solve *Kamitsu* (extreme crowding) in metropolitan areas and *Kaso* (extreme dispersion) in non-metropolitan areas became a prime concern for regional policy-makers and planners of the national and prefectural governments. Thus, the importance of a geographical approach to population analysis has been well recognized by them.

Further, the concentration of population in the metropolitan areas brought the rapid expansion of residential areas toward the outskirts of the metropolitan area, causing sectoral difference within the area. Tachi and Hama (1963) found, together with the concentric pattern of change in population distribution of metropolitan areas, the radial expansion along the routes of the transportation networks.

Beside these studies on urbanization and metropolitanization of population, a great number of researches on internal migration of the population were undertaken. They included not only analyses of volume and intensity of movement of the population between regions, but also those of the relationships of migration with distance and other causes and of the regional differences in the population structure of migrants.

With the progress of researches in population geography, attempts to establish population geography as an independent subject in human geography were undertaken by Kawabe (1964) and Kishimoto (1968). Above all, Kawabe insisted that population geography should include within its scope population change, the product of the elements of movement (birth, death and migration), as well as population distribution.

Population geography during the 1970s and thereafter

Population movement between regions during the 1970s involved diversified patterns which were different from the simple ones in the previous decades. In the 1970s the movement from metropolitan areas to non-metropolitan areas has been recognizable, rather than the stream from non-metropolitan areas to metropolitan areas. On the other hand, during this decade the migratory flow from the metropolitan core to its suburban areas was observed as being the same as for the previous decade. Based on such findings related to the transition in internal migration, there have been controversies whether the change in direction of the main flow in internal migration of the population should have been called a 'U-turn' phenomenon or not, and debates whether the reverse migration from the metropolitan areas to non-metropolitan areas was a return migration or not (Otomo, 1980).

In parallel with the studies of trends and patterns of migration, there have been studies of the factors affecting migration of the population, including distance and socio-economic factors. Above all, Otomo (1982) disclosed, for the first time, the main reasons for the overall flows of migration of population for the whole country and for various inter-regional flows, the analyses being based on reliable statistical data.

Studies of spatial distribution of the population during this period were of two sorts. The first related to regional populations and their changes in the context of the redistribution of the national population. In this respect, Hama (1978) revealed that the change in the pattern of population distribution after 1970 was caused mainly by the transition of internal migration trends which could be explained by regional development, the economic depression after 1974, the change in supply of labour force and the transformation in consciousness of younger people into inclination toward living in rural areas rather than in urban areas. The second type of study on the spatial distribution of population concerned urbanization, urban structure and metropolitanization.

The salient feature of researches in population geography during this period is the increased number of studies of demographic changes, of fertility and mortality, and of demographic structures of the regional populations. Among those studies, one by Yamaguchi and Itoh (1977) revealed that the reproductivity of Japanese women tended to decline not only in urban areas but also in rural areas and the urban-rural differential was becoming smaller. Moreover, according to Hama (1978), in the 1970s the aged population imposed only a small burden on the other population in metropolitan areas but it put a great burden on those in non-metropolitan areas.

Another feature of the studies of population geography in Japan during this period has been the applications of quantitative methods, especially by Ishimizu *et al.* (1976) and Suzuki (1980), which have contributed to the development of the field. Furthermore, based on the results of various researches of population geography, projections and estimates of populations by various types of regions and areas have been attempted by a few population geographers since the 1960s (Otomo, 1979). Some of these have contributed to regional policy-making of national and prefectural governments.

In addition to studying the population of Japan, Japanese population geographers have also studied the populations of foreign countries, particularly in Asia, and they are far from insular in approach.

As described earlier, Japanese population geography does not occupy a dominant position in Japanese geography in terms of number of researchers and of volume of research works. However, it can be concluded that there has been much progress, particularly since the 1960s. The extensive volumes on population geography by Kishimoto (1978), Otomo (1979) and Hama (1982), collecting their previous research work, may be appreciated as representatives of recent studies of population geography in Japan.

References

Hama, H. (1976) Geographical studies of population, in *Geography in Japan*, University of Tokyo Press, Tokyo, 205–10.

Hama, H. (1978) Population problems and national development plan in Japan—post-war trends, *Journal of Population Problems*, Institute of Population Problems, Tokyo, 147, 1–23 (in Japanese with English abstract).

Hama, H. (1982) *Nihon Jinkokozo-no Chiikibunseki (Regional Analysis of Japanese Population Structure)*, Chikura Shobo, Tokyo (in Japanese).

Ishimizu, T., Otomo, A. and Isobe, K. (1976) Trend-surface analysis: its significance, applications and problems, *Geographical Review of Japan*, **49**, 455–60 (in Japanese with English abstract).

Kawabe, H. (1964) Some consideration on population geography, *Geographical Review of Japan*, **37**, 1–13 (in Japanese with English abstract).

Kishimoto, M. (1968) *Jinko Chirigaku (Population Geography)*, Taimeido, Tokyo (in Japanese).

Kishimoto, M. (1978) *Jinko Idoron (The Study of Population Movement)*, Taimeido, Tokyo (in Japanese).

Kiuchi, S. (1951) *Toshichirigaku Kenkyu (Urban Geography)*, Kokin Shoin, Tokyo (in Japanese).

Mugitani, T. (1926) On population geography, *Geographical Review of Japan*, **2**, 952–60 (in Japanese).

Ono, T. (1925) *Dainihon Gunshibetsu Jinko Mitsudozu (Population Distribution Map by* Gun *and* Shi *for Japan) 1: 1,500,000*, Fuzanbo, Tokyo (in Japanese).

Otomo, A. (1979) *Nihon Toshijinko Bumpron (Geographical Distribution of Urban Population in Japan)*, Taimeido, Tokyo (in Japanese with English summary).

Otomo, A. (1980) Progress of studies of population geography, *Recent Progress of Natural Sciences in Japan*, **5**, 81–7.

Otomo, A. (1982) Spatial mobility and reasons for migration of Japanese women, Paper delivered to the Symposium on the Role of Women in Population Redistribution, held in Cagliari, Italy.

Suzuki, K. (1980) *Kukan Jinkogaku (Space Demography)*, Taimeido, Tokyo (in Japanese).

Tachi, M. and Hama, H. (1963) Demographic sphere structure in metropolitan area, *Archives of Population Association of Japan*, **4**, 81–91.

Yamaguchi, K. and Itoh, T. (1977) Recent trends in regional distribution of demographic reproductivity by prefectures, *Journal of Population Problems*, Institute of Population Problems, Tokyo, **144**, 30–60 (in Japanese with English abstract).

26

The Chinese Approach to Population Geography

SUN PANSHOU
(Chinese Academy of Sciences, Beijing, China)

China is the world's most populous country. Its total population amounted to 1,008 million in 1982 and still more if Taiwan Province is included. Today the Chinese government thinks greatly of her population problems. The outstanding achievement which resulted in practising all-round birth control is illustrated by the drastic drop of natural increase rate, from 26.19 per thousand in 1969 to 11.66 per thousand in 1979. Since the late 1970s, more and more Chinese specialists in economic, geographical and other circles have engaged in population study. Among the main topics that Chinese geographers are most interested in are the trend of rural population changes, the status and dynamics of urban population, migration between provinces or autonomous regions, and the law of population distribution.

Trend of rural population changes

China's rural population numbered 842 million in 1979; even if the non-agricultural labour force is excluded, it still amounted to 80 per cent of the country's total population. So the perspective change of such a large rural population has become a problem pondered frequently by both social scientists and geographers. The distribution of population among the sections of the national economy of a particular country, especially in agricultural and industrial sections, decides the ratio between urban population and rural population, and exerts great influence on the geographical distribution of the country's population. China's rural population will continue to inflow into cities and towns along with industrial modernization and development of science, education, commerce and public services. According to estimation, however, the number of people migrating to cities and towns from rural areas only amounted to about 20 million during the period of 1949 to 1979 (Sun,

1982), a small portion of the entire rural population. Therefore, the population migrational process will still be very low at least until the end of the century.

The policy suitable to China's actual conditions is to transform surplus manpower to other activities under the premise of taking agricultural production as priority, ensuring sufficient labour force for agricultural activities and rapidly increasing grain yield as well as other farm products. As to other activities rather than agriculture, the existing channel already being opened is to develop commune- or brigade-run enterprises (including forestry stations, tea plantations, orchards, poultry and livestock feed lots, fishing grounds; manufacturing and mining industries; communications and transportation; construction; commerce and services of all kinds, etc). Up to the end of 1980, 1.43 million such enterprises had been founded throughout the country. Staff and workers reached approximately 30 million, being 9.4 per cent of the nation's total rural labour force. The commune- or brigade-run enterprises thus not only offer job opportunities for rural population and increase collective and individual farmers' incomes, but provide large amounts of production means and consumer goods as well as various services to the local people. Currently, this type of enterprise is being developed even more rapidly in densely populated rural areas in the vicinities of large and some medium-sized cities. It is very significant to study the characteristics and processes of such kinds of non-agricultural activities engaged in by farmers in regions of various types, and to study subsequent functional changes in villages and towns, particularly because this is one of the fundamental ways to integrate industry with agriculture, and city with countryside.

Status and dynamics of urban population

China's urban population only accounted for 13.2 per cent of the nation's total in 1979 (excluding agricultural population who live in cities and towns), which is much less than most other countries in the world. The chief reason responsible for this is that the Chinese government has implemented suitable policies to prevent the unauthorized outflow of farmers from countryside to cities. In addition, the absolute number of China's urban population has already exceeded the considerable figure of 130 million, not including rural population within urban areas. This number contrasts with those of the United States and Soviet Union, which account for the largest urban populations in the world, but it is akin to that of India. In fact, China's present urban manpower situation is quite different from what happened in the 1950s when urban manpower fell short of actual needs. To this end, it is necessary to study the age of urban population, labour composition and potential manpower resources. Secondly, China's urban population is unevenly distributed; some 210 cities comprise 67.1 per cent of the nation's entire urban population (45 cities with more than 500,000 inhabitants contain 42.8 per cent), while over 2,870 towns account for only 32.9 per cent. That means that the concentration of urban population in large cities is very obvious. It is essential to analyze population dynamics in cities of different sizes. And lastly, as the new industrial and other key construction projects will be located primarily in small and some of the medium-sized cities, efforts should be taken to control unduly fast population growth rates in these cities so as to reduce relevant investment on housing and associated public services. For this purpose, it is necessary to investigate rural manpower supply conditions in the suburban areas of cities so as to take advantage of the enrolment of new city staff and workers from neighbouring rural areas.

Migration between provinces or autonomous regions

Right after the 1950s a certain number of inhabitants in China's densely populated central and eastern provinces migrated successively to the sparsely populated and remote border provinces and autonomous regions in the northern and western parts of the country, for the sake of accelerating economic development. According to rough estimation, net in-migrants amounted to about 15 million in Heilongjiang, Nei Monggol (Inner Mongolia), Xinjiang, Qinghai and Ningxia provinces or autonomous regions, as well as smaller numbers to provinces like Yunnan, Guizhou, Shaanxi, Gansu, Jilin and Jiangxi from other provinces. The inter-provincial in-migrants mainly consisted of farmers who devoted themselves to reclamation, as well as workers, technicians, cadres and their family members to industry and mining (Qiu, 1981). Most of the farmers migrated spontaneously. And the migration trend is similar to that in earlier times before the 1950s. For example, farmers in Shandong, Henan and northern Anhui and Jiangsu provinces migrate to north-eastern, northern and north-western parts of China, while those in Sichuan and Hunan migrate to Yunnan and Guizhou in the south-west. This migration trend will continue along with further development and utilization of natural resources in those remote border provinces and autonomous regions. The analysis of past migrational characteristics can be taken for future reference.

Law of population distribution

During the past thirty years, China's population migration between rural and urban, and that between eastern and central provinces and remote border provinces and regions has generally been small in proportion, no remarkable changes so far having occurred with regard to basic features of population distribution. Population distribution in China is quite uneven. If the entire territory is equally divided into two parts—the south-eastern and the north-western—population in the former would be 96 per cent of the nation's total and in the latter just 4 per cent (Hu, 1981). So compilation of population maps and the survey of various factors affecting population distribution and carrying capacity of population in different areas, by using the latest census data, are the important topics which need to be studied by geographers.

At the present stage, China's population distribution depends to a great extent on the allocation of agricultural and industrial production, and population distribution in turn may influence production allocation; the latter fact, however, is often neglected. The deltas of Changjiang, Zhujiang and Hanjiang as well as the Chengdu plain are considered to be the most densely populated areas in China, so formed as a result of constant development of production. The situation of established dense population, which may not be changed within a short period, should be taken into account carefully in the case of production allocation. Therefore, topics such as how to deal dialectically with relationships between production allocation and population distribution, and how to make a correct clarification of the objective law of China's population distribution, have become arduous tasks for the geographers to cope with.

Although Chinese geographers are new participants in dealing with widespread and thoroughgoing population investigation and study, yet population geography in China is bound to develop rapidly. Two reasons might be recognized for this. On the one hand, this particular field will gain support from both the government and various social circles. On the other, multi-disciplinary researches associated with population study have also been energetically pursued, with which geographers may coordinate, and through cooperation population studies may be advanced to a new stage.

Acknowledgements

The author wishes to thank Zhang Li for translating this chapter into English, and Professor Wu Chuanjun for reading and revising the English manuscript.

References

Hu Huanyong (1981) An exploratory discussion on China's population problems from population geographical point of view, *Proceedings of Population Study*, East China Normal Univ. Press, 1–9.

Qiu Weizhi (1981) Preliminary study on population migration since the founding of the People's Republic of China. *Population and Economy*, **4**, 8–13.

Sun Jingzhi (1982) On the problem of China's population distribution, *Population Study*, **2**, 10–11.

27

Population Theory and Policy in the Islamic World

MOHAMED E-S. GHALLAB
(Cairo University, Egypt)

This essay is an attempt to outline the origins of muslim attitudes towards population questions, theory and practice in the Muslim World, on the assumption that population geography must take great account of cultural phenomena, ignorance of which can lead to much misinterpretation of population data. Nowhere is this more obvious than in the World of Islam, which is an all-embracing creed and mode of life. Legislature of a special order called Shari'ah is part and parcel of Islamic life, especially laws concerning family matters. However modernized a muslim community is, it is still influenced by Islam in matters of marriage, divorce and inheritance. So it is imperative that some light should be shed on Islamic concepts concerning population in such matters as nuptiality, reproduction and population theory, practice and policy.

Marriage

In Arabia, the cradle of Islam, the ancient institution of marriage was influenced by primary tribal and environmental needs. But eventually Persian traits penetrated into some forms of marriage. According to 'Aisha, the favoured wife of Prophet Mohammad, there were many practices of marriage in pre-Islamic Arabia, some of which were referred to in the Holy Qur'an. Most of these *djahilia* (pre-Islamic) practices were abolished or modified in Islam. Of the former, an ancient Mazdaean (Persian) form was quite alien to tribal genealogical interest. It was called borrowing in, i.e. a strong or intelligent male was called upon to give a child to a lady of a noble family. Adoption was also known very widely before Islam. A form of polyandry was also practised; a woman would host a number of men, who frequented her bed at the same period of time, and she would call upon any one of them to be the father of the fruit of this collective marriage. Polygyny or plural marriages were unlimited. A man could keep as many wives as he could afford economically.

Islam nullified all these forms. The Shari'ah regards many such practices as mere forms of adultery, which Islam denounces and forbids categorically.

Family laws are perhaps at the heart of any social structure. So far as Qur'an contains legislation, it largely regards family relationships. Islam universalized and institutionalized one form of marriage only, which creates the nuclear family—man, wife and children, which was stressed upon as a self-sufficient unit (Hodgson, 1974). Islam insisted on chastity and righteousness: 'They (women) should be chaste, not lustful nor taking paramours' (S. IV, 25)*. The position of the individual adult male was strengthened. The man retained wide authority over the wife to the exclusion of either his family or hers. He was responsible for the maintenance of wife and children. Inheritance was to be primarily within the immediate family except for rare occasions. The degree of relationships within which marriage could not take place were stressed and even multiplied—with the effect that it was less easy for a married couple to be absorbed by multiple ties within the wider household; thus relationship by fosterage was made equal to relationship by blood. At the same time the integrity of the natural family was protected against the introduction of fictive relationships, which Arabs frequently created between adults and which were allowed no status in law. In the case of plural marriages, each marriage must be given equal status with the first up to the number of four and must have the same tight-knit character. Casual unions were strictly forbidden.

Islam recognizes women's right to property. In Islam, part of the male prerogative as provider of the family was the right of divorce, although women also may in certain cases initiate divorce. Man may in no case make use of his wife's property during marriage but has the obligation of maintaining her from his own resources. The insistence on the personal dignity of every individual, male or female, was illustrated in the prohibition of infanticide which had borne especially on infant girls in *djahilia*. This was denounced in Islam.

Islam regards procreation and multiplication as the goal of marriage. The Holy Qur'an states that 'Wealth and sons are allurements of the life of this world' (S.XVIII, 46). On the other hand, it states 'Your riches and your children may be but a trial' (S.LXIV, 15). Infanticide is condemned and strictly forbidden: 'Kill not your children for fear of want. We shall provide sustenance for them as for you. Verily the killing of them is a great sin'

* Quotations from the Holy Qur'an are taken from the English translation accomplished by Abdullah Yousuf Ali, Kutub Khana Ishayat-ul-Islam, Delhi, 5th ed. 1979. The Sura (chapter) is in Roman numerals and the verse in Arabic.

(S.XVII, 31). 'Kill not your children on a place of want; we provide sustenance for you and for them' (S.VI, 151).

Population theory and policy

Ibn Khaldun (1332–1406), a prominent muslim philosopher of history, political thinker and sociologist, stated clearly what we can regard as the Islamic attitude to population questions during the Middle Ages. In his famous *Prolegomena* (English translation by F. Rosenthal, 1959), he stated that a densely settled population was conducive to higher levels of living, since it permitted greater division of labour, more effective use of resources and military and political security. As a political writer, he observed that a state passes through periods of prosperity and decline alternately and that cyclical variations in population numbers occur in rhythm with these economic fluctuations. Favourable economic conditions and political order stimulate population growth by increasing natality and checking mortality. In the wake of these periods of economic progress come luxury, love of easy life, rising taxes and other changes which in succeeding generations produce military weakness, vulnerability to hostile aggression, economic depression and depopulation.

Further, in Chapters 17–19 of the *Prolegomena* he discussed arts and crafts in relation to the numbers of population (Qadir, 1942; Issawi, 1950; Rosenthal, 1962). Industries, arts and crafts in his opinion are varied and multiplied in towns and cities according to their sizes. Luxurious goods in excess of sustenance needs are only found in big cities, such as Baghdad, Cordoba, Kairouan, Basra and Cairo. Indeed, knowledge and culture can only thrive in such populous places. He rightly pointed out the importance of the division of labour, of industrial traditions of accumulative skill and competence in old-established industries located in big cities. One remark is worth noting: the bigger the populations, the more powerful and widespread and influential their language and literature. A language spoken by a small number of people has no opportunity to compete with a language spoken by a large number. Indeed Ibn Khaldun was a shrewd populationist, who advocated the value of big populations in safeguarding strong states, spreading and propagating cultural influence, fostering industries and building economies.

The Islamic World in modern times is facing the population dilemma faced by most developing countries. Very rapid growth of population as a result of declining mortality and very high natality have caused economic difficulties in most Islamic countries. The need for birth control arises in many muslim communities. As happened in Europe and America religious beliefs had to be reconciled, especially where the masses are good adherents to the creed. Some thinkers resorted to Islamic traditions and found rescue in the writings of a well-loved Arab theologian-philosopher, who taught theology at Baghdad, and lectured also in Damascus, Jerusalem and Alexandria between 1091 and 1111. Al-Ghazali (Lat. Algazel) was entitled *Hodjat al Islam* (authority of Islamic tradition). In his famous work, *Ihya Ulum al Din* (Renaissance of Religious Teachings), he devoted a section to discuss marital concerns. After stating that the aim of marriage is procreation and multiplication, he carried on his thesis about wilful prevention of conception. In his opinion this is allowed in three cases: (1) conservation of property, (2) conservation of woman's beauty, (3) fear of want. The first case concerns slave women, property to be acquired by purchase and if need arises to be sold, who could not be sold if they became mothers. This case is obsolete now and exists no more. The second case is worth noting. If a woman fears the loss of her beauty let alone physical fitness and general health by being pregnant too many times, she is allowed to prevent conception. The third case concerns economy. If the couple think that they have enough children and further children would be a burden on their resources they are allowed to prevent conception. The last two cases concern the welfare of population which society seizes upon to check the growth of population.

Al-Ghazali asserted that during the time of Prophet Mohammad, people used to practise the only known means of contraception, i.e. *coitus interruptus*. He cited many of the Prophet's companions telling incidences of this contraceptive means. However, he also cited a hadith calling for small families; the smaller a family the richer it becomes and vice versa. This saying attributed to the Prophet is often quoted in family planning campaigns in Egypt, but Al-Ghazali stated that the saying is uncertain and its authenticity is weak.

The question of the fear of want as an urge for birth control or checking the rapid growth of population is still debatable among doctors of religion. Opponents of birth control on economic grounds base their argument on Qur'anic texts. 'How many are the creatures that carry not their own sustenance? It is God who feeds (both) them and you' (S.XXIX, 60). 'God enlarges the sustenance (which he gives) to whichever of His servants He pleases, and similarly grants by (strict) measures, as He pleases. For God has full knowledge of all things' (S.XXIX, 62). They claim that God, the Benefactor, provides for all people, and it is blasphemous to think otherwise. On the other hand, many doctors of religion, on the grounds of Al-Ghazali's argument stated above, allow the use of contraceptives. Nevertheless, there is consensus regarding prohibition of abortion, unless on medical grounds. Abortion, as a means of checking natality, is regarded as infanticide which is strictly prohibited in Islam.

Some empirical evidence from Islamic countries

During the past few years the Cairo Demographic Centre (C.D.C.) has carried out micro-surveys and case studies of family and marriage in a number of communities representing muslim societies from different environments. The collected material was supplemented by published or available material supplied by respective countries. The representative samples included rural and urban societies in Egypt, Sudan, Syria, Jordan, Kuwait, Bangladesh and Indonesia. It is important to bear in mind that there exists a conspicuous lack of data relating to nuptiality, age of marriage, remarriage or multiple marriages.

Table 27.1, which shows percentages of never married and the median age of marriage by sex in some Islamic countries, indicates that marriage starts quite early in life especially for females. This reflects the importance of the institution of marriage in Islam. The median age of marriage for men is observed to vary round early to mid-twenties and is lower in rural areas. It is to be noted in this context that in the various areas a significant proportion of males in the age group 25–29 have yet to get married. When such persons complete their marriage, the final median age of marriage will be considerably higher than recorded. This observation is also valid for females.

The female median age of marriage is particularly low (15–17) in rural areas. By the age of nineteen, 70 per cent of Shibpur (Bangladesh) girls and 57 per cent of Jarash (Jordan) girls are married. In the course of the next five years nearly every girl in these two places will get married, thus showing much

TABLE 27.1. *Percentage never married in selected age groups and median age at marriage by sex*

Data Source	Male			Median Age at Marriage	Female			Median Age at Marriage
	20–24	25–29	40–44		15–19	20–24	40–44	
Urban								
Egypt (Cairo)	98.3	81.4	3.9	27.2	97.6	78.5	6.3	19.9
Syria (Damascus)	94.4	54.3	6.7	26.2	89.1	57.3	6.9	18.5
Rural								
Egypt (Bishla)	72.4	31.4	2.9	23.2	69.2	14.7	0.8	16.5
Jordan (Jarash)	34.8	9.6	0.0	20.6	43.2	5.2	2.2	16.2
Sudan (Gezira)	86.0	59.2	5.5	24.8	74.6	49.4	2.4	16.7
Sudan (Darfur)	60.2	14.9	1.1	22.7	68.3	16.6	0.0	16.7
Bangladesh (Shibpur)	67.5	18.9	1.5	23.4	30.0	5.9	0.8	15.1
National								
Kuwait	71.9	30.8	4.3	24.0	71.4	32.0	2.1	18.4
Tunisia	90.2	49.4	4.3	27.0	93.9	51.5	1.7	21.5
Indonesia	58.6	18.5	2.1	—	62.6	18.5	1.2	15.8

Source: This and subsequent tables are based on the work of the following students supervised by the C.D.C. faculty: Cairo (L. Nawar), Damascus (H. Baradie), Bishla (B. Al Deeb), Jarash (N. Gheita), Gezira (H. Yousuf), Darfur (A. Sharif), Shibpur (N. Ahmad), Kuwait (F. Turki), Tunisia (A. Auni), and Indonesia (K. Abdullah).

lower female age at marriage in these two places compared with other places studied.

Considerably higher figures for the two surveyed capital cities (Cairo and Damascus) as for Kuwait and especially Tunisia as a whole seem to reflect a recently rising trend in age at marriage in response to expansion of female education in particular and increasing modernization in general. It is noteworthy that in the Cairo study about four-fifths of males aged 25–29 and females aged 20–24 are still single, compared with about half or more of the respective populations in Damascus and Tunisia and rather surprisingly in rural Gezira (Sudan) as well.

Multiple marriage occurs because of two broad reasons—polygyny and the remarriage of the widowed and divorced. Polygyny in Islam, as stated above, is allowed albeit limited to the number of four wives. In practice, it is extremely rare in Arab and Asiatic countries, except perhaps the Sudan which is affected by the more common African type of polygyny. On the other hand, Tunisia is an exceptional case, having passed a law prohibiting polygyny based on some interpretation of the Maliki school of Shari'ah (Malik was one of the four great teachers of Sunni Muslims). However, this is not theoretically accepted in other muslim countries, although Egypt in the 1970s also passed a law restricting polygyny, and Turkey ceased adhering to Shari'ah altogether since 1923.

Tables 27.2–27.4 provide comparative data on the phenomena of multiple marriage and polygyny. The predominant majority of the populations—males and females—are reported to be married only once (Table 27.2). Only in the case of Darfur is the majority of ever-married males found to have married

TABLE 27.2. *Ever-married persons by sex and number of times married*

	Males					Females				
	Total Ever-	Times Married				Total Ever-	Times Married			
Data Source	Married	1	2	3+	2+	Married	1	2	3+	2+
Urban										
Egypt (Cairo)	837	89.5	8.7	1.8	10.5	1024	94.6	3.8	1.7	5.5
Syria (Damascus)	1108	92.8	6.1	1.1	7.2	1258	96.2	2.8	1.0	3.8
Rural										
Egypt (Bishla)	1122	84.5	11.3	4.2	15.5	1484	90.4	7.3	2.3	9.6
Jordan (Jarash)	1139	88.9	8.7	2.4	11.1	1278	96.0	2.1	1.9	4.0
Sudan (Gezira)	941	73.6	—	—	26.4	1152	84.5	—	—	15.5
Sudan (Darfur)	800	45.6	30.6	23.8	54.4	1059	82.2	15.2	2.6	17.8
Bangladesh (Shibpur)	969	70.0	18.1	11.9	30.0	1239	81.8	14.0	4.2	18.2
National										
Kuwait	—	71.5	20.6	7.9	28.5	—	91.6	7.3	1.1	8.4
Indonesia	—	—	—	—	—	—	68.3	21.1	10.6	31.7

TABLE 27.3. *Percentage of ever-married persons with polygynous background by sex and age*

Data Source	Males					Females				
	Total Polygynous	Less than 30	30–49	50+	Total	Total Polygynous	Less than 30	30–49	50+	Total
Urban										
Egypt (Cairo)	22	0.0	1.9	4.0	2.6	40	1.4	4.8	4.1	3.9
Syria (Damascus)	15	0.8	1.2	2.2	1.3	20	1.5	1.6	1.7	1.6
Rural										
Egypt (Bishla)	59	0.4	4.4	9.7	5.3	98	3.4	6.9	9.9	6.6
Jordan (Jarash)	65	1.1	3.8	16.2	5.7	94	3.4	9.6	13.0	7.4
Sudan (Gezira)	154	2.2	10.5	30.8	16.4	139	9.3	12.4	16.6	12.2
Sudan (Darfur)	384	12.6	46.0	70.0	48.0	444	27.5	49.1	52.0	41.9
Bangladesh (Shibpur)	68	4.9	5.3	11.3	7.0	64	4.7	5.1	6.3	5.2

more than once. With this exception, which is affected by African traditions, the incidence of marriage beyond a second time is rather rare.

Without exception, multiple marriage is considerably less frequent among females compared to males, and in urban areas compared to rural ones. Apart from Darfur noted above, most cases show low percentages of multiple marriages, ranging from 7 per cent in the case of Damascus males to 30 per cent for rural Bangladesh represented by Shibpur. As for male multiple marriages, in all cases it is rather infrequent, ranging from 4 to 8 per cent of the respective totals.

Remarriage in muslim societies now is not a very common phenomenon. Its occurrence is perhaps strikingly low in some muslim populations, especially in urban areas and among females (Huzayyin and Ascadi, 1976, Chap. 26).

Table 27.3 refutes the notion encountered in popular literature that polygyny is a widespread phenomenon among muslims. With the exception of Sudan, the overall proportion of males with a polygynous background is far below 8 per cent of the total, ranging between one per cent in Damascus to 7 per cent in Shibpur (Bangladesh). At the age of 50 and over, this phenomenon

TABLE 27.4. *Percentage of ever-married persons, married more than once, by sex, education and socio-economic status*

Data Source	Total Ever-married	Education			Socio-Economic Status		
		High	Medium	Low+None	High	Medium	Low
		Males					
Urban							
Egypt (Cairo)	837	6.4	10.6	15.3	—	—	—
Syria (Damascus)	1108	4.7	5.4	13.1	—	—	—
Rural							
Egypt (Bishla)	1122	—	—	—	10.9	14.3	18.0
Jordan (Jarash)	1139	—	—	—	8.5	11.3	13.2
Sudan (Darfur)	800	—	—	—	54.4	55.5	53.6
Bangladesh (Shibpur)	969	—	—	—	25.0	28.5	32.0
National							
Kuwait	—	5.4	13.2	29.7	—	—	—
		Females					
Urban							
Egypt (Cairo)	1024	7.3	4.1	5.4	—	—	—
Syria (Damascus)	1258	2.1	2.4	7.1	—	—	—
Rural							
Egypt (Bishla)	1484	—	—	—	6.5	9.3	10.8
Syria (Jarash)	1278	—	—	—	3.8	4.6	4.5
Sudan (Darfur)	1059	—	—	—	22.8	15.3	17.7
Bangladesh (Shibpur)	1239	—	—	—	11.4	12.5	22.8
National							
Kuwait	—	0.9	1.7	7.0	—	—	—

represents only 2 per cent in Damascus, 4 per cent in Cairo and about 10 per cent in rural Egypt.

On the whole, it appears that both education and socio-economic status are inversely associated with multiple marriage (Table 27.4). In other words, marriage beyond the first one seems to be more frequently associated with lower educational and socio-economic status. This is also true considering polygyny, although this pattern is contrary to what is often found among African populations south of the Sahara, where the incidence of polygyny is generally believed to be higher among the richer people.

Conclusions

In pre-Islamic Arabia certain measures were developed to check the growth of population such as infanticide and a form of polyandry. The reason for this was apparently environmental. Islam strictly abolished these devices. The nuclear family is the cornerstone of muslim society. Marriage is encouraged and procreation is highly esteemed. Nevertheless self-interest and the legitimate urge for the betterment of life are good reasons to allow family planning. There is no universal theory of population in Islam; in muslim countries to-day all attitudes towards population concerns are expressed. Polygyny, however, is fading away in modern muslim societies as socio-economic conditions are influencing nuptiality, as well as fertility and mortality.

References

Al-Ghazali, (1965) *Ihya Ulum al Din*, Kitab Al-Sha'ab edition Cairo (in Arabic).

Hodgson, M.G.S. (1974) *The Venture of Islam*, vol. 1, University of Chicago Press.

Huzayyin S.A. and Ascadi, G.T. (1976) *Family and Marriage in Some African and Asiatic Countries*, Cairo Demographic Centre, Research Monograph Series No. 6.

Ibn Khaldun (1966) *Prolegomena*, Kitab Al Sha'ab edition, Cairo (in Arabic).

Issawi, C. (1950) *An Arab Philosopher of History*: Selections from the Prolegomena of Ibn Khaldun of Tunis, (1332–1400) Translated and arranged by C.P. Issawi, London.

Qadir, M. Abdul (1942) The economic ideas of Ibn Khaldun, *Indian Journal of Economics*, Allahabad, India, **22**, 898–907.

Rosenthal, E.I.J. (1962) *Political Thought in Medieval Islam, An Introductory Outline*, Cambridge University Press.

Index